BASILISKS

BASILISKS AND BEOWULF

Monsters in the Anglo-Saxon World

TIM FLIGHT

REAKTION BOOKS

For my mother, Mary Flight, who had her own Beowulfian fight with cancer while this book was being written, and my wife, Martina Wise, the blue to my claret.

In memory of Michael Francis Patrick Lowe (1929–2017)

Eadig bið se þe eaþmod leofaþ; cymeð him seo ar of heofonum

Published by
REAKTION BOOKS LTD
Unit 32, Waterside
44–48 Wharf Road
London N1 7UX, UK
www.reaktionbooks.co.uk

First published 2021
First published in paperback 2023

Printed and bound in Great Britain by TJ Books Limited, Padstow, Cornwall

A catalogue record for this book is available from the British Library

ISBN 978 1 78914 774 2

CONTENTS

INTRODUCTION

The Anglo-Saxon period lasted around seven hundred years, from the fifth to the early twelfth century AD. With so many changes and events taking place in that time, the task of the historian is unenviable. Moreover, the vast majority of voices that have survived are those of the cultural elite, which means we must be extremely careful when talking of the defining beliefs and character of the Anglo-Saxons more generally. With these limitations in mind, let us briefly review what we know of the period as a whole before examining the importance of monsters to such a long, rich and varied culture.

Who Were the Anglo-Saxons?

The term 'Anglo-Saxons' is given to the Continental Germanic tribes who arrived and settled in what was then known as Britannia from the mid-fifth century onwards. Despite what the name might suggest, these tribes also included Angles, Jutes, Saxons, Batavians, Friesians and Franks among their number. Although the Anglo-Saxon period is usually given a start date of about AD 450, Germanic people had been living in small numbers in Britannia since the early fourth century, having been employed as soldiers by the Roman rulers of Britain.

In the traditional narrative, following the sixth-century Welsh monk Gildas, the Anglo-Saxons were employed as mercenaries by British kings ('like timid chickens') left vulnerable to the attacks of the Picts and Scots after the fall of Rome, and then rather ungratefully turned on their employers to conquer the island. Gildas had a thoroughly anti-Anglo-Saxon agenda and described the event in no uncertain terms in his *De excidio et conquestu Britanniae* (On the Ruin and Conquest of Britain): 'The means of destruction [the British kings devised] for our country [Britannia] was to admit the vile Saxons of nefarious name, despised by God and men, into the island, like wolves in the sheepfold, to drive back the northern nations.'[1] According to Gildas, these 'wolves' then set about slaughtering the Britons and leaving the country in ruins, and soon the place was overrun by countless ferocious immigrants.

However, while there can be no doubt that the large-scale arrival of the Germanic tribes changed the country forever, Gildas's version of events has been challenged by archaeology over the last century. The archaeologist Heinrich Härke estimates that 100,000–200,000 Germanic people migrated to Britannia but that they did so over the course of about a century, and wider archaeological evidence simply does not support Gildas's claims of widespread slaughter. While we cannot say for certain why the Anglo-Saxons came to Britannia, it seems that the immigrants settled relatively peacefully, establishing themselves as the new elite, and that the native Britons, by and large, simply adapted to this.[2]

The Germanic immigrants brought with them their own religious practices and pantheon, which in part explains the Christian Gildas's open hostility. We have to tread very carefully with the idea of pre-conversion religious practices, however. While we know that the early Anglo-Saxons worshipped Tiw, Woden and Thor (as the English names for Tuesday, Wednesday and Thursday memorialize), it is a grave error to assume that this meant that their religion was identical with the more familiar Scandinavian tradition of Germanic paganism. The pre-conversion Anglo-Saxons were illiterate and left no written account of their beliefs and practices, and the later Anglo-Saxon Church did its best to eradicate all trace of heathenism, leaving a gaping lacuna in our knowledge. In any event, as well as being foreign, Norse myths went unrecorded until the early thirteenth century, by which time the beliefs were no longer current, leaving Christian writers such as Snorri Sturluson to offer their own systemization of a complex and largely oral religion. It is dangerous to assume that these problematic Scandinavian records represent the earlier beliefs of the Anglo-Saxons. Though there are, nonetheless, remnants of Anglo-Saxon paganism in place names, a limited body of artefacts and literary allusions, the beliefs and practices specific to it remain a will-o'-the-wisp upon which we cannot rely.[3]

By far the biggest change in Anglo-Saxon England came in 597, when the missionary Augustine of Canterbury landed on Thanet, an island off the coast of Kent, following a long and arduous journey from Rome. Sent by Pope Gregory I – after he was shocked to learn that the beautiful Anglo-Saxon slaves he saw at a market were pagans, so folklore has it – Augustine slowly made inroads with the Kentish kings and established his monastery at Canterbury. The conversion of the English did not happen overnight but took centuries, and it is clear even from the late tenth-century writings of Ælfric of Eynsham that pockets of paganism survived long after Augustine's arrival. Within a couple of hundred years of the Gregorian mission, however, Anglo-Saxon England was predominantly Christian. In the early eighth century, Bede was able to write his *Historia ecclesiastica gentis Anglorum* (History of the English Church and People), which traced Anglo-Saxon history up to his day, from the migration through the conversion.[4]

What made the process of conversion especially tough for Augustine and those who succeeded him after his death in 604 was the fact that Anglo-Saxon England was by no means a unified country. It was divided between warring kingdoms, most notably Wessex, Mercia and Northumbria, which preserved their own unique identities and fought ferociously to expand their territories. There was no single ruler to demand the entire population change their religion, and individual kingdoms occasionally returned to their original beliefs long after their official conversion.[5] The Roman mission was helped, at first, by the Celtic Church, which sent its own missionaries to northern England to convert the kings of Northumbria, but disputes over the specifics of practice and observation led to a clash at the Synod of Whitby in 664, from which the Roman Church emerged triumphant.

The new religion brought with it learning. Christianity is a religion of the book, and monks were encouraged to read widely and ponder the Bible in exacting detail. While most Anglo-Saxons were illiterate, within a century of Augustine's arrival on Thanet, Anglo-Saxon England had produced a poet who was without doubt one of the best-educated men in Europe: Aldhelm, Abbot of Malmesbury (*c.* 639–709). Aldhelm was as au fait with Virgil as he was with patristic theology, and wrote witty and complex literature in Latin that still exercises scholars to this day. Aldhelm was also in frequent contact with people on the Continent, and this brings us neatly to another advantage of the new religion: intellectual networks. Christianity tuned the Anglo-Saxons into the latest developments of thought in Europe, and encouraged exchanges of books, ideas and outstanding individuals with distant nations. Although long-distance travel was very limited by modern standards, the minority of the Anglo-Saxon population who were able to visit Europe became so numerous that a permanent hostel, the Schola Saxonum, was established for English pilgrims in Rome. Anglo-Saxon England had a Greek Archbishop of Canterbury, Theodore of Tarsus, in the seventh century and produced scholars famous across the Continent for their learning in Aldhelm, Bede and Alcuin. Christianity's influence on the

Anglo-Saxon period also extended to language: although most people spoke versions of Old English, the corpus of Anglo-Latin texts positively dwarfs the surviving poetry and prose in the native tongue.

Anglo-Saxon England's fertile intellectual environment was disrupted in 793. That year, the Viking Age noisily began with the sack of Lindisfarne monastery. Opportunistic coastal raids developed over the coming decades into country-wide mass immigration and conquest, which ceased only after the campaigns of Alfred the Great, king of Wessex (*c.* 847–899). Alfred managed to defeat the so-called Great Heathen Army after severe early setbacks and forced the Viking leader Guthrum to sign the Treaty of Wedmore, which saw the latter baptized and permanently banished from Wessex. Although the Vikings were allowed to stay in a part of the country renamed the Danelaw, the period saw the first use of the term 'Anglo-Saxon' to describe the non-Scandinavian population.[6] Alfred set about re-educating the nation, whose libraries had been destroyed and religious observances disrupted by the Vikings. This effort involved translating Latin texts, including those of Boethius, Augustine of Hippo, Orosius and Bede, into Old English. Whether Alfred produced these translations himself or simply commissioned them is a matter of fierce debate. As well as making the texts available to a population whose grasp of Latin had severely diminished, Alfred was simultaneously investing his people with a new, collective identity based upon learning, building more successfully on Bede's attempts to create an 'English Church and People'. He signed charters using the title 'rex Angul-Saxonum' (King of the Anglo-Saxons) and further urged collective identity through his creation of the *Anglo-Saxon Chronicle*, which covered history from Julius Caesar's invasion of Britain onwards.[7] The first king of England as we would recognize him, however, was Alfred's grandson Æthelstan (*c.* 894–939), who conquered the Danelaw in the tenth century.

Æthelstan's good work was undone by the notorious King Æthelred (*c.* 966–1016), an impotent ruler whose tactic of paying off a new wave of Viking invaders every time they attacked unsurprisingly encouraged them to keep causing trouble. He was temporarily toppled by King Sweyn of Denmark, whose son Cnut took the throne in 1016 after Æthelred's son Edmund Ironside briefly succeeded his inept father. Æthelred's popular nickname, 'The Unready', is anachronistic. The sobriquet he was given was actually *unræd*, which means 'evil counsel', a pun on 'Æthelred', which translates to 'noble counsel'. Æthelred's seventh son, Edward the Confessor, succeeded Cnut's short-reigning sons, Harold Harefoot and Harthacnut, and died childless in 1066. Although Edward was later canonized, chastity was not a very becoming trait for a king, and the resulting confusion saw both a Saxon earl, Harold Godwineson, and the Duke of Normandy, William the Bastard (later known as 'the Conqueror'), claim to have been named heir to the throne. Harold seized the crown and braced himself for a Norman invasion through the summer of 1066. Inopportunely for poor Harold, the last Anglo-Saxon king, the Vikings proved once again to be a thorn in England's side, as the ferocious king of Norway, Harald Hardrada, invaded the north of England and disrupted Godwineson's plans to intercept William's army as soon as it landed. Shortly after a hard-won victory over a much larger army at Stamford Bridge, near York, Harold received the perhaps inevitable news that William had landed in Sussex. After marching around 320 kilometres (200 mi.) from Stamford Bridge to London in a matter of days, Harold hurriedly mustered a severely diminished, inexperienced army and met William at Senlac Ridge, near Hastings. Fatigue and ill-discipline cost the Anglo-Saxons the day, and Harold his life.

But Anglo-Saxon England did not quite end on 14 October 1066. Historians tend to give the year 1100 as the end of the period, by which time the Norman kings had firmly established their own hegemony. The *Anglo-Saxon Chronicle* continued to be updated until 1154, and Old English merged with Old Norman to create the new dialect Anglo-Norman. Many of our most important words come from Old English: love (*lufu*), king (*cyning*), church (*cirice*) and, perhaps most aptly for England itself, terms for the weather, such as *frost* and *sumer*. We also derive our legal system, parliament and most place names from the Anglo-Saxons: perhaps the xenophobic French rebuke *les Anglo-Saxons* isn't all that far wide of the mark after all.

Nature Red in Tooth and Claw

> All things, visible and invisible, still and unstill, take from that still and that constant and that single God order and appearance and regulation. And it was thus created because he knows why he created all that he created. Nothing that he created is useless to him.[8]

For the Anglo-Saxons, God's Creation was inherently perfect, because God made it. As the quotation above illustrates, nothing existed without God's permission, and nothing that he made was without purpose. This position was, of course, chiefly derived from the Bible, where Genesis 1:31 states that 'God saw all the things that he had made, and they were very good,'[9] but was buttressed by the musings of Church Fathers such as Augustine, Ambrose and Jerome. Having a predominantly agricultural economy, the Anglo-Saxons were well placed to witness the wonder of Creation at first hand, as seeds became plentiful crops and lambs grew into delicious, fat sheep according to the regular four seasons.

But though there could be no doubt that the world was perfect, at times this must have seemed an instance of the Lord working in mysterious ways. Life in God's Creation could be exceptionally hard. Part of man's punishment for original sin in Christian theology was the essentially tough nature of life, as Adam reflects in the Anglo-Saxon version of Genesis, *Genesis A*:

> How shall we two now live or exist in this land, if the wind comes here from west or east, south or north? A cloud will go up, a shower of hail will come, touching the sky, frost will go in its midst, it will be horribly cold. Sometimes heat will shine from the heavens, the bright sun will dazzle, and we two will stand here bare, unprotected with clothes.[10]

Part of the punishment for postlapsarian man – ordained, of course, by God – was to suffer bodily pain, illness, sadness and, ultimately, death. Though man's divinely prescribed punishment could not be questioned, it also could not be borne heroically by any but the most pious and detached.

Adam's lament in *Genesis A* about the natural world he must endure is an addition to the biblical story and demonstrates how the Anglo-Saxons interpreted man's punishment. More than any other early medieval culture, the Anglo-Saxons saw the natural world as hostile to mankind.[11] When they left a field fallow for a year, nature soon tried to take it over with weeds, saplings and thick vegetation; after ten years of neglect, a once fertile field would be near impossible to recover. Those same fields were at the mercy of the climate, which, though following a rough general plan, could spring the odd surprise drought or flood that could be the difference between life and death. Moreover, the climate of Anglo-Saxon England was not only colder and wetter than today's but suffered greater extremes of temperature, with disastrous consequences for even the most zealous and capable of farmers.[12] Sickness could strike a single domestic animal without warning and soon wipe out the entire herd. But it was not just crops and livestock that suffered under the yoke of original sin in Anglo-Saxon England. The vast majority of Anglo-Saxon edifices were constructed from wood: the verb to build, *getimbran*, literally meant 'to make of wood'. Only the most important buildings, such as churches and a few mead halls, were made of stone: Anglo-Saxon domestic architecture for most people consisted of a single-room dwelling that was subject to draughts, damp and rot, which a meagre wood fire could do little to ameliorate. This meant that inhabitants were rarely safe from the vicissitudes of the weather, and disease was subsequently common. Even communal buildings such as halls could survive only two or three generations with regular maintenance and repairs. Life, therefore, was a constant battle against the whims of nature.

The topography of the country was also much different from today's England of closely managed countryside and urban development. Although the idea of a country overrun with thick, primordial forest that the Anglo-Saxons had to clear has been widely disproved over the last fifty years, Anglo-Saxon England was still more wooded than today's landscape. Roughly 15 per cent of England was woodland, compared with 10 per cent today, and the nature of these areas was also significantly different.[13] On

The Great Hall at West Stow, a reconstructed Anglo-Saxon village.

average, the climate was 1°C warmer, despite the extremes of cold, which would have made woodland home to swarms of mosquitoes, probably carrying malaria (a menace that lingered even in nineteenth-century England).[14] Though the timber industry was a vital part of the Anglo-Saxon economy, it is not hard to see how a culture that felt in awe of nature's power over man would see vast woods such as The Weald as an imminent danger.[15]

Early medieval England was also characterized by large tracts of fen – another home for mosquitoes – which were not only intimidating for their lack of apparent human infrastructure but genuinely dangerous to the unwary traveller who strayed from the path. Though partially cultivated and drained in the seventh century, fens inspired enough fear to be associated with all manner of hostile and dangerous creatures. Moorland and mountains, for all our medical and navigational technology, still claim the lives of hikers under certain circumstances in the twenty-first century, and so we need not belabour how intimidating a jaunt across such terrain would have been to an Anglo-Saxon. Surrounding the hazardous island was the sea, perhaps the strongest expression of man's helplessness in the face of nature known to the Anglo-Saxons, which was simultaneously a vital means of communication and a source of food.

Anglo-Saxon England was home to large carnivores potentially hazardous to man, in the form of the Eurasian brown bear (*Ursus arctos arctos*) and the wolf (*Canis lupus*). While the brown bear is thought to have died out relatively early in the Anglo-Saxon period, if not before, the country's population did not know this, and doubtless old tales of terrifying ursine foes would have kept alive the looming threat of the bruin in the woods. We will discuss wolves in their own chapter, so for now we need only mention that the wolf was just as despised, feared and mythologized then as it is today. The secretive Eurasian lynx (*Lynx lynx*) may have existed on the fringes of Britain in a tiny population, and, despite looking

One of the 'Master of Animals' plaques from the Sutton Hoo purse-lid.

like a tubby moggy, the European wildcat (*Felis silvestris*) was widespread and potentially harmful if cornered. Other common creatures that posed a threat to life included the venomous common adder (*Vipera berus*), whose bite can kill if left untreated, and the wild boar (*Sus scrofa*), whose bulk, aggression and sharp tusks were braved for its delicious flesh.

Nature, then, to an Anglo-Saxon was a dangerous and openly hostile entity that would not baulk at killing you. Anglo-Saxon poetry shows an appreciation for the landscape only under very select circumstances, which we will discuss later in this book, and nature for the most part is feared and vilified. A startling illustration of this view was excavated at Sutton Hoo, Suffolk, in the form of a purse-lid. An exquisite seventh-century artefact of gold, garnet and millefiori glass, the lid was found in the famous Mound 1, the burial of an East Anglian king in a treasure-filled ship. Part of the artefact is composed of two identical plaques depicting a man between two canines.[16] The image is an ancient one known as the 'Master of Animals', which in ancient Mesopotamia represented a god with responsibility for man's success in hunting. Later in its development, the image morphed into a depiction of Daniel in the lion's den, miraculously saved from the voracious creatures by God.[17]

The Sutton Hoo Master, however, is far from the motif's dominant force: between the two animals, usually identified as wolves, his legs are restrained by the creatures' hind limbs and tails, their prominently clawed paws grasping towards his worried face. With their jaws agape, it is clear that the beasts are in the act of eating the unfortunate man. Analogues from Scandinavia of a similar period depict the Master fighting off the flanking beasts, in one case stabbing a bear through the stomach, but the overall impression of the Sutton Hoo example is of man's powerlessness in the face of overwhelming, hostile nature. The central figure, arms crossed in defensive posture, is positively dwarfed by the wolves. Despite the antiquity of the Master of Animals motif, this is a characteristically Anglo-Saxon rendering of the subject, and it makes a powerful statement about the danger and ferocity of nature.

Man's task, unambiguously, was to fight back against the natural world. Punishment or not, everyone in the postlapsarian world had to both survive and find salvation, rather than roll over and die unredeemed. So what on earth could the Anglo-Saxons do?

Order, Order

> [Medieval man] was an organizer, a codifier, a builder of systems. He wanted 'a place for everything, and everything in the right place'. Distinction, definition, tabulation were his delight . . . there was nothing which medieval people liked better, or did better, than sorting out and tidying up.[18]

Unable to defeat nature – it was, after all, God's punishment, foreordained long before any Anglo-Saxon was born – the Anglo-Saxon response was to learn, name, define and situate the hostile elements of the natural world. By identifying the natural order in their punitive habitat, they not only worked to see God's hand in everything but protected themselves from it: to name and to reckon something, after all, is to circumscribe its power. The Anglo-Saxons sought the inherent order in everything and saw the world as divided up into binary places.

After the coming of Christianity, the best example of this dividing impulse was the monastery. Copying Roman models, early medieval monasteries were surrounded by a *vallum*, an encircling wall or embankment that separated the sacred space within the enclosure from the profane without. Within the wall or embankment was a place where God was worshipped and contacted through prayer, and a graveyard for the elect permitted entry.[19] It is clear from Bede's *Historia* that the physical land could itself be made sacred by the work of man: when St Oswald dropped dead, the very ground that his holy body touched became inscribed with miraculous healing power.[20] The enclosure of a religious house was simultaneously a practical concern, protecting the cloistered monks from the diverting temptations of the world at large, but even within this limiting of access there was a philosophical message: only the elect, elevated over those excluded, had power over what lay within.

Perhaps the greatest philosophical contrast in the early medieval world was that between wilderness and civilization. The New Testament uses the image of the ideal city, the Heavenly Jerusalem, to depict heaven in the Book of Revelation, and in the early fifth century Augustine of Hippo adapted the motif for one of Anglo-Saxon England's favourite texts, *De civitate dei contra paganos* (Concerning the City of God against the Pagans). Augustine here was additionally influenced by the writings of ancient Greece and Rome, which contrasted the sophistication and finery of urban life against the pragmatic humdrum of rural existence: the derisive term 'pagan' actually derives from the Latin *paganus*, meaning 'country dweller'. Christianity was inseparable from civilization in the Roman Church, paganism from nature: most Christians had little regard for the natural world. Civilization, as represented by cities and towns, bore the stamp of man's power over the land

and imitated the Heavenly Jerusalem. Within the city you were protected from nature by both architecture and the presence of churches and holy men, but without you were very much on your own. Solidifying this contrast was the Anglo-Saxon habit of incorporating churches into city walls, making them a moral cordon protecting those within from the evil beyond the wall in a manner analogous to the monastery. Minor Anglo-Saxon settlements surrounded by ditches and banks of earth probably represent a smaller-scale attempt to divide civilization and wilderness.[21] To the traveller, too, cities and towns in the Anglo-Saxon landscape were a powerful visual image of civilization, contrasted to the surrounding wilderness, as preserved in an Old English proverb: 'cities are visible from far away . . . wondrous works of building-stones.'[22]

The profane and uncivilized, sacred and civilized, were intrinsically linked. An example of this way of thinking comes from the seventh-century *Life of St Wilfrid*, a biography of one of the key figures at the Synod of Whitby. During one of his numerous banishments from ecclesiastical office – Wilfrid did not suffer fools, or make friends, very often – the bishop is forced to travel to 'an area of Sussex which dense forests and rocky coast had saved from conquest by other kingdoms. Up to this time it had remained persistently heathen, and thither God, when all human aid failed, directed our good bishop's steps.'[23] Topography and profanity are inextricable: the land that Wilfrid encounters has remained heathen because of its physical characteristics. Just as nature could fight back against man, as Old English poems lamented of the Roman ruins dotting the landscape, so too could man fight back against nature, redefining a wilderness area as civilization. After converting the pagans of Sussex, Wilfrid founded Selsey Abbey, again linking the morality of people with their environment, as the physical appearance of the area was altered with the religious foundation, and wilderness turned to civilization.

Just as pagans had their place in the wilderness away from Christianity and civilization, so too did the animal kingdom. Animals were inextricably linked with certain habitats, characteristically far from the civilized centres of the Anglo-Saxon world. *Maxims* II, a collection of poetic aphorisms explaining the order of the world, locates fauna in their God-appointed habitat with a confidently imperative mood: 'the fish must be in the water, conceiving family . . . the bear must be on the heath, old and terrifying.'[24] *Maxims* II gives a comforting image of *stabilitas* in the world, especially in the case of the old bear haunting an uncivilized space. Though creatures might, occasionally, move away from their defining habitats, this was a temporary aberration, and even tamed wildlife, such as hawks, could not escape the part of their nature that yearned for their proper place in the world: 'birds of the woods, though they be well and thoroughly tamed, if they come to the trees in the middle of a copse, their teachers are quickly despised, though before they tamed and nourished them for a long time.'[25] God's ordered universe, in which everything had its rightful place, could only temporarily be disrupted.

The Anglo-Saxon world, then, was one of strict boundaries between binary states. Perhaps the most helpful way of visualizing this concept is to think – ignoring the anachronism – of a later Gothic cathedral. These astounding feats of medieval ingenuity were built on as grand a scale as possible, with many withstanding iconoclasm and the test of time to dominate today's European cities. Characteristically, the Gothic cathedral's exterior was bedecked with gargoyles and grotesques in the form of inconceivable beasts, hybrids, devils and sinful humans engaged in hideous acts. The great cost in financial and temporal terms hints at the important role of such carvings: they mark where the profane ends and the sacred begins. Notwithstanding the odd depiction of Hell as part of an Apocalypse wall painting, or a Judas getting his just deserts, within the thick walls of the cathedral only divine matters are permitted. The grotesque carvings huddle around the very boundary of the sacred centre, as if lusting to be permitted entrance. Although nothing on the scale of a Gothic cathedral existed in Anglo-Saxon England, the impulse to divide and define sacred and profane, Christian and pagan, civilization and wilderness was very much alive, as the body of surviving evidence attests.[26]

Another useful demonstration of the concept of boundaries, of people and things being in their proper place, comes from the evidence of charters. The Anglo-Saxons were zealous administrators, and their desire to impose order on the chaos of the postlapsarian world finds dogmatic expression in the legal organization of space. Anglo-Saxon charters, of which an astonishing 1,875 surviving examples are listed in the authoritative Sawyer catalogue, work to give the specific extent of private property in agonizing detail.[27] Many charters were bilingual, with the administrative rubric in Latin and the local, topographical detail in the Old English spoken by those who lived in the place described. To give but one abbreviated example, we have preserved the grant of twenty hides of land at Crediton, Devon, to Bishop Forthhere in 739:

> *of suran apuldran on grenan weg. of grenan wege on wulfpyt . . . of hlypan on byrccumbes heafod . . . of bradan aesce on fox-cumbes heafod . . . of caines aecere on wulfcombes heafod. þanon on stanbeorg . . . of swincumbe on egesan treow.*
>
> [the land extends] from the sour apple tree to the green way; from the green way to the wolf-pit . . . from the leap to Birch Combe Head . . . from the broad ash to Fox Combe Head . . . from Cain's Acre to Wolf Combe Head, thence to the stone-barrow . . . from Swine Combe to Egesa's Tree.[28]

This description of the land's boundaries in Old English offers an intriguing glimpse of how ordinary people viewed and defined the world around them. We have wild animals associated with a particular feature of the land, a barrow or burial mound that is worthy of note, a field associated for some reason with the fratricidal son of Adam and Eve, and individual trees. Landscapes were infused with different meanings from diverse sources, and this reminds us that the Anglo-Saxons experienced the physical world in a very different way to people in the twenty-first century. They moved through landscapes slowly, never experiencing a bird's-eye view of them, and without the benefit of signposts or maps had to use semi-mythical associations and features such as trees as mnemonics to orientate themselves.

One can only imagine how many more charters once existed. The picture we get of Anglo-Saxon England from the extant charter corpus is of a land bisected by complex boundaries and thresholds, controlling the movement of people across territories. Learning these boundaries was important: people from a certain settlement might have the right to gather sticks and kindling from a wood belonging to one landowner, but doing the same thing on land directly bordering it could result in a fine or physical harm. The ideological is never too far from the literal in these charters, and some even place curses on anyone who ignores the boundaries delineated. The overweening desire to keep people and things in their appointed places takes on a sinister aspect in the late seventh-century laws of King Ine of Wessex.

> If a man from afar or a foreigner goes through a wood apart from the highway and neither shouts nor blows a horn, because of this he is to be regarded as a thief, [and] either slain or held for ransom.[29]

Ine's laws exhibit a fear of boundaries being crossed, and it is no surprise that they continued to influence subsequent legal codes for the next few centuries.

A final aspect of physical boundaries that is important to mention is the use of earthen banks to designate territory. By far the most famous of these is Offa's Dyke, a great earthwork spanning part of the border between the Kingdom of Mercia and Wales. Though long assumed to be a military embankment, or an Anglo-Saxon version of Hadrian's Wall, since it was excavated by Sir Cyril Fox in the 1930s the consensus has been that the dyke was a purely ideological endeavour.[30] It has broad gaps between some sections; at around 103 kilometres (64 mi.) long, it is far too big to defend, and its height never exceeds 3.5 metres (12 ft). Instead, it is clear that the dyke was constructed to intimidate and subjugate those from outside Mercia. Dug entirely by hand, it is a monument to the formidable power of the Mercian king who ordered its construction (though Offa in the eighth century is assumed to have done so, there is no archaeological or contemporary written evidence to support this). The motive behind Offa's Dyke later found bourgeois expression in the great banks of earth surrounding late Anglo-Saxon estates, many of which can still be seen today and

A section of Offa's Dyke in Montgomery, Wales, seen from the English border in Shropshire, showing the ditch and embankment.

which once served not just to designate private property but as reminders of the serious repercussions for those who did not respect their boundaries.[31]

Of Monsters and Men

Borders and boundaries defined the Anglo-Saxon world-view, from the philosophical and theological epistemology of learned ecclesiastics to the serf trying to walk a short distance without prosecution. But within this very rigidity, the imagination of the Anglo-Saxons – their fears of a chaotic, threatening natural world – found room for the existence of monsters. Their own experience of natural phenomena and oral legends told them that the world was teeming with bizarre and usually deadly creatures they might never have seen but whose existence they had on good authority. Where civilized people did not dwell, wilderness prospered and provided a perfect home for monsters: the wilderness, symbolically charged with sin, paganism and the misanthropic values of the natural world, may have discouraged humans, but for this very reason it supported colonies of their adversaries, the monstrous races. Terrifyingly, the world had an awful lot of room for monsters to live in, without violating the idea of sacred and profane, civilization and wilderness. Even the most learned had travelled but a short way, perhaps as far as Rome or to the motherland of northern Europe on missionary work, and most people barely left the village in which they were born: 'that part of this world that men inhabit is very nearly a pin-prick compared to the rest', cautions the *Old English Boethius*, a tenth-century translation of Boethius' *Consolation of Philosophy*.[32] This was, indeed, fortunate: the Anglo-Saxons had to accommodate monsters from Christian and classical writings, those they had inherited from their pagan past, and even the bizarre creatures that were thought to roam Britannia long before the first hired sword crossed the North Sea.

Beyond symbolic motivations, the ascription of monsters to the wilderness came from a deep psychological source. Psychologists have found that biophobia, the fear of certain environments, is hard-wired into the human mind. We all have an instinct to fear thick woodland, for early in our evolutionary history this environment could conceal ambush predators such as big cats. Woodlands, in general, loom large in the human psyche and make us feel vulnerable, whether they are commercially managed timber businesses or the impenetrable slopes of the Carpathian Mountains. We have an inbuilt fear of such landscapes for the same reason that many people are born with a fear of snakes and spiders: natural selection favoured individuals with a healthy wariness of certain situations. Under test conditions, subjects in several studies display a marked dislike of visually restricted natural environments and a consequent preference for savannah-like landscapes such as golf courses, in which predators are unable to secrete themselves but where occasional shelter can be sought. Intriguingly, biophobia is far harder to treat than the culturally conditioned aversions related to modern life, such as live electrical wires or firearms. Pareidolia, the tendency to identify faces or patterns in inanimate objects, is a related evolutionary development that enabled humans to identify concealed danger. Seeing things that are not really there is most common in landscapes wherein we are instinctively afraid. Beyond the cultural associations of Christianity, therefore, defining the wilderness as the homeland of monsters satisfied one of mankind's primeval urges.[33]

There are two important definitions of monsters of which we know the Anglo-Saxons were aware, based on surviving manuscripts, library catalogues and citations. These came from Augustine of Hippo and Isidore of Seville, in texts that were among the most popular in Anglo-Saxon England. Augustine's influential discussion of monsters appears in *De civitate dei*:

> It is also asked whether we are to believe that certain monstrous kinds of men which history recounts are descended from the sons of Noah, or rather from that single man from which these men arose [Adam]? [For] it is attested that one type has an eye in the middle of its forehead . . . others do not have a mouth and only breathe through their nostrils . . . some have no head and their eyes in their shoulders . . . But it is not necessary to believe in all of these kinds of people that are said to exist. Truly, whoever is born a man anywhere – that is, a rational, mortal animal – however extraordinary to our understanding the form of the body he carries, or his colour or his movement or his sound, or whatever part or power or quality in his nature, no one of the faithful might doubt that he draws his origin from that single protoplast [Adam].[34]

In trying to decide whether certain races of monsters were, in fact, human, Augustine highlights rationality and ancestry as the deciding factors. His response to the question is circumscribed, but in refusing to rule out the possibility that certain things that look like monsters are actually human, Augustine opened up an intriguing line of thought that contributed to the Anglo-Saxon definition of the monster. Augustine's argument suggests that the boundary between man and monster was uncomfortably fluid, and this troubling possibility influenced how the Anglo-Saxons viewed monstrous creatures and even themselves.

The second source for monster lore comes in Isidore's encyclopaedic *Etymologiae*, written and compiled in the early seventh century. Taking a different approach, Isidore ponders the etymology of the word 'monster' in an attempt to uncover its true meaning, a common method of understanding the world in the medieval period. The Latin root of the word 'monster', *monstrare*, means 'to show':

> Varro says that portents are births that appear to have taken place contrary to nature: but they are not contrary to nature, because they are made by divine volition, for the nature of all things is the volition of the Creator. A portent, therefore, is not made contrary to nature, but contrary to known nature. Portents, signs, monsters [*monstra*] and prodigies are so-called because they are seen to portend and exhibit, show [*monstrare*] and predict things in the future . . . Just as there are certain monstrous people in single races, thus there are certain monstrous races in the whole of mankind, like Giants [*Gigantes*], Cynocephali, Cyclopes, et cetera.[35]

This definition carries several important implications for our discussion. First, Isidore argues on the basis of etymology that a monster is supposed to carry a message from God, who created them. That is, they are meant to tell, or de*monstra*te, something to us: Anglo-Saxon monsters, as we shall see, often carry a message in the form of a moral lesson or pose an unwelcome question for beholders. Second, adapting a line of discussion in Pliny the Elder's *Historia naturalis*, Isidore refuses to discount tales of monstrous creatures in nature on the basis that God is omnipotent and imperfectly understood by mankind. This line of thought – that nothing is impossible to God – explains why unusual creatures were reckoned among nature by the Anglo-Saxons. They had no concept of the supernatural, just God's inscrutable powers, and so many real creatures were explicitly defined as monsters. To an Anglo-Saxon reading Latin authors such as Virgil, Augustine and Pliny, there was just as much evidence for the existence of a basilisk or satyr as for a camel or elephant, and certainly enough unexplored land to accommodate them. Finally, Isidore makes it clear that monsters can occur as single instances in otherwise normal human races: as for Augustine, the troubling conclusion the Spaniard draws is that human birth does not guarantee the security of conventional humanity.

The specifics of Anglo-Saxon monsters, and how much these venerable sources influenced them, will become clear. In brief, however, Anglo-Saxon monsters fit a very strict taxonomy. They live only in the wilderness and both represent and define the values of this uncivilized space. They have strong associations in particular with paganism and the Devil. All are overwhelmingly hostile to man and civilization, and work to maintain the boundary between wilderness and civilization, monster and man, by killing or fleeing from people who enter their designated territory. They could equally be real or mythical creatures, and most posed uncomfortable questions for the Anglo-Saxons who obsessed over them.

By nature, the monster is a creature of margins, and it is therefore unsurprising that it looms so large in Anglo-Saxon thought and culture. The mighty pantheon of monsters fascinated monkish scholar and illiterate swineherd alike, whether challenging intellectual conventions or threatening the integrity and well-being of an isolated village. Lurking in the subconscious, they were feared and loathed in equal measure, and though considered physically far from centres of civilization, they often probed those divinely ordained boundaries. Over the course of this book we will discover how monsters operated in both the intellectual and physical realms, taking in the perceptions of both the learned and ordinary Anglo-Saxon as far as possible, and even consider some putative explanations for why creatures such as dragons, giants and incorporeal demons were thought to inhabit the local landscape.

In the first chapter, we will be travelling far from Anglo-Saxon England to the limits of the known world in the East. We will then return to the wild places of England to meet the wolf, an ordinary animal infused with monstrous characteristics. Chapter Three will do battle with the dragon or basilisk across the fields of literature and scripture and in local place names. We will then join the saints Cuthbert and Guthlac far from the warmth and peace of the mead hall to suffer the torments of local demons, before confronting the whale, the demon of the deep, on its home turf. Across two chapters, we will next face the disturbing questions posed by *Beowulf* of whether Grendel really is a monster, and how firm the boundary is between man and monster. To conclude, we will return from our voyage into the past to confront our own twenty-first-century monsters.

I
THE MAP MONSTERS

The Anglo-Saxons identified boundaries to understand the world around them. Just as Anglo-Saxon England was criss-crossed with borders of both physical and spiritual import, so too the Anglo-Saxons' place in the world was determined by geographical and ideological boundaries. The monster, as a symbol of anti-civilization, took on a key role in this process of national self-definition.

The Tradition of Map Monsters

'Map monsters' is the name we will use to describe the bizarre creatures thought to populate the furthest uncivilized reaches of the earth, marking where the known world ends. The tradition is ancient, dating back to the classical period of Greece and Rome. As both great civilizations pushed their dominions ever further beyond the visible horizon, it was vital to their imperial model of rule that Athens and Rome respectively remained both the seat of power and the definition of the cultural status quo. To achieve this, subjects living in each empire were governed by laws and codes of ethics enshrined at its distant capital. Native cultures were seen as inferior and their inhabitants defined as uncivilized, barbaric and lucky to have been conquered. Non-Greek and non-Roman gods, clothing, agriculture and technology were considered absurd, inefficient and, crucially, to pale in comparison to the correct imperial way of doing things. By this logic, the further someone lived from Athens or Rome, the stranger and more barbaric they and their homeland were.[1]

From this xenophobic mire came all manner of ludicrous and revolting creatures. Map monsters, by definition, lived at the eastern limits of the known world, and over the course of imperial history obligingly moved further from Athens and Rome as the respective empires conquered more lands and imperial boundaries expanded. The earliest descriptions of these monsters came in the writings of Ctesias (*fl.* fifth–fourth century BC). In some capacity, Ctesias found himself at the Persian court, and he set about writing a history of Persia and India. Like many later Westerners who travelled to 'the East', Ctesias was struck with wonder at more or less everything he saw, and was equally taken with the locals' strange customs and culture and the previously unheard of natural fauna, not all of which he encountered at first hand. He was the first Western writer to describe the fabled unicorn, manticore and numerous other strange monsters that were destined to play an important part in Western culture.

The king of map monsters was without doubt the Roman author Pliny the Elder (AD 23–79). Pliny was a philosopher and naturalist best known in the medieval period for his monumental work on the natural world, the *Historia naturalis*. Like the Anglo-Saxons, Pliny saw no difference between beasts that existed and monsters known only through well-placed sources, and in describing all manner of living things he tried to identify a purpose: 'in the contemplation of Nature nothing can possibly be perceived useless.'[2] Following the model of Ctesias and Megasthenes (*c.* 350–*c.* 290 BC), Pliny located his map monsters far from the civilized world of Rome in the conquered lands of the empire's uncivilized foreign subjects. Most importantly for our discussion, Pliny was key in transmitting the Greek writings of Ctesias and others on monsters to the

Latin-literate medieval West. Such is his role in the formation of the medieval monster canon that certain monsters, which we will meet presently, are sometimes called the 'Plinian races'. The Anglo-Saxons knew Pliny's work both directly and through quotations in works such as Isidore of Seville's *Etymologiae*.

The Graeco-Roman model of the civilized centre surrounded by inferior and inconceivably strange people and creatures was readily adopted by Christianity. We have already seen in the Introduction how Augustine of Hippo, a Roman by birth, constructed his magnum opus around the idea of a central Christian city populated by the elect, but in so doing he shifted the definitive civilized centre from Rome to Jerusalem. This had biblical precedent: 'but God is our king before ages: he hath wrought salvation in the midst of the earth [Jerusalem]' (Psalms 73:12).[3] Jerusalem was seen as the geographical and spiritual centre of the world, surrounded by uncivilized lands that only worsened, and gave home to more monsters, the further from the Holy City they were located. As such, the original Greek and Roman model was adapted slightly to place greater emphasis on the heathen nature of the inferior places where monsters and savages roamed. The ease with which the centre of the earth was re-established as Rome as the Catholic Church increased in power through the early Middle Ages hardly needs stressing.

The 'Far East', the furthest known point from Jerusalem and Rome, was thought to be radically, almost ineffably, different. This is clear from Augustine's musings on geography: 'if you divide the world in two parts, East and West, Asia will be in one, Europe and Africa in the other.'[4] Knowing that Jerusalem and, beyond that, Asia, lay in the East allowed Western culture to situate itself both geographically and spiritually. The modern verb to 'orient' oneself comes from the placement of church altars to face east, in the direction of sunrise and towards the part of the world once commonly called 'the Orient'.

Defining the furthest eastern fringes of the world as radically different, barbarous and the home of monsters characterized Western thought from the time of Ctesias onwards, through medieval texts about monsters to Marco Polo to the East India Company. In the words of the pioneering post-colonial scholar Edward Said, 'the Orient was almost a European invention, and had been since antiquity a place of romance, exotic beings, haunting memories and landscapes, remarkable experiences.'[5] The Anglo-Saxons and other cultures throughout the Middle Ages knew that 'the East' was different, and learning about what, allegedly, made it different allowed them to define and assert their own 'superior' culture. Focusing chiefly on three crucial texts discussing map monsters, we will now find out what the Anglo-Saxons thought they were not.

The Wonders of the East

By and large, Old English texts are unique, preserved in a single manuscript with, at best, faint echoes in other texts that some academics spend their careers trying to prove show a wider audience than just the scriptorium that committed it to vellum. However, we have an astonishing three extant manuscripts of the prose text known to modern scholars as *The Wonders of the East*. The text is a description of the strange animals, monsters and peoples native to the uncivilized wastes of the East that Ctesias and Megasthenes would have recognized. Equally remarkable is that each of these manuscript versions is illustrated, another rarity in Old English texts. That *Wonders* survives in three separate illustrated versions is an essential piece of evidence for the Anglo-Saxon obsession with monsters.

It is crucial to contextualize any medieval text within the manuscript in which it is contained, in order to determine something about how it was supposed to be read. In the case of *Wonders*, our oldest version is contained in the late tenth- to early eleventh-century Nowell Codex, named after a former owner and also known as the '*Beowulf* manuscript'. The Nowell Codex is the second of two codices that make up the manuscript known as Cotton MS Vitellius A XV. This Old English version of *Wonders* sits alongside a mixture of prose and poetic items in a manuscript whose assembly has been convincingly attributed to the compiler's interest in monstrosity, and where it is the only illustrated item.[6] We will be discussing or referring to all of the texts contained in the *Beowulf* manuscript over the course of this book. The next manuscript, Cotton MS Tiberius B. V, Part I, was produced in the mid-eleventh century and contains both a Latin and an Old English version of the text, with additional marvels not found in Vitellius. There is no direct relationship between the Vitellius and Tiberius versions, and the illustrations too are independent, suggesting that the *Wonders* text was more popular than even the surviving versions can evidence. Cotton Tiberius B. V offers a vastly different context for *Wonders*, for the other texts bound with it include a variety of scientific, ecclesiastical and geographical material, which suggests that it was deemed an important and factual description of the East. The final manuscript, MS Bodley 614 (in the Bodleian Library, Oxford), dates from about 1120–40 and is based on both the text and images of the Tiberius version.[7] In a sign of the times, however, the Old English text has gone altogether and only the Latin remains, reflecting the victorious Normans' attempts to quash the culture of Anglo-Saxon England. The Bodleian manuscript places *Wonders* alongside a church calendar and a treatise on astronomy, again suggesting the reverence in which this catalogue of 'Oriental' monsters was held.

With these contexts in mind, we can begin our exploration of the East. In line with the contexts of the two later manuscripts, the text itself clearly has aspirations to accuracy, presenting the marvels in a cold, factual manner and including extraordinarily precise geographical measurements for an unknown region. We begin in Antimolima (a place that has never been identified but which is possibly a corruption of Antioch), located '168 of the lesser measurement called *stadia*, and 115 in the greater called *leuuae*' from Babylon, whose chief wonders would not have been inconceivable to the Anglo-Saxon reader: 'there are rams as big as oxen born there.'[8] The Anglo-Saxons farmed both sheep and cows, and so while they would never have seen a sheep of such great size, the giant rams of Antimolima would not have been unimaginable. The accompanying illustrations of the creatures in Tiberius and Vitellius therefore seem a waste of valuable ink. Proceeding further from Antimolima, we get to the first proper wonder, in a place called Lentibelsinea: 'there are hens born there, like those with us, of a red colour. And if someone wishes to catch them or touches them, then they will immediately burn up all his body. That is unheard-of witchcraft.'[9] Like the sheep, the hens' appearance would be familiar to the Anglo-Saxons, but once again there are what seem initially to be pointless illustrations of the creatures in Tiberius and Vitellius to help readers recall what a chicken looks like. The illustration of the burning hen in Vitellius, however, is troubling on closer inspection. Whereas the sheep were depicted snugly within illustrative borders, the Vitellius chicken is only enclosed by a border on three sides. The border, where it exists, has a charred, blackened appearance, and the bird's glorious tail even brushes the text describing it, threatening to burn that up, too.[10] This chicken, in effect, challenges the very borders and text intended to delimit it, just as the *ungefregelicu lyblac* (unheard-of witchcraft) that gives it its curious nature resists easy categorization and understanding. The burning hens exist beyond the physical boundaries of Anglo-Saxon England, and beyond the borders of Anglo-Saxon learning, in equal measure.

Another possible reason for the illustrator deciding to depict rather mundane-looking livestock is to remind the reader of what is normal, for we are swiftly on to weirder things in the next marvel as we move yet further away from the civilized known world. The next marvels are simply called *wildor*, a generic noun meaning 'wild beasts', which have eight feet, two heads and *wælkyrian eagan* (valkyrie eyes).[11] The reader here must use their imagination to conceive what these monsters look like, since the accompanying Tiberius and Vitellius illustrations offer no help whatsoever by depicting what appear to be a couple of dogs standing one in front of the other. The *wildor* remind us again of the importance of physical and epistemological boundaries to the Anglo-Saxon mindset. Not content with just living in the uncivilized places far from men, these beasts are the first of many we will encounter that actively participate in the maintenance of this dual-purpose boundary: 'when they hear a man's voice, they flee without hesitation.'[12] Like the hens, too, the *wildor* will set fire to anyone who tries to touch them, and their elusiveness is indicated in the Vitellius illustration by another imperfect boundary, which allows them to leer with protruding tongues at the surrounding text.

From this point on, the marvels come thick and fast as we make our way progressively further from civilization. Notably odd are the red and black ants as big as dogs, who use their grasshopper-feet to dig up gold. The method of hunting them is appropriately absurd:

> Those men who are brave enough to take that gold take with them male camels and females with their foals. They tie up the foals before they cross over the river. They pack that gold on the females and sit on them themselves and leave the males there. When the ants find them, and while the ants are busy with the males, then the men cross over the river with the females and the gold.[13]

Interestingly, the monstrous gold-mining ants are far more conceivable to the Anglo-Saxons than the camels. To them, this account describes how an aberration of a familiar animal is lured

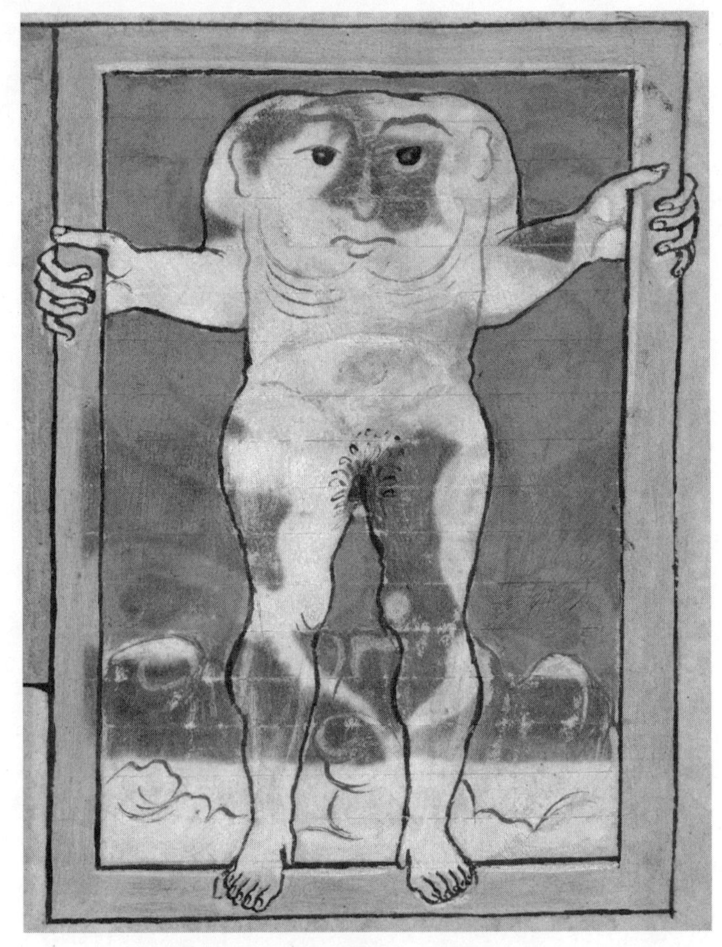

Blemmyae, Cotton Tiberius B. V, Part I, f. 82.

and robbed by one they have also never seen. The method of stealing the gold is utterly baffling – what is the point of bringing the foals, and how does the females' maternal state protect them from the ants? – but represents another instance of the East being, quite literally, another world, and full of strange people.

The East of *Wonders* is crawling with map monsters, many of which were discussed earlier by Pliny, including the Blemmyae, who reappear, unnamed, in the *Wonders*: 'Then there is another island south from the Brixontes on which men are born without heads, that have their eyes and mouth on their breasts. They are eight feet tall and eight feet wide.'[14] The Blemmyae diverge radically from norms concerning the human body. Although there is no detail given about their ferocity towards people or particular sinfulness, the weirdness of the creature's body would have been particularly horrific to the Christian audience reading *Wonders*. They have the requisite human parts, just not arranged in the normal manner. In Genesis 1:26, when God makes man, he states: 'Let us make man to our image and likeness.' Any deviation from the norm of the human body was deemed an abomination, and certain Anglo-Saxon law codes prescribed bodily mutilation as a permanent punishment for criminals. The Tiberius Blemmyae is a particularly disturbing illustration, its slightly conceited smirk almost inviting the disgust of the reader. It is depicted as a biped, albeit with its recognizably human face in its breast, and with human hands it grips around the back of the frame that is supposed to contain it, as if the illustrator's attempt to confine it was but an illusion. The Blemmyae walks the boundary between what is human and what is monstrous, and the Tiberius illustration clearly shows how futile such a distinction may be in practice.[15]

Another apparently physically harmless Plinian map monster is the Panoti:

> East from thence there are men born that are fifteen feet long and ten feet broad in size. They have large heads and ears like fans. At night they spread one ear under them, and cover themselves with the other. Their ears are very light and their bodies are as white as milk. And if they see or are sensible of a man in those lands, then they flee with their ears in their hands and depart so speedily that someone might suppose that they flew.[16]

The Panoti is also a monster that flees from men, as if trying to maintain the firm boundary between them. Although called 'men' by the *Wonders* author, their enormous sleeping-bag ears are another corruption of God's design for the human body. Perhaps also, their desire to maintain a firm boundary between human and monster is because they are conscious of the confusing boundaries themselves: after all, an eight-legged, valkyrie-eyed beast could hardly be mistaken for a human, but a jet-heeled, jug-eared coward like the Panoti might well be, and so they may equally wish to avoid the confusion of seeing a similar creature to themselves too close for comfort.

And what of the explicitly human inhabitants of the East in *Wonders*? In accordance with the Anglo-Saxon paradigm of uncivilized people in profane, monstrous places, they are almost all far removed from the status quo of Christendom:

> In a certain land men are born that are six feet long in length. They have beards to the side of their knees and the hair of their heads to their heels. They are called Homodubii, that is, 'doubtful ones', and they live off the raw fish that they eat.[17]

The Homodubii are particularly disturbing because they subvert Anglo-Saxon norms. Though they are not given an illustration, there is no mention of clothes, and their unkempt and scruffy appearance suggests a wildness: long hair and a beard symbolize a lack of cultivation that went very much against what we know of Anglo-Saxon grooming habits. They are doubly uncivilized for their diet of raw fish, which again was not the done thing in Anglo-Saxon England. Defining people as uncivilized on the basis of diet is a relic of the cultural hegemony imposed by the Greek and Roman empires, and as late as the colonial period in the West it was being used to justify the brutal treatment of conquered subjects.[18] If we follow the Anglo-Saxon logic here, however, these hirsute pescatarians are just the sort of odd and barely human inhabitants one would expect to share the uncivilized world with monsters and strange beasts.

Monsters are often read allegorically as signs of something else, based on the tradition advanced by Isidore. Though some Old English scholars have tried to define all the monsters of *Wonders* as each providing a moral lesson for readers, it is hard to see quite what the *wildor* or dog-sized ants have to tell us, beyond how uncivilized their homeland must be, or God's inconceivable power over Creation and ability to make whatever he pleases. The more human wonders, however, do carry another more pertinent message. Take, for example, the monstrous Hostes:

> Beyond the River Brixontes, east from thence, men are born long and great that have feet and shanks twelve feet long, sides with chests seven feet long. They are black of colour and are named Hostes. As certainly as they seize a man, they consume him.[19]

The Hostes live beyond one natural boundary, the River Brixontes, and strive to protect another, the boundary between man and monster, by devouring anyone who strays into their territory. While the Panoti and valkyrie-eyed beasts are content to re-establish the boundary separating them from men further afield by fleeing, the Hostes go one step further, eliminating any memory of a trespassing human altogether by devouring him and defending their territory in the process. Again, however, they are called 'men', but their size, colour and cannibalism equally show them to be more monster than human, along with what is implied by their habitat. Eating what are effectively guests in your homeland is not a very Christian act, and cannibalism is of course a taboo that goes far beyond Christianity. Their immoral manner of defending the boundary between man and monster demonstrates conclusively on which side they lurk, and cautions readers that such transgressive behaviour will force them into the ideological land of the Hostes.

Other humans living in the East include pagan sun-worshippers and a group simply called *ða wyrstan men ⁊ þa ellreordigestan* (the worst and the most barbarous people),[20] without any specific crimes being listed; their homeland, it seems, is enough to define them as such. The most subversive of people however live even further away than the pagans and *þa ellreordigestan*:

> Around that place women are born, that have beards down to their breast, and have made their garments from horse's hides. They are named great huntresses, and in the place of hounds they nourish tigers and leopards that are the fiercest of beasts. And they hunt all the kinds of wild beasts that are born on the mountain.[21]

The huntresses seem, for all intents and purposes, human, and yet they confound the accepted forms of difference between men and women in the early Middle Ages. They have beards, an otherwise masculine trait and thus a corruption of God's design for human beings. Hunting in the Anglo-Saxon period was another characteristically male activity that women seem not to have indulged in, and so such behaviour would have been deemed strange and unnatural. Their ability to tame and train *kenestan deor* (the fiercest of beasts) perversely suggests that they are stronger than Anglo-Saxon men. Their clothing is also uncivilized, but what is perhaps the greatest threat to the accepted order of things is the apparent absence of men where the huntresses live. Though we are told that the huntresses are born (*akenned*), the dearth of men asks serious and disturbing questions about how they are conceived and brought into this world. After all, only God was known to impregnate women without mortal male involvement. The Tiberius huntress has more than a suggestion of masculinity, with a long jet-black beard dangling over her exposed breastless chest. She stands alone, feeding her hunting cats in an arid, rocky wilderness. In deviating from nature and what was thought to define the male and female genders, these women are monstrous and very much at home in the East, far from the secure world of Anglo-Saxon England.

The *Letter of Alexander to Aristotle*

By and large, *Wonders of the East* is a dispassionate catalogue of wondrous things and creatures that live in the 'Orient'. The *Letter of Alexander to Aristotle*, however, offers a withering, markedly colonial view of the lands of the East. As its title suggests, the *Letter* purports to be a missive sent by Alexander the Great to his former tutor, the great philosopher Aristotle. Although clearly fictional, the *Letter* is based on a grain of truth, for Aristotle was indeed Alexander's tutor, and it was actually the philosopher who encouraged the king to expand his empire east and to treat 'the barbarians as a despot but the Greeks as a leader'.[22] The Old English version is a translation of a lost Latin original, and survives without illustrations in a single manuscript, the Nowell Codex of Cotton Vitellius A XV, which also contains the older version of *Wonders*. It is widely accepted that the text was included in Vitellius on the basis of the monsters it describes in great detail.

In the *Letter*, Alexander describes his voyage of conquest and discovery in India. Like *Wonders*, with its arbitrarily precise units of measurement, the text attempts to anticipate any potential scepticism among its readers, however unlikely, at the beginning, with Alexander noting that 'I would not have believed the declarations of any man that so many wonderful things might be before I myself saw them with my own eyes.'[23] Immediately, the Anglo-Saxon reader is alerted to the fact that the *Letter* will push the limits of credulity, but they have the word of a famous king who empathizes with their own possible scepticism across the centuries, and moreover an individual who claims, earlier in the *Letter*, to have taught the great Aristotle about astronomy in previous correspondence.

After the epistolary preamble, Alexander launches into a description of his crushing victories over King Darius of Persia and King Porus of 'Fasiacen'. At this stage, on the limits of Western geographical knowledge, the sole wonders described are *feower hund elpenda* (four hundred elephants) that are captured – monstrous creatures known only by repute to an Anglo-Saxon.[24] Alexander is also very taken with Porus' beautiful palace and soon decides to explore the further parts of India, but is given a dire warning by the locals at the Caspian Gates: 'we should ourselves take heed of the various kinds of serpents and ferocious wild beasts, lest we come upon them. Many live in the downs and valleys and woods and fields, and hide themselves in holes in the rocks.'[25] These topographical features were all familiar to the Anglo-Saxons as uncivilized places where monsters were known to live, with the exception of 'fields', which perhaps suggests the inherent, overwhelming wildness and monstrosity of the region. Alexander is not to be dissuaded, and intends also to find and kill King Porus, who has evaded capture after being defeated, before he can *on þa westenu middangeardes gefluge* (flee to the wildernesses of the middle-earth).[26]

It is some time before monsters make their appearance. Alexander first details the organization of the expedition, battles with dehydration and enforced urine-quaffing, and an encounter with people living at the edge of the uncivilized part of the known world. Appropriately, the people are *healf nacode* (half-naked) and behave like the beasts of *Wonders* by fleeing as soon as they catch sight of Alexander and his enormous army. Giving chase, unfortunately, requires Alexander's men to swim across a river full of monsters:

> A great number of water-monsters [*nicras*] appeared, larger and fiercer in their aspect than the elephants, that plunged the men in the midst of the waves of the water to the bottom of the river and tore and bloodied them with their mouths and destroyed them all, so that none of us knew where any of them had gone.[27]

These water-monsters, clearly hippopotamuses, are defending the natural boundary from men. While the half-naked Indians are content to flee, the hippopotamuses obliterate any trace of men ever having breached their boundary. Although the text is describing a real animal, the noun applied to them, *nicras*, is a catch-all term for enormous monsters that live in any body of water, which demonstrates again why real animals and monsters were conflated in the Anglo-Saxon mindset: a monstrous, carnivorous beast that lived in water known by hearsay must be along the same lines as those known to live around the British Isles.

Nature in India is unspeakably hostile and dangerous, and gets still worse the further the Greek army travels from the West. In search of fresh water on the same day as the hippopotamus encounter, Alexander and his army are constantly attacked by 'lions and bears and tigers and leopards and wolves'.[28] When they finally find water and make camp, Alexander tries in vain to counter the terror of the land: 'I also commanded that fires be kindled from the trees that had been felled . . . I did this so that if something unknown came to us we had light and help from the fire.'[29] We can picture here the same action being taken by travellers back in Anglo-Saxon England, fearful of what was lurking in the wood in which they were compelled to spend the night. Unfortunately, as comforting as the presence of the great fire must have been, the place is still the uncivilized home of monsters, not men, and the army is beset by scorpions and the multitude of serpents they were warned of back at the Caspian Gates. The link between monsters and their environment is literal when Alexander describes how the land itself took on the behaviour of the serpents: 'all of that land sounded [*hleoðrade*] with the hissing of the serpents.'[30] Further serpents of different kinds come, including some resembling dragons or basilisks: 'the breath and breathing of the serpents was extremely deadly and poisonous, and many men died because of their pestiferous breath.'[31] Like the bad-breathed serpents, the land itself later emits a poisonous vapour. Further beasts defying the accepted rules of nature launch their attack, including bull-sized lions and bats with human teeth.

Another beast familiar to us, but unequivocally a monster to the Anglo-Saxons, makes an appearance at the dreaded watering hole, and its behaviour is comically aggressive:

> Suddenly there came an exceedingly great wild beast bigger than any other thing. That wild beast had three horns on the front of its head and was terrifyingly armed with the horns. The Indians call that wild beast *dentes tyrannum* [teeth tyrant]. That wild beast had a head like a horse and was black of colour. When this wild beast had drunk the water, it saw our camp, and suddenly charged at us and our camp. It did not hesitate because of the burning flames and the heat of the fire that faced it, but it went and walked over everything . . . it at once slew 26 of my thanes in one charge, and trampled 52 . . . with great trouble we shot it with arrows and also with long-shafted spears, and slew and killed it.[32]

This creature – a rhinoceros, of course – is indubitably a monster. It is bigger than even the hippopotamuses from the earlier river, fears neither man nor man's technology, and its strange body is equipped with horns in an unnatural place quite different from the horned beasts known to the Anglo-Saxons, such as sheep, cows and deer. Moreover, it does not make any attempt to eat anyone at the camp, and so its brief moment of thought after spying the men suggests that it is motivated entirely by malice and the desire to buttress the physical boundary between man and monster, civilization and wilderness.

Alexander's journey through the Indian wilderness also takes in a battle with savage people who inhabit the land in isolated pockets, and who behave in a manner similar to the various monsters that also live in the uncivilized realm. On the literal level, the *Letter* tells of a European bringing culture and civilization to a world badly in need of it, a process lamentably to be repeated and celebrated countless times over the coming centuries. But is Alexander the right man to bring civilization to the savage ends of the earth?

A strong case can be made for the text taking a very dim view of Alexander.[33] In the first instance, he is a pagan and not only sets up graven idols of Hercules and Bacchus but, at the end of the text, prays at a *godcundan bearo* (divine grove).[34] Worship at sacred groves is one of the few facts about Insular paganism that we can glean from Anglo-Saxon sources; whether this was true or an invention of the Christians who wrote the descriptions is unimportant, as it was clearly deemed factual.[35] To an Anglo-Saxon concerned with all manner of boundaries, the line drawn between paganism and Christianity was one of the most important, and Alexander, in occupying the wrong side of the threshold, would not have been received in a positive fashion. Alexander is also markedly cruel to his guides: after the hippopotamus debacle, he throws 150 of them into the river, and they are promptly eaten. He similarly blames the remaining guides for the night of the serpents, and organizes a particularly grisly execution: 'I ordered my guides to be bound and their bones and legs broken . . . and also that their hands be cut off,' before leaving them to be eaten alive by the serpents on their way to the watering hole.[36] Equally, he is monstrously proud of his achievements and rages at a perceived slight in the most obnoxious terms: 'my power stretches from the east of the middle-earth to the west, and now these senile barbarians are insulting me.'[37] This negative portrayal of Alexander probably comes from the Roman historian Orosius, whose early fifth-century *Historiae adversus Paganos* (History against the Pagans) was an important and widely read source in Anglo-Saxon England. From Orosius, the Anglo-Saxons knew Alexander as a tyrannical megalomaniac whose vainglorious campaigns caused widespread suffering.

Arrogant, cruel and pagan, Alexander is not a suitable representative of the civilized West to conquer the East. Alexander's success in India should perhaps not come as such a surprise, therefore. Pagans and savages are the only humans who live in that fetid, uncivilized land alongside ferocious monsters, and Alexander is very much at home among them. The monsters he fights and usually slays work to ask questions of the king's worthiness and even humanity, and ultimately they have the last laugh in showing him not only to be at ease among them, but perhaps even one of their number.

Liber monstrorum

The *Liber monstrorum* (Book of Monsters) is one of the most astonishingly learned monuments of Anglo-Saxon literature. Across its three books, the *Liber monstrorum* demonstrates thorough knowledge of Lucan, Virgil, Pliny, Greek mythology and Christian theology in producing its catalogue of around 120 different monstrosities. Based on orthography, we can identify the *Liber monstrorum* as the work of an Englishman or Irishman living in England between about 650 and 750.[38] It was immensely popular in its time and survives in five manuscripts from the ninth and tenth centuries. The wealth of references all indicate that whoever wrote *Liber monstrorum* had access to the same library as Aldhelm of Malmesbury, and a case can even be made for Anglo-Saxon England's first great poet himself being the author.[39] In its manuscript contexts, *Liber monstrorum* tends to appear alongside classical Latin literature, suggesting the esteem in which it was held.

Like *Wonders of the East* and the *Letter of Alexander*, the *Liber monstrorum* is characterized by the Anglo-Saxon obsession with boundaries and with things being in their proper, ordained place:

> You have asked about the secret placement of the lands of the earth and if as many types of monsters are to be believed as are shown in the concealed parts of the world, suckled through the deserts [*desertum*] and the islands of the Ocean and in the lairs of the most distant mountains.[40]

Liber monstrorum makes it clear at the outset that it will chiefly be concerned with map monsters, those that lurk in distant, uncivilized places, or *occulto orbis terrarium* (the hidden parts of the world). The author has even given some thought to the impact civilization's expansion has had on monsters:

> Now the human race has multiplied and the lands of the earth have been filled, under the stars fewer monsters are brought forth, and we read that in very many of the angles of the earth they have been totally rooted out and destroyed by them, and now, plucked out from the shores, they are hurled violently down to the waves.[41]

Monsters and civilized men cannot live together, and the encroachment of one on the territory of the other will naturally lead to corresponding depopulation. As we saw in *Wonders* and the *Letter*, the monsters themselves seem happy with the arrangement keeping them from people, and preserve their boundaries by running away from interlopers, killing them or simply devouring them whole.

As we would perhaps expect, however anachronistically, of a work of such formidable learning, *Liber monstrorum* exhibits a marked scepticism not seen in *Wonders* or *Letter*: 'only certain things in these wonders are believed true.'[42] Despite establishing a rational distance from the topic of monsters, however, the author is soon discussing wonders he has himself seen: 'Truly I attest in the beginning of this work that I was acquainted with a human being of both genders who appeared more virile than feminine in their face and breast . . . but loved female activities and beguiled ignorant men in the way of a prostitute.'[43] By modern standards, this gender-ambiguous individual would certainly not be reckoned a monster, but, as we have previously discussed, the disorder of the human body was seen as sinful, for it corrupted man made in the image of God. Like the female huntresses of *Wonders*, what makes this person monstrous is their defiance of the normal order of things: clothed, this person looked like a man, yet 'loved female activities' and, it was assumed, had female genitalia. This monstrosity, which presumably lived among men, violated the sacred boundaries that exist to differentiate men and women, led others into sin and thus challenged the integrity of the Anglo-Saxon world-view.

Though *Liber monstrorum* does not operate on the same geographical lines as *Wonders* and the *Letter* – that is, with a steady progression across the world marked by a consequent increase in the weirdness of the monsters described – an equivalent intensification of oddities does characterize the monstrous races of Book One. The first monster mentioned is one known to the author, presumably from England or Ireland, and those immediately following are of either incredible stature or, in the case of the people with six digits on their hands and feet, disfigured. From these sufferers of polydactyly we arrive immediately at hybrids, including fauns, sirens and hippocentaurs. That these classical oddities are listed alongside instances of deformity is revealing: clearly, the boundary between humans and monsters was not as firm as we would like to think, and for the author an extra finger made one monstrous as much as did goat legs or a fish's lower half.

Although there is no direct link between the *Wonders*, *Letter* and *Liber monstrorum*, the last lists many of the same monsters as the other texts in its Book One, suggesting that the author worked from similar source material. We see again our old friends the Blemmyae, the Panoti and hairy fish-eaters. Another monster mentioned in *Liber monstrorum* that was to prove popular throughout the Middle Ages is the Sciapod:

> And they report there is a race of men that the Greeks call Sciapods because, lying flat, they defend themselves from the brightness of the sun by the shadow of their feet. Truly they are of a very fast nature. They have only a single leg for their feet and their knees harden in an inflexible fastening.[44]

This description of the Sciapod is worth quoting in full, as it is a classic map monster. Mentioned in Pliny's *Historia naturalis*, it lives on the edge of the civilized world, has peculiar habits, and its bizarre physiognomy defies all logic. It would not have taken a sophisticated understanding of anatomy to know that a one-legged man would be anything but fast-moving, and yet the peculiar Sciapod is noted for its pace. The Sciapod offers nothing in the way of a moral message beyond being a corruption of the perfect image of man but, like most of the map monsters we have described, stood as a symbol for the danger and weirdness of the East, which is best defined for our purposes as Where Anglo-Saxon England Wasn't.

Book Two of the *Liber monstrorum* contains descriptions of beasts unfamiliar to an Anglo-Saxon, including everything from the tiger to the hippopotamus and fearsome Chimera, in line with the Anglo-Saxons' incorporation of monsters into the natural world. The description of a rhinoceros is particularly interesting as it gives a short precis of Alexander's encounter with it, and the author is under the impression that it was a single beast that no longer exists: 'there was besides a certain beast in the boundaries of India . . . Alexander, when 26 soldiers were dead, at length penetrated it with hunting-spears [and] killed it.'[45] One can hardly blame *Liber monstrorum*'s author for thinking that the gigantic triple-horned *dentes tyrannum* was a one-off. Book Three is a description of serpents, from the snakes that attacked Alexander in India to the Hydra of classical literature.

The *Liber monstrorum*, then, is a vast and informative catalogue of monsters, a category that for its author included deformed humans, exotic beasts and serpents of varying kinds. It was written by someone who was not only extremely well read but clearly preoccupied with their subject, given the obscurity of some of the sources they cite for certain beasts. Despite the text being peppered with sceptical comments, the author has thought long and hard about the monsters and their rightful place in the world, and does not dismiss all of the absurd creatures they describe as falsehoods. For the author, monsters – notwithstanding the odd physical aberration like the hermaphrodite, which Isidore mentions can occur in otherwise normal races of men – live by nature away from people in the hidden and unpleasant parts of the world, marking where the civilized world ends, and, crucially, they stay there.

Man and Monster: The Cynocephalus

Of all the map monsters, one stands head and shoulders above the rest as the most popular and well evidenced in the Anglo-Saxon world-view. This is a beast known as the Cynocephalus, or 'doghead', and the near-identical creatures called Conopenae. These are very much beasts of the East and are discussed in all of the texts we have examined in this chapter. *Wonders* details a colony living in southern Egypt: 'also there are born Half-Dogs [*healfhundingas*] that are called Conopenae. They have horses' manes, wild boars' tusks and dogs' heads, and their breath is like the flame of a fire.'[46] The Conopenae and Cynocephali were thought to be monstrous hybrids of human and canine: they had the body of a human but the head of a dog. In the *Letter* they receive only a customary mention, perhaps relying on the reader's existing knowledge of what they looked like, but are described as markedly more dangerous than their Egyptian cousins and as living in the woods, a notoriously monstrous habitat.

> Then after that we saw between the woodland groves and trees a great multitude of Half-Dogs [*healfhundinga*] that came because they wished to wound us. And we shot them with arrows, and they soon fled away and went again to the woods.[47]

The *healfhundingas* of India have a monstrous, anti-human nature to match their monstrous outward appearance. In the *Liber monstrorum* they get several mentions, both as Cynocephali and Conopenae:

> Cynocephali are asserted to be born in India, which have dogs' heads, and corrupt, intermixed with barks, all words that are uttered, and in the raw meat they chew they imitate not people but the beasts themselves.[48]

> And they teach that there are beasts in Persis which they call Conopeni, below the canine heads of which an equine mane hangs down from the neck, and from their mouth and nostrils they exhale fire and flames.[49]

Taken together, we have a relatively full description of the *healfhunding*. It is a dog-headed human that lives in the East and can communicate only in barks. It is hostile to people, sometimes breathes fire and lives on a truly canine diet of raw meat. These details all conform to the idea of the map monster.

However, while the *healfhunding* may seem like another simple map monster of the world's end, in fact it posed a particularly difficult problem for the Anglo-Saxon world-view, for one of the Church's most important martyrs, St Christopher, was widely believed to have himself been a Cynocephalus. This tradition, inherited from the Byzantine Church, may have arisen from a mistranslation of the Latin *Cananeus* (Canaanite), which describes someone from the land of Canaan and is superficially similar to *canineus* (canine). When this tale was heard in the West, people simply remembered the writings of Ctesias, Megasthenes and Pliny on the Cynocephalus, and logically ascribed Christopher to the race of dog-heads. Christopher was a revered saint in Anglo-Saxon England, and there is a definite record of his relics being held at Exeter (though, sadly, we are not told whether these were human or canine bones).[50] We also have three separate Old English texts (a fragmentary life in the Nowell Codex, a now lost homily by Ælfric and the text that follows) and a Latin version that survives in several manuscripts, all depicting him as a Cynocephalus. The description of Christopher in the *Old English Martyrology*, a hagiographical compilation from the late eighth or early ninth century, is unflinching:

> On the same day is the passion of the great martyr St Christopher; he came in the days of the Caesar Decius to the city that is called Samos, from the nation where people have the head of dogs, and from the land in which men eat each other. He had the head of a dog, and his locks [of hair] were to his side, beyond measure, and his eyes shone

> as bright as the morning star, and his teeth were as sharp as a wild boar's tusks. He was faithful to God in his heart, but he could not speak like a man.[51]

Christopher is more monstrous than any of the other *healfhundingas* we have seen in descriptions of barbarous places: to the accumulated list of horrible things about dog-headed people, the *Martyrology*'s author has added the heinous and unspeakable crime of cannibalism. And yet, Christopher is unequivocally a man; after all, how else could he become a saint? The standard hagiography has Christopher given the power of speech, arrested for preaching the Christian faith, refusing to convert to paganism even after being tortured, and finally having his head lopped off by the Roman emperor Decius. It is fascinating to note, however, that although Christopher is given the ability to talk rather than bark in order to spread the word of God, his physical appearance is not altered. In other words, despite his monstrous appearance, he was already human.

The perceived facts of Christopher's appearance were a serious blow to the measured Anglo-Saxon sense of what defined a man. As we have already discussed, the Bible told them that God made man in the image of himself, and the examples of the hermaphrodite and people with extra fingers and toes in the *Liber monstrorum* attest to how strictly a man was defined in opposition to a monster. So how could a man with a dog's head, who communicated only in barks until divine intervention gave him human speech, possibly be reckoned a man rather than a monster? A direct answer, fortunately, lay in the famous monster passage of Augustine's *De civitate dei*:

> What shall I say of the Cynocephali, whose canine head and barking show them to be rather beasts than men? . . . Truly, whoever is born a man anywhere – that is, a rational, mortal animal – however extraordinary to our

> understanding the form of the body he carries, or his colour or his movement or his sound, or whatever part or power or quality in his nature: no one of the faithful might doubt that he draws his origin from that single protoplast [Adam] . . . God is the Creator of everything, who knows himself where and when a creature ought to be created, or have been created, choosing in his knowledge the various parts from whose similarities and differences he weaves the beauty of the universe.[52]

Christopher's faith in God reveals him to be a rational being, and therefore human. His unusual appearance in all this is irrelevant; indeed it is something to be celebrated. Thus when the *Martyrology* author got to work on the entry for Christopher, they saw no reason to hold back on the monstrosity of his appearance, for this proclaimed one of the inscrutably beautiful parts of God's marvellous Creation, and, moreover, it provided a harsh lesson for any mortal men having the arrogance to suppose that they could understand God's ineffable purpose in what he made. Indeed, the central point of the Christopher martyrdom is that appearances can be deceptive and will lead the unthinking person astray. The emperor Decius looks, for all intents and purposes, like a human, and yet he not only rejects the true religion but subjects one of its adherents to abhorrent physical pain and, finally, death. His adversary, a hairy, dog-headed monster from a race of cannibals, is faithful to God and subjects himself to martyrdom. Decius is clearly the monster in this particular story.[53]

There are traces of the Christopher narrative and Augustine's discussion of monsters in an illustration from the Vitellius *Wonders*. Cotton Vitellius A XV itself contains three texts that include dog-heads (although the *Passion of St Christopher*, in the Nowell Codex, does not explicitly call the saint a Cynocephalus, the beginning of the text was lost in a fire and this is where his physical appearance

Conopenae, Cotton Vitellius A XV, f. 100.

would have been discussed, and moreover the surviving part gives his height at a truly monstrous 'twelve fathoms'[54]), and so perhaps it is no wonder that considerable trouble has been taken over the drawing of the Conopenae. The head aside, this illustration clearly depicts a man. The creature is bedecked in men's garments, stands on two feet and wears shoes. To press the point further, it has been noted that the Conopenae's appearance is distinctly royal. The Conopenae is carrying an orb – the regal symbol of dominion over the world – and a king's sceptre, and the red colour of his luxurious robes connotes imperial authority. His pointed shoes and hose were the very height of fashion when the Nowell Codex was made around the year 1000.[55] This is a provoking image and, like the story of Christopher's martyrdom, reminds the Anglo-Saxon reader not to be misled by appearances or to adhere too dogmatically to the conventional man-made way of deciphering God's Creation, which is only truly understood by him.

At the Ends of the Earth

Despite the troubling example of the Cynocephalus, an Anglo-Saxon could quite happily read any of the above texts with a feeling of relative security. The intellectual tradition, as represented by Isidore, held that the *Liber monstrorum*'s hermaphrodite and six-fingered people could occur in any group of otherwise normal men and women. The East and its dangerous, revolting monsters were a long way from northern Europe, and so whether or not they challenged the very definition of a man, this was not something that the Anglo-Saxons would have to deal with at home. The map monsters of the *Wonders*, *Letter* and *Liber monstrorum* in this sense did their job: they lived in the pagan, uncivilized extremes of the world, defining both the places as such and themselves along the same lines, and demonstrated what civilization was not.

Alas, things were not quite so straightforward. The logic of defining the East as a wilderness populated by monsters was legitimized by its great distance from Jerusalem and Rome. Unfortunately, it was not just the East that was far from these holy centres of civilization, but other places in different geographical directions, including England itself. In 23 BC, Horace says that Britain is located *in ultimo orbis* (at the end of the world) in his 35th Ode. Gaius Julius Solinus, the third-century Roman writer, describes Britain as *paene orbis alterius* (almost another world). This miserable geographical position was worsened by the imperial dictates of the Roman Empire, which defined all colonies as not only inferior to Rome but more so the further from the Eternal City they were located: Pomponius Mela in the first century AD calls the inhabitants of Britain *inculti omnes . . . ita magnis aliarum opum ignari* (all uncivilized . . . [and] moreover ignorant of a great many things).[56]

During the Anglo-Saxon period, one of its most popular authors, Isidore of Seville, not only follows the Roman tradition of locating Britain at the very edge of the world in his *Etymologiae*, but even increases its isolation: 'Britannia is an island in the Ocean, separated from the whole world by the intervening sea.'[57]

Learned people living in the British Isles knew this tradition and concurred wholeheartedly because of the great reverence traditionally shown to Roman learning. The Welsh monk Gildas, for example, gives a damning assessment of Britannia's location in *De excidio*: 'the island of Britannia lies almost on the extreme limit of the earth . . . an island frozen stiff with frost and withdrawn, like in a remote part of the earth's surface, from the visible sun.'[58] Although the sun, here equating to the message of Christ, did eventually arrive in Britain, Gildas endorses the Roman link between the island's remoteness and its naturally ignorant, uncivilized nature.

There was no attempt to quibble with classical geography from the Anglo-Saxons either, who like Gildas were familiar with Latin learning. Bede begins his *Historia ecclesiastica* by locating Britain in its usual far-flung place: 'Britain is an island of the Ocean . . . located between the north and west, opposite Germany, Gaul and Spain, which form the larger part of Europe, though a great distance from them . . . [it] lies nearly under the North Pole.'[59] In Bede's account of the Synod of Whitby of 664, Bishop Wilfrid calls the British Isles 'the two most remote islands of the Ocean'.[60] On the only surviving Anglo-Saxon map of the world – included in the mid-eleventh-century Cotton Tiberius B. V, Part I, one of our manuscript sources for the *Wonders* – a remarkably accurate outline of Britain is located in the far corner of the world, a long way from both Rome and Jerusalem, which are also displayed.[61]

THE ANGLO-SAXONS HAD NO doubt, then, of their peripheral location at the edge of the world. By the logic they applied to the

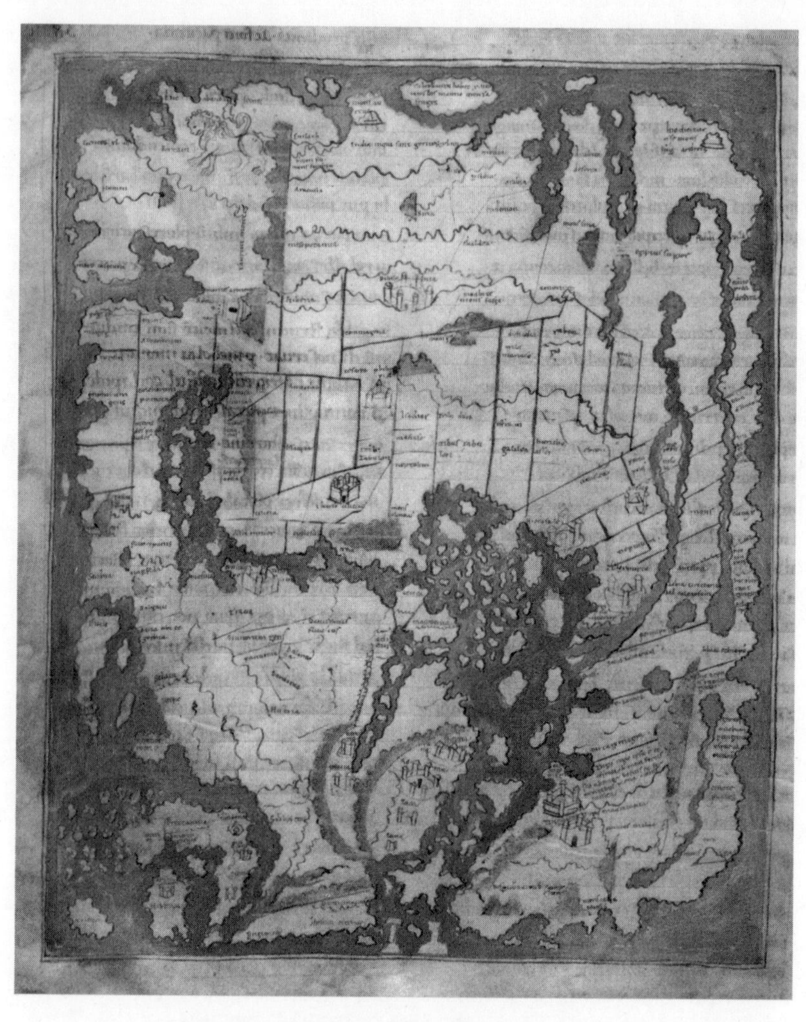

Map of the world, Cotton Tiberius B. V, Part I, f. 56v.
The British Isles are in the bottom left corner.

East, their island was crawling with monsters and uncivilized people. However, as the *Liber monstrorum* states, where people expand, monsters can no longer flourish, so it was not impossible for civilization to bloom in such a location. After all, even in the monstrous Orient described by *Wonders* there are a few pleasant groups of people surviving against the odds in certain isolated places: 'there is another kingdom in the land of Babylon . . . [where] there are decent people who have power and royal authority over the Red Sea.'[62] The map monsters could be defeated or resisted, therefore, and good could flourish in wild places converted to civilization.

But monsters formed part of the natural fauna of uncivilized places at the edge of the world. Inevitably, alongside the more prosaic birds and mammals we know today, parts of England were home to all manner of nefarious monsters that threatened to reclaim their former territory from the interloping Christians. Over the rest of this book, we will be examining those monsters with whom the Anglo-Saxons shared their island home *in ultimo orbis* and how the population coped with living alongside them.

II
OF WOLF AND MAN

Among the multitude of monsters that beset Alexander in the *Letter*, only two could have been directly known to the Anglo-Saxons: the bears and wolves that attack the Macedonian army alongside lions, tigers and leopards. Since it would be anachronistic to separate real animals from mythical creatures in Anglo-Saxon accounts, we must reckon the bear and the wolf as early medieval monsters. But perhaps because of its scarcity, or even extinction, there is little monster lore surrounding the bear. The wolf, on the other hand, was a fully fledged monster with a rich accompanying body of thought and legend, and one deemed to pose a great threat to livestock, people and even the soul.[1]

Guardians of the Uncivilized

Wulf sceal on bearowe.[2]
The wolf must be in the woods.

A defining characteristic of the Anglo-Saxon monster was its preference for wild, uncivilized places, where man would not choose to live or had yet to get around to colonizing. As the quotation above suggests, the wolf was thought to conform to this very criterion. *Maxims* II, a poetic catalogue of proverbial sayings preserved in the mid-eleventh-century Cotton Tiberius B. I, depicts the world as an ordered place with everything confined to its proper habitat, and is as certain that wolves live in the woods as it is that fish live in water. Despite the economic importance of the timber industry to Anglo-Saxon England, the woods stood in direct symbolic opposition to the cities and monasteries they often neighboured. Where mankind is psychologically programmed to fear and can only cross by staying on well-worn pathways, wild animals can move and navigate at will and lurk unseen by the pedestrian. In a further contrast to Christian civilization, the woods were believed to be sacred to pagans, such as Alexander the Great in the previous chapter. The woods to the Anglo-Saxons were a heathen, much-feared place best suited to wild animals and, more specifically within the animal kingdom, monsters.

Maxims II is far from the only reference to the monstrous habitat of these monstrous canids. The Franks Casket, an early eighth-century whalebone box from Northumbria, also portrays

The left side panel of the Franks Casket, showing the story of Romulus and Remus.

wolves in their natural environment.[3] The left-hand panel depicts the Roman tale of Romulus and Remus, specifically the moment when the boys are discovered being suckled by a she-wolf. The legend was already known in Britain before the Anglo-Saxons arrived and proved popular throughout the period, with East Anglian kings adopting the motif of the twins suckled by the wolf on their coins. The most fascinating detail of the carving is the woodland setting itself. There can be no doubt which scene from the legend is depicted: the accompanying runic inscription reads 'Romulus and Remus, two brothers, a she-wolf nourished them in Rome city, far from their native land'.[4] The woodland setting however is unique to this version of the legend. Clearly, the wolf was so firmly linked to the woods in Anglo-Saxon culture that any depiction of a narrative scene involving the creatures simply could not do without the surrounding trees. The contrast between wilderness and civilization is demonstrated in the way that the wolves and shepherds interact with the woods. While the men are depicted on the near side of the trees, a close examination of the second wolf (again, not attested in any other version of the legend) shows that it is partially obscured by its nearest tree, almost absorbed by its environment and far more at home. The pose of the she-wolf is also notable: recumbent, she has found a place between two trees that acts almost like a chaise longue, allowing her to rest both her head and tail against them. Monsters are at home in the woods; men are not.

Another wood-dwelling wolf plays an important role in the martyrdom of St Edmund, after whose shrine Bury St Edmunds in Suffolk is named. In Ælfric's late tenth-century *Lives of the Saints*, the unfortunate king of East Anglia is captured by a Viking army after refusing to accept defeat. The Vikings shoot Edmund with so many arrows that they look *swilce igles byrsta* (like a hedgehog's bristles), then cut off his head and chuck it in a thicket of brambles for good measure.[5] Edmund's men go in search of the severed head and after hearing its miraculous cries come upon a wonder: a hungry wolf guarding the holy head, naturally *on wuda* (in the woods). The wolf's traditional habitat is widely attested elsewhere in Anglo-Saxon literature. In the poem *Elene*, an account of Helena, the mother of the Roman emperor Constantine, finding the True Cross, written by the poet Cynewulf and preserved in the late tenth-century Vercelli Book, the wolf is said to live *on wealde* (in the wold, literally 'high land covered with woods') and is later described in stronger terms as *holtes gehleða* (companion of the woods).[6] The Old English poem *Battle of Brunanburh*, preserved in the *Anglo-Saxon Chronicle* entry for the year 937, repeats the former description precisely, *wulf on wealde*, and it appears again in the Nowell Codex poem *Judith* with a variant spelling, *wulf in walde*.[7]

Further evidence for the link between wolves and woodland comes from place names. In their definitive study of places named with reference to wolves – and there are indeed several – C. Aybes and D. W. Yalden found that most, or 26 per cent, referred to woodland, either a clearing in one (such as Wooley in Derbyshire; *wulfa* + *leah* meaning 'wolves' clearing') or woods themselves (such as Woolgraves, West Yorkshire; *wulf* + *græfe* meaning 'wolf copse').[8] Place name evidence proves the strength of this identification, whether wolves were commonly seen in these woodland locations or these were deemed to be suitable lupine habitats. Although, as the percentage above suggests, wolves were not exclusively associated with woods, other places and features named after them are similarly wild, such as hills, valleys, caves, marshes and natural pools. Likewise, *Fortunes of Men*, an Old English poem from the largest surviving manuscript of Old English poetry, the Exeter Book, created circa 975 in southern England, muses on the diverse fates that await people, and dubs the wolf *har hæðstapa* (the grey heath-stepper).[9]

The wolf's most common Anglo-Saxon habitat is, however, at odds with modern wolf biology. Researchers have documented wolves existing in all manner of strange places that seem to defy this apparent confinement to the woods, and even the wilderness at large. Many modern wolves have adapted to urban life, such as a pack in Romania that not only enters a city at night to scavenge in bins but has learned the train timetable in order to cross a railway line safely.[10] There are even numerous examples from around the world of wolves denning, unnoticed, in abandoned houses. Their natural range takes in all manner of habitats, from Arctic tundra to desert; think, for instance, of the wolf's former range across the whole of North America, from frostbitten Alaska to the scorching Texan border with Mexico. So why were they ascribed so firmly to the woods in Anglo-Saxon England?

The most important determining factor in wolf habitat is the availability of wild ungulates, such as deer.[11] The wolves inhabiting abandoned houses do so because of the scarcity of their natural prey and the availability of alternative sustenance in urban areas. Most modern wolves studied by zoologists will actively avoid people and exhibit fear when they detect a human presence, and only when prey is in severely short supply will they adopt such a drastic change in habitat.[12] The habitat of the wolf's natural quarry in England, the roe deer and red deer, would have naturally confined it to wild, unpopulated places, for deer are notoriously flighty and scared of people. When we consider that the most common species of deer in Anglo-Saxon England, the roe, is a cervid that inhabits woodland and forest clearings, the association between wolves and the woods may not have been so far from the truth after all.

But what may have been a perfectly natural behaviour in the wolf was charged with ideological significance. In choosing the wildest and most heavily wooded places in England, by definition far from the centres of town and monastery, the wolf was telegraphing its opposition to humanity. Like the monsters of the *Wonders* and *Letter*, the wolf lived away from men by choice and, assuming Anglo-Saxon England's wolves were not too dissimilar to their modern descendants, would most often flee at the sight or sound of men encroaching on their territory. That is, the wolf, like all monsters, was concerned about maintaining the boundary between man and monster. In the Old English *Exodus*, a poem composed around the eighth century and preserved in MS Junius 11 of circa 1000, and based on the biblical account of the Crossing of the Red Sea, wolves are configured in just such a way: 'the border-guardians [*mearcweardas*] screamed in the middle of the night.'[13] The *mearc* that the wolves guard is not just a literal environmental division between civilization and wilderness, but the ideological place where the world of men ends and the land of monsters begins. To say that *wulf sceal on bearowe* (the wolf must be in the woods), therefore, was not merely a reflection of a possible ecological reality but also literary shorthand for saying that the wolf was a monster that could exist only in that terrestrial apotheosis of the heathen, anti-human wilderness: the woods.

Counting Sheep

In the Anglo-Saxon period, as today, one of the alleged defining characteristics of the wolf was its unbridled lust for the flesh of sheep. Sheep farming was common across Anglo-Saxon England, which was home to around a million sheep at the time the Domesday Book was written in 1086, and unfortunately for the wolf, its danger to such flocks was set in scripture:

> Beware of false prophets, who come to you in the clothing of sheep, but inwardly they are ravening wolves. (Matthew 7:15)

> Behold I send you as sheep in the midst of wolves. (Matthew 10:16)

> I am the good shepherd. The good shepherd giveth his life for his sheep. But the hireling and he that is not the shepherd, whose own the sheep are not, seeth the wolf coming and leaveth the sheep, and flieth: and the wolf catcheth, and scattereth the sheep. (John 10:11–12)

> I know that, after my departure, ravening wolves will enter in among you, not sparing the flock. (Acts 20:29)

Like Anglo-Saxon England, the biblical Middle East was a pastoral economy where sheep were reared and herded for milk, wool and meat. Many of the Bible's key metaphors – the Good Shepherd, Christians as the flock threatened by wolves – were hence readily comprehensible to the Anglo-Saxons converted after Augustine's mission in 597.

The image of the helpless flock threatened by 'ravening wolves' was thus seized upon by Anglo-Saxon Christianity. In the *Historia*, Bede describes how, in the early seventh century, Laurence, the second Archbishop of Canterbury, was tempted to leave England altogether after facing overwhelming hostility from pagans stubbornly refusing to convert. As he prepared to flee, Laurence received an inspirational visitation from the Apostle Peter, who asked 'to which shepherds he was sending away Christ's sheep, that were placed in the midst of wolves, by his fleeing'.[14] Needless to say, Laurence decided to stay. The reference was broad in appeal: to the learned such as Bede and Aldhelm, the image referred to the teaching of Christ, from whom came all the biblical passages quoted above, and so would remind learned (and usually ecclesiastical) readers of their pastoral duties. But the wolf–sheep paradigm was also a powerful image of imminent, snarling danger that even the most ignorant Anglo-Saxon could understand. We can only assume that the wolf–sheep image was disseminated from the pulpit and consequently widely known in the period.

Whether because of the Bible's anti-wolf rhetoric or personal experiences, it seems that for the Anglo-Saxons, real wolves were considered a constant danger to sheep. Although we should not take Ælfric's tenth-century *Colloquy* as a serious account of Anglo-Saxon shepherding practices, we can assume that the facts of its rather bland statements preserve accepted beliefs. The text, which takes the form of a dialogue, was intended to help pupils learn Latin and so could not be obtuse or illogical. One of the fictional pupils in the *Colloquy* is a shepherd, who gives an account of his daily routine: 'in the early morning I drive my sheep to their pasture and stand over them with dogs in heat and cold, lest wolves devour them.'[15] The description is straightforward and uncontroversial, as is usually the case with school texts. People have used dogs as lookouts and security for thousands of years, and large pastoral breeds such as the Pyrenean Mountain Dog and Hungarian Komondor still guard today's flocks against opportunistic predators such as wolves.

However, it seems likely that this shepherd's constant vigilance against wolves was largely a waste of time. Modern studies of wolves preying on domestic livestock have suggested that such incidents are rare, being sensibly avoided by wolves except in times of desperation. For example, in northern Portugal, where wild ungulates are extremely scarce, wolves prey almost exclusively on domestic livestock out of necessity, whereas packs of wolves in the wilds of North America regularly trot past herds of livestock on their way to hunt the abundant deer that still roam the continent.[16] Archaeology tells us that in Anglo-Saxon England wild animals were only very rarely hunted for food by humans, who instead lived almost entirely off domestic livestock such as sheep, cattle and pigs.[17] Hunting deer, the wolf's favoured prey, would have been time-consuming and comparatively inefficient. Based on what we know of today's wolves, it is likely that the population of deer, left largely unmolested by man, would for the most part have been high enough to discourage wolves from risking life and limb to get at the sheep zealously watched over by men and dogs.[18]

But another thing we can learn from modern wolves is the lasting impact of livestock predation on the people that own the animals. The preferred hunting method of the wolf is not for the faint of heart: working as a team, wolves chase and harry their prey to tire it before pulling it to the ground as soon as they can get a proper grip on the rear, nose or throat. Though they target the neck to kill their prey, death often takes minutes as the unfortunate creature dies from exhaustion, blood loss or asphyxiation. It is also not uncommon for an animal to be literally torn to pieces while still alive. The wolf's method of killing leaves a great mess of blood and fur, especially if the animal is consumed where it falls. Witnesses to such an attack would not soon forget the sound of the panicked flock, the snarling of the wolves and the quarry's shrieks as its life ended in the most horrific fashion. Losing livestock in this manner can be extremely distressing: Olivier Maurin, a French farmer interviewed by the *Sunday Times* in 2018, explained that 'when the wolves come for your sheep, it feels personal . . . it is like they are killing your family.'[19]

Worse still, wolves are known to indulge in surplus killing: they slaughter far more prey than they can possibly eat, and simply leave bloodied carcasses wherever they fall. This phenomenon is well attested. According to leading wolf experts L. David Mech and Rolf O. Peterson, surplus killing is a natural response to an unnatural situation: 'programmed to kill whenever possible because it is rarely possible to kill, wolves automatically take advantage of an unusual opportunity.'[20] This behaviour would have been deemed monstrous by the Anglo-Saxons, who lacked our knowledge of zoology and ethology. At best, surplus killing would seem greedy, and at worst motivated by extreme malice, cruelty and unconscionable monstrosity. Depending on flock size, which in Anglo-Saxon England could vary from a couple of dozen to around a thousand animals, surplus killing by wolves could pack a severe economic punch in addition to causing psychological trauma. On a single night in the late twentieth century in Minnesota, for example, a pack of wolves killed or injured 34 sheep and two hundred turkeys;[21] a similar feat would have been enough to wipe out an entire flock in parts of Anglo-Saxon England. A single surplus killing, however distant in the memory of the oldest members of a village, could have a wide-reaching impact on how wolves were viewed. What other than a monster could wreak such wanton destruction?

As well as enacting one of Christ's favourite metaphors, in leaving the woods or wilderness and entering land farmed by humans, the wolf was crossing a boundary it was supposed to maintain. The wolf of the wilderness entering farmland takes us to the root of the Latin word for 'uncivilized', *incultus*. It means, literally, 'uncultivated', the very opposite of *cultus*, 'cultivated'. Farmland is by definition cultivated, and pastoral farming at its very essence is an attempt to impose man's order on the natural world. Sheep and cattle are confined to a single place, repressing their natural instinct to move across broader areas in search of food. Keeping livestock in farm buildings protects them from the natural vicissitudes of the weather and predators. The arrival of a wolf in a fold not only breaks a crucial boundary between *cultus* and *incultus*, therefore, but reverts the cultivated land to its natural state – chaos and wilderness – for as long as it remains there. Indeed, the wolf was even believed to sully physically anything it touched: the Anglo-Saxon *Pontifical of Egbert* (*c*. 750) stated that 'if a wolf shall attack cattle of any kind, and the animal attacked shall die in consequence, no Christian shall touch it.'[22] Isidore of Seville goes further in *Etymologiae* and states that 'anything they touch with their feet does not live.'[23] As an animal deeply symbolic of the wilderness, the wolf entering the human world had truly monstrous powers of transformation and, like all monsters, threatened what man had toiled to carve from the cruelties of the natural world.

Wolf and the Devil

As the words of Olivier Maurin suggest, losing one's sheep to predators is a harrowing experience. Think, however, of the pious Anglo-Saxon shepherd waking one morning to find that a lamb had been killed. Wolves typically target the weakest member of a herd and when hunting domestic livestock do not scruple to slaughter any lambs that fall in their path. The lamb, however, was a universal Christian symbol for Jesus: 'Behold the Lamb of God [*agnus Dei*]. Behold him who taketh away the sin of the world' (John 1:29). Christ was often portrayed as a literal lamb across Christendom, and a series of rings and coins bearing the Lamb of God survive from the Anglo-Saxon period. The Anglo-Saxon Mass from the eighth century onwards included the invocation 'Agnus Dei, qui tollis peccata mundi, miserere nobis' (The Lamb of God, who takes away the sins of the world, have mercy upon us) during the most sacred part of the service, the breaking of the Eucharist, the body of Christ. In killing a lamb, the wolf unwittingly added another crime to its charge of monstrosity: satanic opposition to God.

Beyond symbolic deicide, the wolf's association with the Devil is also strongly evident in the Bible. In Christ's allegories, the Good Shepherd is variously himself or a religious official tasked with caring for the spiritual health of his flock (congregation). The threat to the flock is codified as the wolf, which is then logically equated with Satan. The link is made explicit in the poem collection in the Exeter Book known as *Christ I*: 'the accursed-wolf [*se awyrgda wulf*], the bold death-shadow [*dædscua*], Lord, has dispersed your flock, driven [them] widely in different directions . . . the wicked one [Satan] sorely oppresses [the flock] and takes them captive.'[24]

Here, Satan is unequivocally a wolf. Two Anglo-Saxon charters place a curse on anyone who opposes the estate boundaries and the associated duties they outline, along the same lines: 'may he be separated from the fellowship of our Lord Jesus Christ and placed with greedy wolves [*lupis rapacibus*].'[25] These charters seize upon the reputation of wolves as insatiably gluttonous and make it a diabolical characteristic. Indeed, homily XVII of the Blickling Homilies, an anonymous Old English text from the end of the tenth century, casts the demonic inhabitants of Hell as decidedly lupine: 'devils in the likeness of water-monsters [*nicras*, the same noun used for the hippopotamuses in the *Letter of Alexander*] were gripping [the damned souls] like greedy wolves [*swa swa grædig wulf*].'[26]

The alleged greed of the wolf was a key part of its monstrosity. Wolves' status as monsters, intensified by their connection with Satan, fits neatly with the Anglo-Saxon view of the world as made up of boundaries and things in their proper place. As we will see, the wilderness was also the natural home of demons: the wolf is both a monster and a diabolical creature. But, as a monster opposed to Christendom, the wolf's hostility to mankind did not end with its natural habitat and occasional taste for symbolically charged livestock.

Wolves and Men

The threat posed to humans by wolves is as controversial today as it has ever been. Like many of their descendants in the twenty-first century, the Anglo-Saxons were in no doubt that wolves killed and ate people as a matter of course. The *Fortunes of Men* in the Exeter Book, for example, includes being eaten by a wolf in its understated catalogue of the eventualities that may befall one: 'the wolf, the grey heath-stepper, will eat him; then the mother mourns the death.' Another Old English poem from the same manuscript, *The Wanderer*, mentions the fate in a similar list of unfortunate demises: 'one the grey wolf dismembered in death'.[27] Ælfric's homily 'In letania maiore' (On the Greater Litany) describes the harrowing ordeal of Vienna: 'There befell a great earthquake [*eorð-styrung*] in a city, which is called Vienna, and churches and houses fell down, and wild bears and wolves came and devoured a great part of the people.'[28] In line with the equation of wolves with the Devil, Ælfric gives this disturbing account at the very beginning of a sermon ascribing these events to the sinfulness of the Viennese: after three days of penitential fast, God ended the *gedreccednys* (affliction). God allowed Satan and his infernal forces to roam the world, tempting and testing people, as per the tribulations of Job in the Old Testament, and the wolves of Vienna fulfil the same purpose. It is clear, however, that although the wolves were eating people, as was customary for them, in entering the city they breached the boundary they were supposed to observe, making the visitation extremely disturbing for Ælfric's parishioners.

There are also artefacts of the period that depict wolves attacking or eating people. The Sutton Hoo purse-lid, discussed in the Introduction, has two wolves mauling an apparently helpless and unarmed man. The wolves' hind legs grip their victim, while their forelegs lunge at his vulnerable throat. The animals are depicted at the moment of delivering the final blow, a bite to either side of the man's head. Another wolf attack is depicted on a fragmentary narrative frieze from Old Minster, Winchester (the predecessor of the current cathedral), dating from between 980 and 1094.[29] Preserved on the fragment is a prostrate man, shown from the shoulders up, with what is unmistakably a wolf worrying his face. The animal has a dew-claw and once had the upright prick-ears characteristic of wolves. Its paw, three toes of which are visible, pins the man's chin down, while its elaborately tongued muzzle pushes into his face. The beginnings of a mane also suggest that this animal is a wolf, not a domestic dog. Oddly, the wolf's tongue seems to be in the man's mouth: whether this is an aesthetic choice or perhaps the ravenous beast tasting its victim is unclear, with so much of the panel missing and what remains damaged. The specific story that the frieze depicts is unknown, though a strong case has been made for an incident in the Old Norse *Völsunga saga* (Saga of the Völsungs), when the fettered hero Sigmund kills a

Carving from Old Minster, Winchester, showing a man being devoured by a wolf.

wolf, sent to eat him alive, by biting off its tongue.[30] Regardless of its source, this sculpture is further evidence of the belief that wolves preyed upon people.

And yet, literary and artistic depictions aside, there are no records of wolves eating people in any other Anglo-Saxon source. The much-quoted claim that January was known as 'wolf month' (*wulf monaþ*) because the cold weather made wolves more troublesome than usual, owing to the scarcity of their prey, is a myth. This actually originates with the sixteenth-century writer Richard Verstegan and has no corroboration in any Anglo-Saxon source, rendering it extremely dubious.[31] We would perhaps expect that the extant charter corpus might contain a reference to a place where a wolf killed a man among its thousands of local toponyms, or that the *Anglo-Saxon Chronicle*, which recorded important deaths and other notable events, might have an entry. There is likewise no evidence of laws being passed against wolves for their predation of people. This absence suggests one of two things: either wolves killed so many people that such deaths were not thought to be worth recording, or wolf predation of humans was extremely rare.

We have no choice but to refer again to modern studies of wolves. There can be no doubt that wolves do kill and eat people, on occasion. State and communal archives from northern Italy record 440 people killed by wolves between the fourteenth and nineteenth centuries, while in Russia, 1875 alone saw 161 people killed by wolves. It is impossible, however, to say how many of these attacks were perpetrated by feral dogs or wolf–dog hybrids.[32] Most dangerous of all are rabid wolves, which attack in a frenzied state and can withstand multiple injuries before being killed or driven off. A rabid wolf in eighteenth-century France killed an old woman and severely disfigured seven armed men in a matter of minutes before finally being overwhelmed.[33] It is possible that rabies existed in Anglo-Saxon England, since *Bald's Leechbook*, a medical text written circa 900, has a remedy *wiþ wede-hundes slite* (against the bite of a mad-dog), which may refer to the disease.[34] Again, however, a rabid wolf that killed or injured scores of people would surely be something worth recording somewhere, and so either rabies or wolves cannot have been widespread.

We should however be wary of expecting Anglo-Saxon wolves to conform to modern scientific data or later historical accounts. Researchers have noted a dramatic fall in the number of wolf attacks from the late twentieth century onwards, and some have suggested that this may be because the greater availability of firearms, unavailable in Europe until the fourteenth century, has given wolves an even stronger fear of people. Since the Anglo-Saxons had no firearms with which to defend themselves, it is possible that the wolves they encountered were much bolder than today's animals.[35] On the other hand, the environmental conditions of Russia, to take one example, are vastly different from Anglo-Saxon England. Russian wolves are especially dangerous when prey becomes scarce during the country's harsh winters, and though the climate of Anglo-Saxon England was far from tropical, it was hardly comparable to Siberia. The overall consensus of biologists is that wolf attacks and predation of people are rare and abnormal, if not unheralded, which seems a sensibly moderate position to take for their Anglo-Saxon ancestors.[36]

Although the wolves of Anglo-Saxon England enjoyed a bounteous provision of their natural prey, the deer, and rabies does not seem to have been common, there are a number of factors that might have brought wolves into potentially deadly contact with people. Modern wolves have adapted to raiding urban rubbish dumps, and it is likely that some Anglo-Saxon packs took to visiting villages under the cover of darkness to scavenge on the detritus of communal living. Though the remains of wolves are especially rare finds in archaeological digs, excavated Anglo-Saxon rubbish dumps contain bones and offcuts from animal butchery which would have attracted wolves and other scavengers from a wide radius. Wolves will also happily feast on human corpses, and so flourish during times of strife. In fact, this habit was widely known to the Anglo-Saxons, who incorporated the wolf into a poetic feature known to modern scholars as the Beasts of Battle motif. These Beasts of Battle are always depicted just before a battle starts, looking on with greedy eyes in anticipation of the inevitable pile of corpses there will be when it ends: 'the lean one, the wolf in the wold, rejoiced, and the dusky raven, the bird eager to prey on the dead. They both knew that the great men intended to give them a feast of doomed men.'[37] The wolf and its companion the raven have an almost preternatural knowledge of the banquet to come. Although a poetic device intended to increase the terror and tension before a battle is described, it is likely that the Beasts of Battle were based on first-hand experience. Given the various battles fought between kingdoms in the early Anglo-Saxon period, and against the Vikings from the ninth century onwards, this particular trope probably came from observation of real wolves. The Anglo-Saxons would also have heard of wolves digging up corpses from graves, a disquieting habit that involved these wilderness-dwelling beasts of ill repute desecrating sacred ground.

Whether scavenging on the dead in graves and the battlefield or rooting around a refuse pile just outside a village, wolves that indulged in this sort of behaviour would become habituated to people. That is, they would learn to associate people and their erstwhile frightening scent with food, and not with danger, creating an increasingly bold animal that would not only defend its meal aggressively but even proceed to viewing the living as quarry. In 1439, for example, a notorious pack of wolves began killing people in the outskirts of Paris, sometimes even dragging them from their homes, having grown accustomed to eating the corpses left by the Plague and the Hundred Years War.[38] While we have no reports of such fearful packs in the British Isles, the potential for wolves to learn to view men as prey certainly existed in Anglo-Saxon England.

A final circumstance in which a wolf might attack and eat a human is when the animal is solitary. Wolves are natural pack animals, and their ability to capture their favoured prey is contingent upon working together as a pack, both because of the size of a deer and its ingenuity in escaping predators. A lone wolf is therefore unable to capture its usual quarry and has to resort to desperate measures to get the several kilograms of meat it requires per day. Far smaller animals, such as mice and frogs, are added to the menu alongside high-risk but slow-moving quarry such as livestock and humans. This may explain a curious feature of the wolf described in *Maxims II*: 'the wolf must be in the woods, wretched and solitary [*anhaga*].' Many have puzzled over the designation of a characteristically gregarious animal as solitary, but perhaps most of the wolves bold enough to enter an Anglo-Saxon village or farmstead – and thus the most commonly seen – were of the desperate lone variety.

It is likely that Anglo-Saxon settlements took measures against nuisance wolves. Anglo-Saxon charters and place names make reference to wolf pits (*wulfpyt*, of which the place name Woolpit is a derivation), which some scholars have interpreted as a pest-control measure in the form of a deep hole in the ground.[39] However, no Anglo-Saxon wolf pit has ever been identified, let alone studied, and all that survives in the textual corpus is the name, rather than any description of its purpose or application. The evidence for the existence of wolf pits for lupine trapping is somewhat undermined by references to other pits associated with supernatural creatures, such as giant pits (*þyrspyt*), sometimes even located in the same place as a wolf pit. Some scholars still cite a document detailing the foundation of a hospital in Flixton, North Yorkshire, to protect travellers from wolves in the late Anglo-Saxon period. The briefest glance at the actual source, however, gives us several good reasons to discount it. The document, which claims the hospital was established in the reign of Æthelstan, dates from the mid-fifteenth century, more than half a millennium after the alleged foundation. The story, moreover, is recorded to support a contested claim for the ownership of some land, which in the absence of legal documentation relies entirely upon the allegedly ancient date of its foundation. Finally, even when taken at face value, the reference itself – 'lupos et alias bestias voraces et silvestres' (wolves and other beasts voracious and wild) – makes it clear that wolves were but one of many threats to travellers in this part of Yorkshire, and not the sole reason for the hospital's probably mythical establishment.[40]

In sum, it is probable that wolves did kill people in Anglo-Saxon England, but it seems overwhelmingly likely that attacks were rare. Most important to note, however, is the severe psychological impact of a wolf attack on a community and even the history of a region. Wolves kill people in much the same way that they kill their other prey. Since the archaeological evidence does not suggest that wolves were frequent visitors to villages, let us consider the plight of a lone traveller passing through a great wood or moor, destined to become a wolf pack's next meal. The wolves would track him or her across incredible distances, if necessary, and as they neared, noses to the ground, he would have perhaps heard their imminent approach. He may have heard snarls, yelps and perhaps even the terrifying howl of the wolves as they communicated with one another across the terrain. Knowing that he was in the home of monsters, he would realize his utter peril and futilely pick up his pace. Hearing the footfall of paws on the turf or forest floor, he may well have run for his life, but there would be little point: wolves have been measured running at speeds of 60 kilometres per hour and will often chase prey for a day at a time. When they caught up with him, the wolves would have taken bites out of the doomed traveller, nimbly avoiding all blows, until one finally pulled the weakened victim to the ground, whence, if luck was on his side, he would have been dispatched with a wound to the neck before being ripped to pieces. The grisly remains of people feasted on by wolves cannot be unseen: exposed bones, internal organs, great clumps of blood and gore congealed with scraps of clothing and jewellery, the impotent ephemera of civilization.

Imagine coming upon such a scene. Large, clawed paw prints would identify the culprit, and the carnage would seem the work of a monster, confirming everything you had heard recently in church about the wolf's demonic nature. Word would spread, and without the benefit of modern man's understanding of wolf biology it would be abundantly clear that wolves killed people as a matter of course. Given the likely rarity of such an event, its unfamiliarity would only magnify the horror, and people who had never seen a wolf, let alone a person eaten by one, would exaggerate the already gruesome details with every telling. It is not hard to see how the actions of one rogue animal or a desperate pack could define wolves in perpetuity as monsters who eat people.

Despite the wolf's nefarious reputation as a satanic, wilderness-dwelling, man-eating monster, a surprising number of Anglo-Saxons bore names containing the element *wulf*. Why on earth would anyone wish to associate themselves with a monster that stood diametrically opposed to everything that civilized man was supposed to be? It is generally agreed that naming people after wolves originated with the pagan Germanic tribes of the Continent, who had the wolf among their totem animals. Displaying the wolf on weapons and armour, and even wearing wolfskins, seems to have been thought to pass on something of the wolf's ferocity and strength to their owner. In a tumultuous period of war and violence, this was a boon. But one would expect that once the Anglo-Saxons, bearing all manner of *wulf* compounds as first names and even tribal monikers (for example the Wuffing, or 'Little Wolf', dynasty of East Anglia), were converted to the lupophobic Christian faith, these bestial monikers would have died out altogether. Such was not the case. In the Domesday Book there were still Saxons named

Acwulf (*ac* + *wulf*, 'oak-wolf'), Æscwulf (*æsc* + *wulf*, 'spear-wolf') and numerous other lupine compounds. The most famous Anglo-Saxon 'wolf', moreover, was a high-ranking priest: Wulfstan (*wulf* + *stan*, 'wolf-stone'), Archbishop of York from 1002 to 1023. A famous homilist, Wulfstan is best remembered for his *Sermo Lupi ad Anglos* (Sermon of the Wolf to the English), a diatribe that blames the early eleventh-century Viking raids on the sinfulness of the English people. Despite the monstrous associations of his name, Wulfstan embraced it wholeheartedly, and often signed documents as 'Lupus', the Wolf.

Archbishop Wulfstan perhaps wanted to evoke fear in his congregation through being the self-styled Lupus, but the reason for the continuity of *wulf* names seems to run a little deeper. The Anglo-Saxons, as we know from Bede's *Historia*, were fully aware of their pagan origins, and post-conversion some aristocrats continued to trace their ancestry back to Woden, the chief god of the Germanic pantheon. Woden's divine status was hastily reconfigured as earthly prowess, however, as in Æthelweard's late tenth-century *Chronicle*: 'Woden, who was king of many nations, and whom some pagans now worship as a god'.[41] So while they were proud of their ancestors' deeds, they were also aware of their sinful paganism and did not let themselves forget it. Perhaps keeping names that were originally pagan was a way for Anglo-Saxons to remind themselves of the dangers of slipping back into the immorality of their forefathers, the natural sinful state of the Germanic people. But *wulf* names go further in this by evoking not only a pagan past but a monster of the present: perhaps their persistence suggests that wolves and men were not quite as different as they seemed at first glance.

Wolves and Outlaws

Wineleas, wonsælig mon genimeð him wulfas to geferan, / felafæcne deor.[42]
Friendless, the unfortunate man takes wolves for companions, very treacherous wild-beasts.

In Anglo-Saxon poetry, only death is worse than exile. From a theological standpoint, all men are exiles from the Kingdom of God, having been cast from his beatific presence in the Garden of Eden, but many poems focus upon the more specific fate of those exiled from the community of men. *The Wanderer*, for example, is an elegy imagining the feelings of an exiled man yearning for the community he has lost, and contains a particularly moving description of the exile's loneliness: 'sorrow is renewed when the memory of kinsmen passes through his mind; he greets [them] joyfully, eagerly surveys the companions of men. They often swim away.'[43] In one sense, despite his mental torment and grief at what he has lost, the narrator of *The Wanderer* is fortunate, for his exile has come only from the death of his former lord, not as a result of personal shortcomings. But while some exiles were the victims of circumstance, others were banished by their lord and legally condemned to live far away from the world of men as outlaws.

Although today the idea of an outlaw brings to mind Robin Hood and his Merry Men, life for an Anglo-Saxon outlaw was far from a romantic ideal. The outlaw was banished for having committed a heinous crime against their community – such as murder, grave-robbing, refusing to participate in the law of the land or failing to keep the peace – and sent to live far from where people were supposed to dwell. This was effectively a death sentence: the outlaw was not permitted to live communally, their life no longer protected by the laws of man, meaning that anyone could kill them without repercussions. In committing their antisocial crimes, the outlaw had effectively crossed a boundary defining what was acceptable behaviour for a human, and had lost their humanity in the process. No longer in their proper place within the bounds of civilization, the outlaw was forced to live in the profane and dangerous wilds; having crossed the moral boundary, the outlaw was made to cross its corresponding physical threshold, too.

As we have seen, the uncivilized places of Anglo-Saxon England were crawling with monsters, including wolves. The *wineleas* man of the quotation from *Maxims I*, another Exeter Book poem, above is likely an outlaw, and his fate is grim:

> Very often the companion [a wolf] tears him . . . it howls with hunger, by no means grievously mourning: the grey wolf does not weep for the slaughter, the murder of a man, by any means, but it always wishes for more.[44]

The rightful place for an outlaw is among the wolves, who show themselves to be monsters by killing him. Having eaten, the wolf's monstrous appetite is not sated, and it laments the fact that it has finished devouring the man's delicious flesh. The remorseless wolf's crime against its new companion mirrors the outlaw's crime against his community, demonstrating why they must live together in the wilderness. Outlaws and wolves were in fact so closely linked in the Anglo-Saxon mind, owing to their shared habitat, that when receiving their sentence, the outlaw was said to carry a wolf's head, and the conceit was enshrined in law, including one passed by Edward the Confessor (r. 1042–66):

> *lupinum enim capud gerit a die utlagationis sue, quod ab Anglis wluesheued nominataur.*[45]
> From the day of his outlawry he carries a wolf's head, which is called *wluesheued* by the English.

This strange expression derives from an ancient Germanic law in which the outlawed person was forced literally to wear a wolf's head around their neck in order to signify to strangers that they were an outlaw and their life forfeit. Since the person in question behaved like a wolf, so too was their life deemed to be worth that of the hated monster of the woods, and they were designated *caput lupinum*, or 'wolf's head'. The loss of humanity equated with becoming an outlaw and close identification with the beast is further indicated by the kenning for 'gallows', *wulfheafedtreo*, literally meaning wolf-head beam or tree.[46]

This association between outlaws, criminals and wolves had an even more literal form than the *caput lupinum*. The *Old English Boethius* suggests that criminals are more beast, or even monster, than man: 'if you meet someone so defiled that he is turned away from good to evil, you may not rightfully call him a man but a beast. If you perceive that someone is avaricious and a robber, you must not call him a man but a wolf.'[47] Linking the sinful with wolves was clearly current beyond the dusty vellum of Anglo-Saxon law. Deeply embedded in the Anglo-Saxon mindset was the total equation of wolf and outlawed criminal in the noun *wearg*, which could mean a criminal, an evil spirit or a wolf.[48] The term is so ancient and ingrained – though it is never used in Anglo-Saxon laws – that its specific meaning, and how one becomes a *wearg*, is unclear. *Maxims II* seems to indicate that a *wearg*'s wrongdoings were at the more extreme end of the outlaw's crimes: 'the *wearg* [*wearh*] will hang, justly pay for the evils he previously committed against mankind [*ær facen dyde manna cynne*]'.[49] *Maxims II* suggests that the *wearg* is someone who sins not just against his immediate community but against the entire human race, meaning that the crime would have to be far more appalling than a simple murder (for which it was usually possible to pay *wergild*, compensation determined by the victim's social status), ignoring legal statutes or failing to keep the peace. What better way to define such an evildoer than to render them indistinguishable from the grey monster of the woods, the wolf? Where the outlaw no longer enjoys the legal protection common to all men and is merely sent to live among wolves, the *wearg* becomes one and must be destroyed.

The tradition of the *wearg* dates back to long before the Anglo-Saxon settlement of Britannia in the mid-fifth century to the bishop Wulfila's fourth-century translation of the Bible into Gothic, in which Christ is shamefully condemned to be crucified as a *gawargjand*.[50] The early sixth-century *Lex salica* (Salic Law), a compilation of Germanic law used by the Franks, may also have some bearing on what it was that made someone a *wearg* in Anglo-Saxon England: 'if anyone disinters or despoils a buried body, let him be a *warg* [*sic*].'[51] Intriguingly, the equation of wolves and criminals is even older than Wulfila's Gothic Bible; in Hittite law from about 1600 BC it is said that if a man elopes with a woman, then kills two or more of the rescuing party, compensation cannot be paid: instead, 'Thou art become a wolf.'[52]

Whatever it was that turned a human into a *wearg*, these monsters were thought so heinous that in the depiction of hell in Blickling Homily XVII, their presence alone is a punishment for sinners: 'under that stone [where the demons tormented the damned souls] was the dwelling of sea-monsters and *weargs*.'[53] Places where *weargs* were executed were local landmarks, and in a boundary clause from 957 in Stanton St Bernard, Wiltshire, *þa wearh roda on wodnes dic*, meaning 'the *wearg* cross or gallows on Woden's Ditch' (modern Wansdyke), helps to delineate an estate. Executing the *wearg* on a landscape feature thought to have been built by a pagan deity is an appropriate end for someone thought to have crossed the boundary beyond what is human and what is monstrous or wolf-like.

The rudiments of the later werewolf tradition are all here in the lore of the man-turned-monster-wolf. The individual deemed a *wearg* lost their status as a human after crossing a moral boundary and, in effectively becoming a wolf, had to be obliterated. However, although there is nothing semantic to separate a wolf and a man designated a *wearg*, there is no evidence that the transformation was thought to be entirely literal. The word 'werewolf' comes from the Anglo-Saxon *wer* (man) + *wulf*, but the only instances in which it is used are clearly not references to people who have physically transformed. Our old friend Wulfstan, appropriately enough, is responsible for its first use as a noun, in the laws he drew up in 1020 for King Cnut:

> Therefore must the shepherds be very watchful and diligently cry out, who have to shield the people against the spoiler; such are bishops and mass-priests, who are to preserve and defend their spiritual flocks with wise instructions, so that the madly audacious werewolf [*wodfreca were-wulf*] does not too widely devastate, nor bite too many of the spiritual flock.[54]

Sadly, Wulfstan here is tautologically cementing the link between evil men doing Satan's bidding, who might corrupt Christians, and the wolf of the metaphor. There was even a ninth-century Mercian priest named Werewolf, described in glowing terms by the Welsh monk Asser as a learned man who assisted Alfred the Great in his educational reforms. The werewolf tradition was to blossom after the Anglo-Saxon period ended, but the associations that would give birth to the northern European idea of a man so bestial he becomes a literal wolf were present in Anglo-Saxon thought.

FOR THE ANGLO-SAXONS, THE wolf was the antithesis of a good, civilized person: violent, hostile to humankind, a monster that lived where civilization ended, a satanic beast whose attributes would be witnessed by the sinful who ended up in darkest hell, and a despoiler of real and symbolic flocks of sheep. However, it is clear that the boundary between man and monster-wolf was not as stable as it may have seemed: men could become indistinguishable from wolves, either by being sentenced to live among them or by being dubbed and executed a *wearg*, all through their wicked deeds. The possibility of becoming a wolf, albeit not literally, was a very real threat. We end with a dire warning from Ælfric's account of St Edmund's martyrdom. Though the wolf that protects the saint's dismembered head is controlled by God, it still shows some spiritual goodness in not eating it. It is not the only wolf in the text, however. Hinguar (Ivar the Boneless), the Viking who tortures and executes the king, *swa swa wulf on lande bestalcode* (went stealthily across the land like a wolf). Like the story of Decius and the dog-headed St Christopher discussed in the previous chapter, the wolf in Ælfric's text poses the disturbing question of which is the real monster: the hideous wolf that guards the saint's holy head, or the Viking who killed that very saint for his own amusement?

III
HIC SUNT DRACONES

Sharing the wilderness of Anglo-Saxon England with the wolves were a far more formidable foe: dragons. There is no doubt that, for all the dragon's symbolic connotations, the Anglo-Saxons believed that the wild places of their island were home to vast fire-breathing serpents with a burning hatred of man. And yet the Anglo-Saxon dragon simply could not do without the human race it threatened and despised.

The Natural History of Dragons

The dragon is remarkably widespread across the world. Even today, dragons are familiar from sources as disparate as China's annual Dragon Boat Festival and the Welsh national flag, and the situation in the first millennium AD was equally ubiquitous. Dragons were present in Mesopotamia, the great ancient civilization that flourished between about 4000 BC and the seventh century AD. In the *Enuma Elish*, the Babylonian creation epic probably composed in the fourteenth century BC, the goddess Tiamat takes the form of a sea-dragon and fights the storm god Marduk, who creates heaven and earth from Tiamat's corpse after defeating her. Tiamat is often depicted in her draconic form and was seen as the mother of all dragons in Mesopotamian cosmology. In East Asian culture, the dragon has traditionally been associated with the forces of nature, especially storms, and consequently crop fertility, and is of a similar antiquity. There are also dragons in the Bible and ancient Greek and Roman culture.

Historians have long puzzled over the presence of dragons in so many disparate cultures. Few believe that they were real creatures, but one popular theory plausibly suggests that the dragon myth originated with people across the world uncovering dinosaur bones at various stages of history and creating narratives to explain them.[1] Alternatively, the anthropologist David E. Jones has linked dragons to humans' inbuilt fear of snakes and apex predators such as big cats, a behavioural relic of evolution, and suggests that these deadly foes were combined into the dragon.[2] While both hypotheses are tenable, and no doubt fossils and people's fear of being poisoned or eaten contributed to dragon mythology, neither theory wholly accounts for the remarkable similarities between, say, a dragon slain by a knight in a fourteenth-century medieval romance and one of Tiamat's children carved on an ancient Mesopotamian temple.

However they reached northern Europe, there were dragons in Anglo-Saxon England. The Anglo-Saxons knew dragons by two Old English words, *draca* (from the Latin *draco*) and *wyrm*. There does not seem to have been any difference between the terms when applied to dragons in the Anglo-Saxon period, although in the later medieval period *wyrm* solely signified wingless, serpentine beasts while the Middle English noun *dragon* denoted the airborne, fire-breathing variety. Old English *wyrm* was a more flexible term than *draca*, though, and beyond a dragon could also mean a snake, such as those that attack Alexander in the *Letter of Alexander to Aristotle*, or even the maggots that devour corpses and frequently appear in homiletic literature, urging people to behave themselves. In Anglo-Latin, *basiliscus*, or basilisk, could also mean dragon, though dragons and basilisks elsewhere have a distinct mythology. In the traditions available through Latin texts to the Anglo-Saxons, the basilisk is a serpent with the power to kill living things with a glance, touch or its revolting breath, leaving the areas around its fetid lair devoid of all life. 'Basilisk' comes from the Greek *basiliscus*, means 'little king', and Pliny and Isidore, while maintaining the beast's deadly nature and kingship over snakes, insist upon its improbably diminutive size: Pliny states twelve inches, Isidore a measly six.[3] Although some of the basilisk's natural history, largely its deadly breath and habit of leaving its surroundings barren, informs the characteristics of the Anglo-Saxon dragon, the basilisk as a distinct entity was familiar in learned Anglo-Saxon circles. The solution to one of Aldhelm's riddles, for instance, is a weasel, and as a clue he mentions the tiny mustelid's unusual reputation as the single animal capable of killing a basilisk, but uses the term *draconem* for their mythical foes.[4] This conflation is also traceable in the vernacular tradition, where *basiliscus* in Latin texts is usually glossed with the Old English *fagwyrm* (coloured-*wyrm*).[5] This verbal link is significant, for parts of the Anglo-Saxon dragon's behaviour – sadly omitting weasels – resemble that of the basilisk, as we shall see later in the chapter. Thus we might use dragon and basilisk interchangeably, and without censure.

Beyond short textual references, we have three main sources for Anglo-Saxon dragons or basilisks: the lengthy description of a dragon in *Beowulf*, the record of dragons spotted over Northumbria in the *Anglo-Saxon Chronicle*'s entry for 793, and Aldhelm's accounts of basilisk-fighting virgins in both the prose and poetic versions of his *De virginitate* (Concerning Virginity). From these sources, we can reconstruct something of the dragon's taxonomy. All three texts agree that the dragon's breath was

Dragon ornament from the shield excavated at Sutton Hoo.

deadly, and they were thought to breathe fire or poison (or both, in the case of Beowulf's final adversary). Although Aldhelm does not mention whether his basilisks could fly, the dragons of *Beowulf* and the *Chronicle* are explicitly airborne, and the beast depicted on the Sutton Hoo shield possesses no fewer than four pairs of wings. Aldhelm mentions the great size of the dragon slain by the holy virgin Victoria, and *Beowulf* states the basilisk's length as *fiftiges fotgemearces* (fifty feet).[6] Aldhelm and the *Beowulf* poet

Christ trampling the beasts, including a dragon, from the Winchcombe Psalter f. 195v.

both mention the dragon's reptilian appearance, with Aldhelm describing its scales (*squamigerum*, scaly) and the *Beowulf* poet its sliminess (*nacod*, smooth).[7] The latter dragon's hide is extremely tough and snaps Beowulf's sword during the fight. Though the *Chronicle* omits any physical description of the dragons it records, we can assume that these too were reptilian, since the dragon in Anglo-Saxon art is always somewhat serpentine or crocodilian. At least some Anglo-Saxon dragons had legs and feet with sharp claws, such as in the Sutton Hoo shield decorations and the depiction of Christ trampling the basilisk in the Winchcombe Psalter of about 1025–50, though neither Aldhelm, the *Chronicle* nor the *Beowulf*-poet explicitly mentions limbs. With the monster's physical appearance in mind, we turn now to its behaviour.

The Anglo-Saxon Dragon

> *Draca sceal on hlæwe, frod, frætwum wlanc.*[8]
> The dragon must be in the burial mound, wise [and] proud with treasures.

Like all Anglo-Saxon monsters, the dragon was thought to be a beast of the wilderness. In *Beowulf*, which devotes almost 1,000 lines to the hero's final fight with a dragon, the monster lives in a 'burial-mound under the earth near the surging of the sea'.[9] This dragon lives at the extreme uncivilized limit of the land, elsewhere called a *westenne* (wilderness),[10] where Beowulf's kingdom gives way to the great sea. The dragon's lair is moreover so distant that only one man knows where it is ('he alone knew the earth-hall').[11] Likewise, the troublesome basilisk ravaging a city in Aldhelm's story of Victoria in the poetic *De virginitate* is banished to its rightful home in *vacuas . . . selebras* (empty wastelands) and *incultis . . . arvis* (uncultivated fields).[12] Describing Cedd's foundation of a monastery in a remote location, Bede gives a biblical quote that cements the association of dragons with wilderness: 'in the dens where dragons dwelt before [*in cubilibus in quibus prius dracones habitabant*], shall rise up the verdure of the reed and the bulrush.'[13] It is clear from both Anglo-Latin and Old English texts that the dragon or basilisk not only defines its home a wilderness by merit of its ideological resonance but subjects the area to a physical transformation. Recalling the basilisk mythology found in Pliny and Isidore – where the beast's gaze and foul breath kill all life in the vicinity – the area around the Anglo-Saxon dragon's home is often polluted, devoid of life and uninhabitable by man. In Tribula, says Aldhelm, 'a deadly dragon [*draco*] belched gusts from its stomach, corrupting the clear air with deadly poisons, so much that the citizens, frenzied in a great panic, now preferred to forsake the city polluted with its exhalations.'[14] Vernacular dragons, such as the following in *Solomon and Saturn* II, an arcane poetic dialogue between the biblical King Solomon and a Chaldean prince named Saturn preserved in a tenth-century portion of Cambridge, Corpus Christi College, MS 422, are equally guilty of polluting their homes: 'on that field he [Wulf] slew 25 dragons at daybreak, and then death destroyed him, because no man can seek that land, no one the border-place [*merc-stede*], nor birds fly there, any more than beasts of the earth.'[15] This befouling effect is also mentioned in *Beowulf*, albeit only after the dragon has been provoked, which we will subsequently discuss in greater detail.

But where the dragons of Aldhelm and Old English poetry diverge is in their specific natural habitat within the wilderness. For as the quotation above, from *Maxims* II, suggests, dragons were widely thought to live in burial mounds. Just as the *Maxims* II dragon lives in a *hlæwe*, Beowulf's final adversary lives in a *stanbeorh steapne* (steep stone barrow).[16] This was the dragon's natural environment, and the *Beowulf* poet goes further in explaining how dragons customarily find a home, echoing the form of *Maxims* II: *he gesecean sceall/ hord on hrusan* (he must seek a [treasure] hoard in the ground, that is, a barrow).[17] Several Anglo-Saxon place names refer to this superstition, such as Drakelow (*draca* + *hlæw*, 'dragon's burial mound') in Derbyshire and Worcestershire, and Wormwood Hill in Cambridgeshire, which was formerly called Wyrmelawe (*wyrm* + *hlæw*).[18] At first glance, this aspect of the dragon's behaviour may seem to run contrary to its association with the wilderness, but there was a very good reason that the monsters chose to live in this particular man-made place.

Anglo-Saxon England was dotted with burial mounds. Many of these were prehistoric in origin, such as Wayland's Smithy in Oxfordshire or the West Kennet Long Barrow in Wiltshire, and were looming over the surrounding landscape long before the first Anglo-Saxons arrived as mercenaries in the fourth century. Their origin was a mystery, but the pagan Anglo-Saxons who permanently settled in Britannia correctly deduced that barrows must be the graves of important people, and from the mid-sixth century onwards chose to emulate the native kings of their new homeland.[19] Sometimes they interred their dead in existing mounds, at other

West Kennet Long Barrow, a Neolithic grave that contains artefacts dated between 3000 and 2600 BC, was standing long before the Anglo-Saxons arrived.

Anglo-Saxon burial mounds at Sutton Hoo.

times they raised new structures. The most famous and dramatic of the copycat Anglo-Saxon burial mounds is Sutton Hoo, which contains eighteen tumuli, including one widely believed to contain King Rædwald of East Anglia (d. *c.* 624).[20] Pre-Anglo-Saxon barrows mostly survived intact in fairly isolated places, as did imitative cemeteries such as Sutton Hoo.

What is crucial to note about these burial mounds, and their Anglo-Saxon imitations, is that they were built by pagans (though the people who buried their dead at Sutton Hoo seem to have been hedging their bets and stuffed the graves with both pagan and Christian artefacts). With the spread of Christianity, the Anglo-Saxons ceased to copy the example of the heathen former inhabitants of Britain and began burying corpses on sanctified ground in a manner more akin to modern funerary practices. Thus from the post-conversion period onwards, people began to view burial mounds with fear and suspicion. Regardless of their age, burial mounds and prehistoric earthworks came to be associated with the dreaded pagan deities the Anglo-Saxons once worshipped. The numerous monuments across southern England, of both prehistoric and Anglo-Saxon origin, known as 'Grim's Ditch' ascribe their construction to Woden, who was sometimes nicknamed Grim, 'the masked one'.[21] Place names we still use today also testify to the supposed malevolent and heathen nature of burial mounds, such as Shuckburgh in Warwickshire (*scucca* + *beorg*, 'demon's burial mound/hill').[22] Burial mounds and earthworks also became common places for judicial executions as an appropriately unchristian punishment for criminals.[23] For example, the sixth-century barrows at Guildown, in Guildford, Surrey, became an execution site in the tenth and eleventh centuries, recalling the '*wearg* gallows on Woden's Ditch' in Wiltshire discussed in the previous chapter.[24]

Another reason for the use of burial mounds as places for capital punishment was their association with boundaries. Barrows of all ages were prominent and well-known features of the landscape, and lent themselves to the demarcation of a territory's perimeter: the charter corpus describes 150 barrows defining the borders of a piece of land, and around 90 per cent of Anglo-Saxon execution sites are at hundred (part of a shire divided for judicial and military purposes) boundaries.[25] With the Anglo-Saxon view of boundaries as both physical and ideological markers, executing wrongdoers on a boundary marker associated with heathenism was a deeply symbolic act.

Thus the dragon, in choosing to live in barrows, announces itself to be a beast of the pagan wilderness, and fits our monster paradigm perfectly. Although the Continental basilisks described by Aldhelm in the poetic *De virginitate* do not live in a burial mound in the wilderness, instead scourging cities close to where they live, it is clear that heathenism remains the motivation behind their choice of habitat. Victoria banishes the basilisk slaughtering people in the town of Tribula in exchange for the locals forsaking their pagan beliefs, and things are even worse in Rome, where a crypt-dwelling specimen scourges the Eternal City because the inhabitants 'disdained to accept the one Christ, thinking that veneration of a horrifying serpent was preferable'.[26] Moreover, Victoria banishes the basilisk of Tribula in the name of Christ. A similar pattern of a dragon worshipped as a false, heathen deity is contained within Ælfric's sermon *De falsis deis* (Concerning False Gods), which describes how the Babylonians brought food and offerings to a dragon that they believed to be divine and which lived in their city. The prophet Daniel feeds it morsels laced with boiling pitch, and the poor basilisk explodes. By merit of their pagan actions, the people of Tribula, Rome and Babylon have transformed the civilization of their physical homes to ideological wilderness (and almost literal wilderness in the case of Tribula, which has been abandoned by its townsfolk), and thus the dragons are attracted to take up residence. Once civilization returns, in the form of Victoria, Silvester and Daniel, to banish heathenism, the local basilisk can no longer thrive.

A Warning to the Curious

The attraction of burial mounds to dragons was not just their heathen and uncivilized nature, however, but the treasure inside. Prehistoric burial mounds contained not just the glorious dead but all manner of treasure and artefacts. Burying the dead with physical objects was a common practice across the ancient world – from the ancient Egyptians interred with treasure to make their way through the next world, to the Bronze Age man laid to rest at Stonehenge with a bow and arrows in preparation for post-mortem battle – and suggests something of the physical nature of the heathen afterlife, if such a broad generalization can be made without censure. The pre-Christian Anglo-Saxons similarly buried their dead with all manner of artefacts, including the wonderful treasure excavated from the ship burial at Sutton Hoo. Since the tradition of interring the dead with weapons, coins and treasure is also known in the ancestral homelands of the Anglo-Saxons, this could have been a tradition imported from the Continent that found pre-Anglo-Saxon analogues in the prehistoric barrows of Britain, as much as another instance of native culture being imitated.

The association of dragons with treasure is likely a pagan tradition. After all, treasure buried in a conspicuous, man-made burial mound would no doubt have attracted thieves. Talk of dragons guarding the treasure in the mound would presumably have worked as a deterrent to potential grave-robbers. It was the dragon's job to protect the gold: in *Beowulf*, the dragon '*hæðen gold / warað wintrum frod*' (guards heathen gold, wise in winters).[27] From this position, it was but a natural development to suggest that the dragon loved the gold that it guarded from thieves. Further, in robbing the dead in a prehistoric or pagan Anglo-Saxon burial, the perpetrator was also crossing the boundary between life and death. While there is precious little evidence about how the afterlife was conceived by the pagan Anglo-Saxons, it is conceivable that, as in many other pagan cosmologies, the centre of the earth had some role to play. Perhaps the barrow was not just a grave but a gateway to the realm of the dead itself, and so in entering the burial mound a living person was crossing the threshold between this world and the next, a taboo and threat to the separation of the two realms. The dragon, in this scenario, was a guardian of the underworld. The Old English poem *Christ and Satan*, at least, has dragons guarding the entrance to the Christian hell: 'dragons [*dracan*] eternally dwell at the doors of hell, hot in their breasts.'[28] Vercelli Homily IV, found in the tenth-century Vercelli book, even configures damnation as being swallowed by a dragon: 'they never return . . . from the gullet of the dragon [*þæs dracan ceolan*] that is named Satan.'[29] Whatever the tradition's origin, dragons are depicted on grave goods from the pagan or early conversion periods, and at Sutton Hoo they are found decorating a shield: dragons were quite literally in the barrows.

There may also be a natural explanation for the dragon's home being in a barrow. Archaeologists have noted that burial mounds were often made of very fine sediment, which sealed the inner chamber from the surrounding environment. Under such conditions, methane-producing bacteria flourish and are able to consume more than just their usual diet of the contents of the interred person's gut. Over time, the amount of methane built up to such an extent that once the barrow was opened a jet of gas would come shooting out. Were the grave being robbed at night, and hence by torch, the resulting explosion when the fire ignited the methane may have led people to assume that a dragon was living within the mound, thereby birthing a tradition.[30] Such an occurrence would no doubt have been memorable, but, like the other theories about the origin of dragons, it must remain a hypothesis. For our purposes, the widespread belief that dragons lived in heathen barrows and the richness of the surrounding lore far outweighs any consideration of how this tradition came to be.

By the time that dragons were written about, the Anglo-Saxons had been converted, but the pagan association of dragons with treasure did not die out. Old English texts make it clear that dragons lived in barrows because they contained treasure. The dragon described in *Maxims* II is 'wise, [and] proud with treasures' (*frod, frætwum wlanc*), and the dragon that fights Beowulf 'guards heathen gold, wise in winters'. In the *Beowulf* account, the dragon sits guarding the *hæðen gold* for three hundred winters, until its hoard is robbed. Unlike the literary wolves of the previous chapter, which stay in the wilderness and attack anyone who crosses the boundary separating it from civilization, people have a very direct role to play in turning a seldom-seen, silent security guard into a deadly monster.

Dragons like the one in *Beowulf* seem to have been content to guard their treasure and avoid people, if left unmolested. When a dragon's hoard was plundered, however, the consequences were dire. In *Beowulf*, the basilisk is provoked when a desperate slave, exiled by his lord, stumbles upon the barrow and steals a *fæted wæge* (gold-plated cup) with which he regains his master's favour, at a terrible cost.[31] Despite the fact that 'there were many other ancient treasures in the earth-hall',the dragon still notices that a single, tiny piece of its hoard has gone.[32] Its behaviour upon finding that it has been burgled is a stark reminder that the dragon was very much a part of nature to the Anglo-Saxons:

> When the dragon [*wyrm*] awoke, hostility was renewed; it sniffed across the stone, the stark-hearted one discovered the enemy's footprints . . . The hoard-guardian sought eagerly along the ground, wished to find the man, he who had sorely harmed him in sleep, hot and troubled in mind it circled around the outside of the burial-mound [*hlæw*] often . . . sometimes it returned to the barrow, sought the costly vessel.[33]

The dragon responds to the presence of man like any wild animal, sniffing and following the interloper's tracks. There is however something rather sad and slightly human about the dragon's occasional returns to the inside of the *hlæw*, as it checks and double-checks whether it has made a mistake in its inventory. Being a dragon, though, it is not long before it unleashes its rage on the surrounding land:

> The hoard-guardian waited with difficulty until evening came; the guardian of the barrow was then swollen with rage [*gebolgen*], the hostile-one wished to requite with fire the beloved drinking cup. Then the day had passed away to the joy of the dragon [*wyrme*]; he did not lie within the wall, [nor] wished to wait, but went with fire, impelled with fire. The beginning was terrible to the people in the land . . . the hated air-flyer did not wish to leave anything there alive.[34]

The basilisk proceeds to burn everything in the vicinity of its barrow indiscriminately with fiery breath, its aim to kill everyone it comes across. Like all monsters, the dragon is protecting the integrity of its wilderness home, and once this is breached by theft and trespass it responds with murderous intent.

Despite the dragon's excessive reaction to a small piece of its copious treasure being taken, it is clear that this is all the fault of a man, and no blame is laid at the dragon's door. In the words of the poem, the dragon peacefully guards the hoard for three hundred years, '*oððæt hyne an abealch / mon on mode*' (until a certain man enraged him in his heart).[35] While the dragon was a protection against thieves and potential otherworld interlopers in the pagan period, after the conversion it clearly operated as a warning against immorality. Grave-robbing in and of itself was a Christian taboo, and in the late Anglo-Saxon law code known as *Walreaf*, stealing from the dead is defined in most serious terms as the action of an outlaw.[36] Moreover, robbing a grave was an act motivated by avarice, a major Christian sin, and it is here that the pagan nature of the treasure is especially important. Grave-robbers broke a taboo in entering and plundering a barrow, made only worse by their goal being heathen, and inherently sinful, gold. The example of the slave in *Beowulf* is a dire warning. The dragon, inextricably linked with heathenism, is a symbol of what will happen to a land harbouring people of such low, pagan morals: it will be turned from civilization to wilderness, just as the basilisk's fire physically turns the cultivated land to a barren tundra. The lasting moral outrage at such symbolically charged behaviour is reflected in place names such as Brokenborough in Wiltshire, which is formed from *brocenan + beorge*, 'broken burial-mound', and memorializes a grave that has been plundered.[37]

Chaos and Cupidity

The dragon is able to fulfil this symbolic role because it is a monster of the pagan wilderness. As *Maxims II* states, 'the dragon must be in the burial mound'; provoking it to leave disrupts the divinely ordained order of the world. Just as the basilisk banished by Victoria in the poetic *De virginitate* has caused the people of Tribula to abandon their town because of its poisonous breath, so too the dragon of *Beowulf* razes the surrounding human dwellings to the ground. This Scandinavian dragon goes even further in its symbolic role as the enemy of civilization by attacking the Geats' great hall: 'then the terror was quickly and truthfully reported to Beowulf, that his own home, the best of buildings, the gift-throne of the Geats [*gifstol Geata*], had melted in burning flames.'[38] The poem makes it clear that this victim of the dragon's rage was no ordinary building. The hall in Anglo-Saxon poetry was symbolic of order and civilization.[39] Beowulf's hall is explicitly described as the 'gift-throne of the Geats', and in heroic poetry the dispensing of treasure was a symbolic act that ensured peace and fellowship in a community. The very symbol of Beowulf's rule and power over his land has been destroyed by the forces of chaos, which on the literal level causes severe disruption to the order in Geatland that Beowulf has laboured so hard to preserve. The dire warning of the poem is that entire civilizations can be brought to chaos and wilderness by the acts of individual men, even a desperate slave plundering the dragon's hoard. Without Christian morality and man's ability to withstand temptation, civilization will revert to wilderness, and basilisks, no longer confined to isolated pagan monuments, will leave their designated homes in this new, disordered world. Aldhelm's worshipped dragons bear the truth of this statement.

It has also been suggested that the dragon in *Beowulf* is a metaphor for war. It launches its attack as retaliation, engaging in a feud like many of the nations mentioned in the poem, and turns the cultivated land to waste, razing buildings and killing countless people in the process. It also destroys the centre of power and legal administration in the form of the hall. For the scholar Kathryn Hume, this all suggests the actions of an invading army.[40] Certainly, the dragon's behaviour does resemble the effects of a bloody invasion, which also involves the crossing of boundaries from one territory to the next, but the dragon's significance, in both *Beowulf* and Anglo-Saxon culture more broadly, is greater. The dragon represents the far more potent forces that can be unleashed simply by man falling into sin, a much greater threat to civilization.

Beowulf, as the representative of the civilization that has been destroyed by the dragon, must fight back. He puts his trust in God – 'for us it must happen at the wall [the dragon's barrow] as Fate, the Creator of all Men, allots for us'[41] – and thus exhibits the qualities that define the Christian world, refusing to shirk his responsibility as king to rid his land of the presence of the dragon. Leaving to one side his eleven retainers and the cup-thief forced to show them the barrow, Beowulf arrives at the basilisk's lair and summons the beast with a mighty bellow. The dragon displays again its enmity to man as it immediately rushes out to attack Beowulf upon hearing *mannes reorde* (the voice of a man).[42] Before it emerges, the dragon shoots a jet of molten fire from the entrance to the barrow, then flies and writhes through the flames towards Beowulf.

We can garner a few specific details about dragons in examining the fight narrative. The dragon's hide is so tough that Beowulf's sword, Nægling, an ancient heirloom that has seen much success in battle, fails to cut through it, and it later snaps entirely when it connects with the monster's skull. In fact, the dragon is so strong that Beowulf only defeats it with the help of his brave young retainer Wiglaf. Wiglaf is the only one of the soldiers Beowulf brings with him to the dragon's lair who actually intervenes when it becomes clear that the monster is going to emerge victorious. He rebukes his cowardly kinsmen, then joins Beowulf in the fray. Unfortunately, the dragon is even more angered by the presence of a second man, and launches the fatal attack on Beowulf:

> Then a third time the people's foe, the terrible fire-dragon, rushed on the brave one, mindful of hostilities, when he was yielded space, hot and battle-grim, clasped him entirely around the neck with sharp fangs; he [Beowulf] became drenched with life-blood, wet with waves of gore.[43]

Beowulf's killer is equally deadly with its fiery breath and sharp teeth. Wiglaf then lunges forward and pierces the dragon through its belly, allowing Beowulf to deliver the *coup de grâce* with a small knife he has strapped to his belt. Alas, the dragon's bite is fatal, and Beowulf's neck *swelan ond swellan* (burned and swelled) and *him on breostum bealoniðe weoll / attor on innan* (the baleful affliction boiled in his breast, the venom within).[44] The dead hero receives a noble burial, but the dragon is rather unceremoniously chucked into the sea. Beyond buttressing our knowledge of how dragons attack, the point of the episode is to highlight the rottenness of Geatland. Wiglaf is the only one of Beowulf's most trusted retainers unwilling to abandon his king to the evil dragon. He reminds them of the promises they had made in exchange for gifts in the hall, but still they refuse to honour the near-sacred bonds of fellowship that make for a peaceful world that can overcome the uncivilized pagan forces represented by the dragon. The dragon, then, tests the mettle of the Geatish forces and finds only Beowulf and Wiglaf worthy. No wonder a grave-robbing thief has been fostered in such a fetid place.

Dragons and the Apocalypse

Leading directly on from the dragon's role as the bringer of chaos, we move now to the association of dragons with the end of the world. In both the pagan and Christian tradition, the dragon is one of the beasts of the Apocalypse. In the Book of Revelation, Satan is described as a dragon:

> And there was seen another sign in heaven: and behold a great red dragon, having seven heads, and ten horns: and on his heads seven diadems . . . And that great dragon was cast out, that old serpent, who is called the devil and Satan, who seduceth the whole world . . . (12:3, 9)

Although he was defeated and exiled from heaven, the dragon then appears again at the Apocalypse: 'I saw a woman [the Whore of Babylon] sitting upon a scarlet coloured beast, full of names of blasphemy, having seven heads and ten horns' (Revelation 17:3). The return of the dragon marked one of the key moments of the Apocalypse, in which Satan, the dragon, is vanquished once and for all by Christ, the lamb. The events of the Apocalypse as told in Revelation were a popular subject for medieval religious art, and Bede records just such a painting installed by Benedict Biscop in his own monastery:

> He carried [from Rome] pictures of sacred likenesses with him to decorate the church of St Peter the Apostle which he had built ... likenesses of the vision of the Apocalypse of St John [Revelation], to decorate the north wall, so that all who entered the church, even though they were ignorant of letters ... having the final moment of the Last Judgement as if before their eyes, [they would] be brought to examine themselves with appropriate severity.[45]

The Apocalypse, as Bede states, was a crucial means to terrify laymen into religious conformity and acceptable behaviour, and the seven-headed dragon was among its most harrowing and memorable moments.

Another dragon, or monstrous water-serpent, has an important role at Ragnarok, the apocalypse of Norse paganism. Among the other fatal battles fought by the gods, Thor, the thunder god, fights Jörmungandr, a serpent so large that it can encircle the earth.[46] Although Thor defeats the beast, it also spells the end for him and brings about the new world that follows the age of Odin (Woden for the Anglo-Saxons). As we have reflected, it is foolhardy to assume that the written facts of Norse paganism committed to the page centuries after the religion more or less died out are identical to the nebulous and little-known beliefs of the pagan Anglo-Saxons, but the parallel is worth noting here. Thor was an important god, in one manifestation or another, to the pre-conversion Anglo-Saxons, and it is not impossible that this particular legend contributed in part to the association of dragons with the end of the world in popular consciousness. The story of Thor's battle with Jörmungandr would at least have been told in Anglo-Saxon England once the Viking settlement began, and a battle between the adversaries is possibly depicted on the tenth-century Gosforth Cross in Cumberland.[47]

Certainly, there is evidence that dragons were interpreted as portents of the end of the world or coming destruction. When he hears the grave news about his hall being burned to cinders by a dragon, Beowulf immediately assumes he has angered God in some way: 'the wise man thought that he had made the Ruler, the Ancient Lord, bitterly swell with rage [*gebulge*] over an ancient law.'[48] The poem, of course, blames the foolhardy thief entirely for the destruction of Geatland, but Beowulf's reaction to the news is telling. Although the dragon has not been sent as a judgment on Beowulf himself, it does bring about his death by merit of a poisonous bite to the shoulder, and the predicted fate of the Geat nation without their heroic leader is nothing short of apocalyptic:

> The Swedish people will attack us, when they learn that our king is dead, he who before preserved our treasure-hoard and kingdom against foes . . . therefore spears, morning-cold, must be many, grasped with palms, lifted in hands. By no means will the sound of the harp wake the warriors, but the dark raven eager for corpses shall speak much, tell the eagle how he succeeded at the meal when he plundered the slaughtered with the wolf.[49]

The messenger who reports the news of Beowulf's death makes it clear that peace and prosperity have gone with the king, and that now the Geats will be slaughtered and left as a feast for the Beasts of Battle, including our old friend the wolf.

The belief that the appearance of dragons foretold destruction is evident elsewhere in Anglo-Saxon texts. In the *Anglo-Saxon Chronicle*, the appearance of dragons in the year 793 is recorded in these lines:

> Here terrible portents came over the land of the Northumbrians and wretchedly frightened the people. These were whirlwinds without measure and flashes of light, and fiery dragons [*fyrenne dracan*] were seen flying in the air. A great famine soon followed these tokens and, a little after that, the same year on the 6th before the Ides of January the harrowing of heathen men wretchedly destroyed God's church on Lindisfarne through plunder and slaughter.[50]

The chronicler is in no doubt that dragons flying over Northumbria warned of the famine and the atrocity on Lindisfarne that swiftly followed. This attack on Lindisfarne was the notorious raid that marked the beginning of the Viking Age in Britain, and it is important to note that the coming of a heathen army was announced by the appearance of the dragon, a pagan monster. The sight of dragons predicting bloody defeat is also evident in *The Battle of Finnsburh* (or the Finnsburh Fragment), an incomplete poem copied from a now-lost manuscript fragment, when King Hnæf, on the eve of battle, reassures his men that *her draca ne fleogeð* (the dragon is not flying here):[51] the mere appearance of dragons would guarantee doom to his army.

Although none of the examples above link to the Apocalypse directly, the result of the dragon's rage would certainly have reminded the Anglo-Saxons of Judgment Day. Across Old English poetry, the sight of a ruined city inspires an elegiac mood and leads to a contemplation of the terrors of the Apocalypse.

> The wise man must understand how terrible it will be when the wealth of all this world stands as wilderness [*weste*], just as now variously throughout this middle-earth walls stand blown against by wind, fallen with frost, the houses ruinous.[52]

Similarly, reading about the dragon of *Beowulf* sweeping with fire the world surrounding its barrow, killing and destroying everything in its wake, would have made an Anglo-Saxon think of the end of days, and this presumably went for contemplating any dragon disturbed from its rest. The dragon's apocalyptic associations in both scripture and popular tradition added to its overall monstrosity.

Man-dragons

The dragon is a monster whose ravages and boundary-crossings are explicitly brought about by sinful people. But the dragon's closeness to people goes further than its role as the punisher of men. As well as repaying the avarice of those who would steal its heathen treasure, the dragon is as guilty of the sin as the most feckless grave-robber. For treasure, in heroic poetry, is supposed to be shared out among people. King Hroðgar in *Beowulf* is the shining example of a good monarch, and his goodness is indicated by the number of epithets referring to his generosity: *brego Beorht-Dana* ('lord of the shining Danes', implying how much treasure they wear) and *goldwine* (gold-friend), for example.[53] When he builds his great mead hall of Heorot, Hroðgar intends 'within there to share all such as God gave him with young and old'.[54] Heorot is called a *gifhealle* (gift-hall) and, like Beowulf, Hroðgar sits upon a *gifstol*.[55] Treasure was given out to retainers to pay for their service or forge friendships, and a good king had therefore to be munificent. After Beowulf kills Grendel and Grendel's mother, Hroðgar is exceptionally generous with the treasure he gives to the young man, both as reward and to ensure future good relations with the hero's native Geatland. In the heroic idiom of the poem, sharing treasure is the mark of a good king and symbolizes peace and fellowship among men.

The dragon, however, is the very opposite of generous. After all, it is the theft of a small cup that inspires the holocaust it brings to innocent people unfortunate enough to live near its barrow. Moreover, even when left in peace, the dragon simply sits upon the enormous pile of treasure, guarding it against thieves, and does nothing else: *ne byð him wihte ðy sel* (he is not at all better than before) for doing so, in the poet's understated criticism.[56] Treasure, which should be shared with others, does no good to anyone, including the dragon, when hoarded like this. The dragon's rage when a small part of its hoard is pilfered, and its disproportionate reaction, are inspired by utter, contemptible greed. The basilisk is a miser, an Anglo-Saxon Ebenezer Scrooge, and an example to men not to be so greedy and avaricious. After Beowulf kills Grendel's mother, Hroðgar gives him lengthy advice on being a good king and mentions an individual named Heremod as a negative exemplum. Heremod's actions are very similar to the dragon's: 'by no means did he give [gold] rings to the Danes according to custom; he remained joyless, suffered misery, long-lasting punishment by his people because of that strife.'[57] Heremod's avarice prevented him from giving treasure to his people, whom he moreover treated cruelly according to other parts of the sermon, and as a result was forced into exile, where he was murdered by his new companions. Like the dragon, he guarded his treasure hoard for a long time, and *ne byð him wihte ðy sel.*

The dragon, in this way, was a monstrous symbol of avarice and a warning to men about the consequences of committing the sin. But despite being a fifty-foot-long, fire-breathing, flying monster, the *Beowulf* dragon is not as inhuman as it first seems. However disproportionate its reaction to being robbed, revenge is a human motive, and *Beowulf* is full of descriptions of feuds between warring nations escalating out of control. Beowulf himself conceives of his many deeds of valour as revenge on several occasions, and even delivers the following maxim: *selre bið æghwæm / þæt he his freond wrece, þonne he fela murne* (it is better for everyone that he avenges his friend than mourns too much).[58] In deciding to seek revenge, the dragon displays rational behaviour more fitting of a person, and its thoughts and reactions to things are described on a number of occasions: awaiting the fall of night, it *wiges gefeh* (rejoiced of battle); the day ends *wyrme on willan* (to the joy of the dragon); during the battle with Beowulf, *wæs hringbogan heorte gefysed* (the coiled-serpent's heart was impelled).[59]

The links between men and dragons go even further than feuding and avarice, however. The dragon lives in a barrow, but this is conceptualized in explicitly human terms: *eorðhuse* (earth-house), *eorðsele* and *eorðreced* (both meaning 'earth-hall').[60] Most disturbingly, both Heorot and the barrow are called a *dryhtsele* (splendid hall).[61] Like the human kings in the poem, the dragon lives in a hall filled with treasures, and it is also important to remember that its *eorðsele* is explicitly a man-made structure. When Beowulf fights the dragon, both are old: the dragon has ruled its hall for three hundred years, and Beowulf his for fifty. Beowulf and the dragon are both described as *stearcheort* (stout-hearted), and furthermore Hroðgar, Beowulf and the dragon are each called a *hordweard* (hoard guardian).[62] Clearly, the solitary, miserly dragon is in stark contrast to the popular and generous Beowulf, but the fight can be read as a deadly battle between two kings.

The threshold between men and dragons may therefore be disturbingly permeable. Early in the poem, after Grendel's death, the *scop* (a court poet) at Heorot compares Beowulf to another Germanic hero:

> After his death-day, great fame arose for Sigmund, after the brave warrior killed the dragon, the guardian of the

> hoard. Under the grey stone, the nobleman's son ventured alone upon the perilous deed, [though] Fitela [his nephew] was not with him. However it happened to him, his sword passed through the wondrous dragon [*wrætlicne wyrm*], so that it stood in the wall, noble iron; the dragon melted in the violent assault. The formidable one [*aglæca*] had won the ring-hoard with courage so that he might enjoy it according to his own judgement.[63]

This is a reference to the story told in the Icelandic *Völsunga saga*, written down in the late thirteenth century. The saga relates the history of the Völsungs, a legendary family that suffers numerous plots and conspiracies connected to the cursed ring Andvaranaut and, along with the closely related *Nibelungenlied*, was the inspiration for Wagner's *Ring* cycle and Tolkien's *The Lord of the Rings*. In the standard Völsung story, the dragon slaying described in *Beowulf* is carried out by the famous hero Sigurd rather than his father, Sigmund (spelled Sigemund in *Beowulf*), who is only credited with this feat in the Old English poem. Most interestingly for our purposes, the dragon killed by Sigurd is called Fafnir and used to be a dwarf, humanoid creatures which shared significant characteristics with people in Norse mythology. Fafnir is the son of the dwarf Hreidmar, whom he kills to gain possession of the cursed gold given to Hreidmar by the treacherous god Loki. Venturing into the wilderness with the gold, Fafnir turns himself into a dragon in order to protect it. Sigurd kills Fafnir at the instigation of the dragon's brother Regin and takes possession of the treasure.

Although the *Beowulf* poet does not name the dragon as Fafnir, and has Sigmund rather than Sigurd kill the beast, there are possible indications that the story later told in *Völsunga saga* was known in Anglo-Saxon England. Although Sigurd's slaying of Fafnir first enters the written record in a skaldic stanza of about 1030, the story of the Völsungs circulated first as an oral tale and is considerably older than its first textual occurrence.[64] Numerous depictions of the fight can be found on stone monuments dating from the Viking Age in Britain, such as the tenth-century Halton cross shaft, which displays specific elements of the later Fafnir story, including Sigurd roasting the dragon's heart.[65] Although it is impossible to reconstruct the precise version of the Fafnir legend known in Anglo-Saxon England and truncated in *Beowulf*, the *Beowulf* poet clearly wants the reader to compare Sigmund to Beowulf by drawing a comparison between the two basilisk-slayers, and the possibility that both dragons were once people is also intriguing.

As we have seen, the dragon that Beowulf slays exhibits human behaviour, and even lives in a den described as a human habitation. Could this comparison have been made because the nameless dragon killed by Sigemund was known to be a man-dragon? Over the years, certain critics have argued that the so-called Last Survivor, who buries the treasure in the barrow,[66] is himself the very same dragon that guards it.[67] It has been tenuously suggested that in the original oral version of *Beowulf* told by pagans, this transformation was made explicit, but that by the time it was written down by a Christian the man-dragon was no longer an acceptable part of the story.[68] This is conjecture, and given the impossibility of constructing the *ur*-version of *Beowulf*, any attempt to discover the truth would be futile. But there is enough in the description of the dragon to suggest that it had human qualities and served as a warning to men about the dangers of avarice and crossing the boundaries of civilized behaviour: excessive covetousness and lack of generosity could turn you into a solitary, murderous dragon. In probing the definition of the human, the *Beowulf* dragon recalls the deeds of some of its fellow Nowell Codex monsters in *Wonders of the East*, the *Letter of Alexander to Aristotle* and the *Passion of St Christopher*.

But whether or not people were believed to transform literally into dragons through sin, the link between dragons and people seems to have been strong enough to be captured in stone sculpture.

The Repton Stone, dating from the late seventh to late eighth century, is a fragment of a stone cross from Repton, Derbyshire, that was unearthed in 1979.[69] It was once part of an important monument in this area of Mercia, estimated to have stood at around 3.6 metres (12 ft) high.[70] The stone is badly damaged and only two faces survive. On the first is a man riding a horse, carrying a sword and shield. A band across the rider's head indicates his rank and sovereignty. He wears a skirt and hose, and his horse's bridle is ornate. The absence of a nimbus indicates that this well-dressed man is a secular figure, a ruler of some distinction.

The other side of the Repton Stone, however, is nothing short of horrific. A coiled serpent with a man's head consumes two people, head first, and stares coldly at the viewer. The head is indubitably a man's: it has two protruding human ears and closely set, forward-facing eyes. Positively dwarfing its human victims, the serpent is clearly a dragon of some sort. What, we may ask, is its possible relation to the wealthy equestrian on the other face? Several of the symbolic dragons we have discussed in this chapter offer plausible answers. Given the example of the *Beowulf* dragon and its emphatic links to human kings, it is not impossible that the extant sculpture shows a king corrupted by worldly power and wealth who turned into a dragon as a result. Unfortunately, the lower part of the stone-face is too badly damaged to show whether the creature is sitting upon a pile of treasure, but the positions of the faces of the rider and dragon, sitting on the same level, seem to demand that the beholder compare the two figures. The transformation from man to dragon need not have been literal – the dragon on the cross could be a physical depiction of the state of a soul corrupted by avarice and greed. Perhaps, in moving from wealthy warrior to man-dragon, viewers of the original cross were shown the true, vile nature of the proud rider.

The evident wealth of the dashing rider in contrast to the hideous basilisk does suggest, at the very least, a homiletic link

Repton Stone face: a proud rider.

between the two surviving cross faces. The Repton Stone's dragon has been interpreted as a Hellmouth, a common image in which the entrance to Hell is depicted as the head of a lion or dragon swallowing the damned. But since no other Anglo-Saxon Hell-mouth has a human head, the Repton man-dragon may just be

Repton Stone face: a man-dragon devouring two men.

one of the *dracan* that the poem *Christ and Satan* says dwell in Hades. Either way, the dragon's victims are wearing near-identical hose to the nattily dressed rider, suggesting the latter's moral turpitude.[71] In this sense, the infernal man-dragon may be eating the sinful rider, now damned to Hell after being adjudged guilty of appropriately draconian avarice, a *contrapasso* punishment recalling another of the basilisk's symbolic roles. If there is a relation between the two faces, as is the case on most Anglo-Saxon stone crosses, it is certainly not complimentary to the rider, who is in some way like the hideous dragon with whom he shares a place on the monument.

WHATEVER THE INTENDED PURPOSE of the original Repton cross, the incorporation of a dragon into an ecclesiastical monument is testament to the monster's symbolic flexibility. The Anglo-Saxon dragon both punished avarice and represented the sin itself. It was associated with the Apocalypse, heathenism, Hell and Satan. It could even be a manifestation of the wilderness, the chaotic pagan threat to civilization. Nonetheless, it remains at heart a typical Anglo-Saxon monster: it lives away from men in an uncivilized, heathen space, which it zealously protects; its entrance into civilization is a matter of great distress and threat to people, and it stands opposed to humankind. But the basilisk, perhaps more so than any other Anglo-Saxon monster, is remarkable for its links to humans. Dwelling in a man-made structure and guarding treasure made and buried by people, it becomes dangerous only when disturbed by man's greed, and not only punishes wrongdoers but reflects back at them the very sin of which they are guilty. Most alarmingly, those who fail to heed the dragon's warning risk becoming dragons themselves.

IV
SAINTS AND *SATANAS*

The Anglo-Saxons shared their world with more than just the monsters of the animal kingdom. Scripture, hagiography and local legend left them in no doubt that parts of Anglo-Saxon England were infested by creatures belonging to another world altogether: demons. Although somewhat different in their strict taxonomy to the flesh-and-blood monsters discussed elsewhere in the book, demons were nonetheless functionally identical to their purely physical cousins. The Anglo-Saxons, after all, had no concept of the supernatural, and it is clear that demons were seen as monsters and thus a part of nature. However, in carrying a satanic mandate to spread sin and turn the world to wilderness, demons may even be the most dangerous monster of all.

Anglo-Saxon Demons

The Anglo-Saxons inherited the vast majority of their demonology from the Christian tradition. Although Satan, famously, makes very few appearances in the Bible, this did not prevent him becoming fundamental to the Christian faith from the early medieval period onwards. The Book of Revelation, for example, allusively describes a war in heaven, which was destined to capture the imaginations of Christians to the present day:

> And there was a great battle in heaven: Michael and his angels fought with the dragon, and the dragon fought, and his angels; And they prevailed not, neither was their place found any more in heaven. And that great dragon was cast out, that old serpent, who is called the devil and Satan, who seduceth the whole world; and he was cast unto the earth, and his angels were thrown down with him. (12:7–9)

These short verses were adapted into a long narrative of Lucifer's arrogance and pride causing war to erupt in heaven. This popular legend set the tone for human history: vengeful and envious, Satan was next responsible for the Temptation in the Garden of Eden, when a serpent convinced Eve to eat of the Tree of Knowledge, and has been persecuting mankind ever since.

The story of the rebel angels is told in the Old English poem known as *Genesis A*, a text based on the first book of the Bible, and the poem interpolated into it known as *Genesis B*. These texts are translations in a specifically medieval sense. Rather than being translated word for word, this type of translation adapted and changed a text so that it would be better understood by a contemporary audience, meaning other relevant material would be added when necessary. Thus although the story of Satan's rebellion is not mentioned in the canonical Genesis, the Anglo-Saxon version adds a lengthy account of it into the story of Creation. *Genesis A* and *B* survive in a single manuscript, the late tenth- to early eleventh-century MS Junius 11, which also contains similarly free Old English translations of Exodus and Daniel, and another poetic account of Lucifer's fate in *Christ and Satan*. Interestingly, the manuscript is named after Franciscus Junius (1591–1677), a former owner and the composite poem's first editor. Junius was a friend of the poet John Milton, and a case has been made for Milton having consulted the Old English account of the war in heaven and its aftermath in the Garden of Eden when writing *Paradise Lost*.[1]

The Fall of Satan, from MS Junius 11, p. 3.

Satan, bound in Hell, sends an emissary to the Garden of Eden, from MS Junius 11, p. 20.

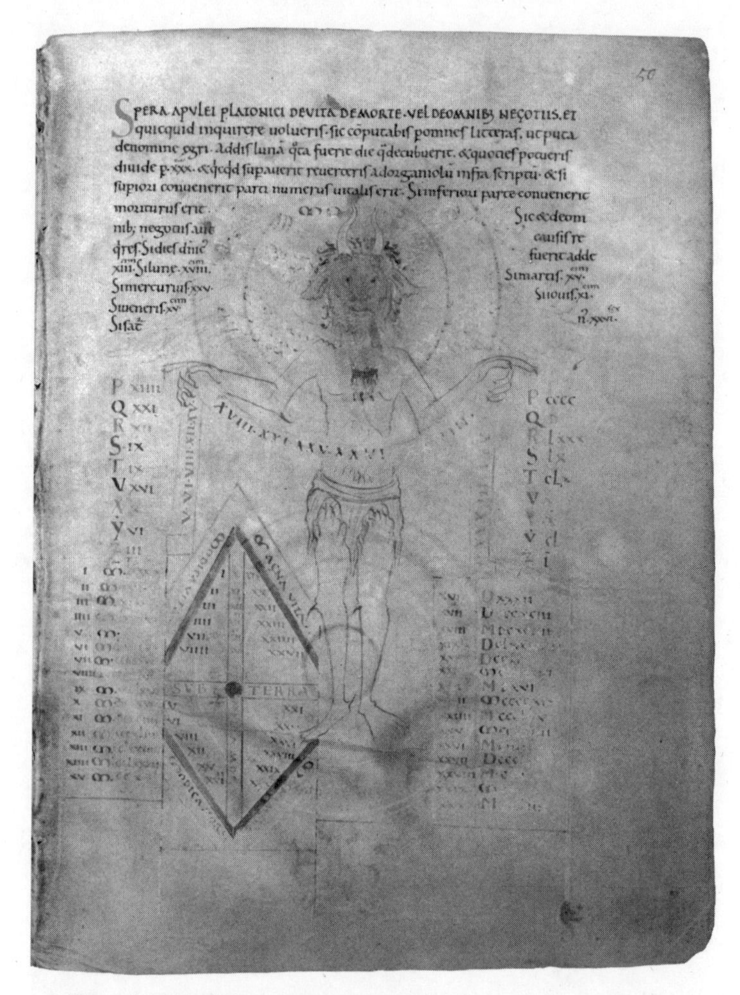

The earliest English rendering of Satan, from the Leofric Missal f. 50r.

Indeed, *Genesis B* is unusual for giving Satan a proto-Miltonic, lengthy speech lamenting his downfall and announcing his resolution to punish mankind. Its inspiration for Milton remains an intriguing possibility.

The portion of the manuscript containing the *Genesis* poems is illustrated and contains depictions of Satan. Reading from top to bottom, a full-page illustration gives a narrative account of Lucifer's glorification, rebellion and banishment to Hell. At the top of the page, Satan is physically no different from the other angels, but stands closest to God in the mansions of heaven. Immediately below, he is depicted with wings and arms outstretched, accepting gifts from other angels, a sure sign of his overweening pride. The next illustration shows the Archangel Michael armed with three spears, casting the rebel angels from heaven. Satan here is depicted reclining in a leonine Hellmouth, bound with ropes to its enormous fangs. His hair has changed to a tangled, serpentine mess of protruding black locks and his fettered hands have prominent claws. His wings are no longer visible, though they may be concealed further inside the Hellmouth's great maw. Satan's evil pride and opposition to God have physically changed him from angel to demon.

By the time the Temptation is depicted, the Devil has changed once more. Bound with elaborate fetters to stakes in the ground, Satan is roasted over a fire and watches as one of his emissaries leaves Hell to enter Eden above. Both Satan and his minion have short horns and wings. In Eden, this demon takes on the form of a serpent. Writhing around a tree, it has a jet-black eye and a basilisk's head with a protruding tongue. Here is depicted the most dreadful moment of Christian history: the serpent persuades Eve, standing nearby, to eat of the forbidden fruit. Beyond mankind's expulsion from Paradise, the event also marks an important point in our history of Anglo-Saxon demons, for it is the first instance of a demon wandering from Hell to tempt mankind. This infernal arrangement, with Satan confined to Hell and his minions carrying out his work on earth, is echoed later in the Junius manuscript by *Christ and Satan*: 'some [demons] must roam throughout the land of men and often stir-up strife in the families of men throughout middle-earth.'[2]

Satan and his followers, post-expulsion, look almost indistinguishable in the Junius manuscript, reflecting the nomenclature of 'devil' and 'demon' commonly ascribed to both. Thus it is worth mentioning the earliest Anglo-Saxon depiction of Satan, which may also be an indication of how the physical appearance of lesser demons was conceived in Insular culture. In the Leofric Missal, a composite illuminated manuscript of liturgical material from several different churches, a portion produced at Glastonbury in the 970s contains a near full-page drawing of the Devil. This particular Satan would be far more recognizable to a modern audience than anything in Junius, for here he is the bipedal, goat-headed beast of popular culture. Smirking defiantly at us from the page, Satan has prominent curved horns atop his head, complete with the floppy ears and cold eyes of a goat. Although the rest of his body is distinctly human, he also has claws, spikes coming out of his knees and heels, and a bestially furry stomach above a ragged loincloth. As a hybrid creature, Satan here challenges our understanding of nature and subverts the harmony of God's Creation, a physical representation of his cunning and rebellious nature. Dragon-like beasts can just about be traced emanating from his striking head, possibly emissaries off to do Lucifer's bidding on earth. Let us meet some of their intended victims.

Hermits and Demons

Directly in the firing line of demons were hermits. Also known as eremites, these pious individuals gave up the pleasures of the world to live alone in the most inhospitable wildernesses, dedicating their lives to worshipping God. The most famous hermit of all, Antony the Great, for instance, gave up everything to live in the Egyptian desert. It is worth dwelling on Antony, and hagiography in general, before we begin our discussion proper, as his life was a direct inspiration to generations of demon-battling hermits in the chillier climes of Anglo-Saxon England.

Antony (*c.* 251–356) inherited vast estates from his wealthy parents at the age of just twenty. But though a comfortable and indulged life beckoned, a chance trip to church one day inspired him to sell all of his possessions and give the proceeds to the poor. Putting his sister in a convent, Antony swore to lead a life of poverty. After passing time with other local ascetics, Antony decided that he could get closer to God by living in the midst of the desert, far from anyone, barely eating and spending all day in prayer. Once installed in the arid wilderness, it is said that there followed a long period of demons attempting to disrupt his devotions and send him back to wallow in the sinful world of other men, which Antony overcame by keeping his faith in God. In fact, devils assailed him even before he went to live alone in the desert. According to the *Life of Antony*, written by Athanasius of Alexandria (*c.* 296–373) and translated from Greek into Latin for Western audiences by Evagrius of Antioch, 'the devil, an enemy of the word Christian, could not bear to see such outstanding virtues in a young man, and so he attacked him with his old wiles.'[3] The trials and temptations for which Antony became famous all took place in the desert, however, and this was to form the essential narrative of hermit saints: a retreat to the wilderness followed by temptation and punishment by demons, and victory over them.

The Antony story was fundamental to Christianity for a number of reasons. First, in Antony's day there were no monasteries, and the earliest such establishments were born when many others copied the example of ascetic hermits and lived near one another in the desert. In Athanasius' memorable description, 'the desert has been made a city by monks who left their own people.'[4] In fact, the lives of Antony and other Desert Fathers, and the rules they imposed on their followers, formed the basis for monasticism.[5] Second, though he was not the first ascetic even in the *Life of Antony*, and though St Jerome claimed that Paul of Thebes was actually the first hermit, his *vita* (hagiography) was the most widely read and influential of all the tales of desert eremites. This second point is perhaps the most important, for eremitism is essentially an act of imitation. Even Antony is inspired to seek the desert because 'a servant of God ought to take as his model the way of life of the great Elijah [Old Testament desert prophet] and to use it as a mirror to organize his own life.'[6] People became hermits in emulation of others, and even pioneers like Antony were copying biblical figures. In the New Testament, John the Baptist's lifestyle made him the model for all subsequent hermits: 'a voice of one crying in the desert . . . clothed in camel's hair, and a leathern girdle about his loins: and he ate locusts and wild honey' (Mark 1:3, 6). Even the idea of being tempted by the Devil (perhaps via one of his minions) in the desert had precedent in the Temptation of Christ. Fasting in the Judaean desert for forty days and forty nights, Jesus is visited by Satan, who attempts to corrupt him through honeyed words. The important demonic element of eremitic life was adapted from the accounts of the Temptation in Matthew, Mark and Luke.

Imitating desert heroes from the Son of God to St Antony, and even repeating their feats, was a tried and tested method for the hermit to please God. This imitative process was taken even further by hagiography, the biographical texts that immortalized the lives of the saints, including hermits. Hagiography deliberately incorporated repetitions of events and miracles associated with prominent saints into narratives about newer or less illustrious figures. This was a form of literary shorthand, emphasizing the subject's sanctity by reference to a better-known figure. For instance, St Edmund the Martyr was said to have been slain by a surfeit of arrows, in a thinly veiled attempt to elevate his miserable death to the status of St Sebastian's near-identical heroic martyrdom in the third century. This double imitation of man and text is vital to bear in mind, for in the rest of this chapter we will be discussing demons chiefly through the hagiography of the two most famous Anglo-Saxon hermit saints, Guthlac of Crowland and Cuthbert of Lindisfarne. Both were inspired to retreat from the world in order to imitate others, and their biographers were similarly at pains to compare them to the same figures. But while the hagiographical method may suggest that some of the events described did not really happen, the texts are vital for demonstrating Anglo-Saxon attitudes towards hermits, the landscape and, most importantly, demons.

'For pride in the wilderness': Guthlac of Crowland

Guthlac of Crowland (*c.* 674–715) was one of the most popular home-grown saints in Anglo-Saxon England. He was included in several litanies, his feast day was widely celebrated, and he had an entry in the *Old English Martyrology*. His life was so remarkable that a Latin *vita* appeared a few years after his death in 715. This text, *Vita sancti Guthlaci*, by an author known only as Felix, was very popular and survives in seven Anglo-Saxon manuscripts among other biographies of more famous saints. An Old English translation of Felix's text and a homily summarizing it have also survived. As further evidence for Guthlac's popularity, two Old English poems about him with little relation to the *Vita* survive in the Exeter Book.[7]

Like Antony, whose life was doubly an influence on both Guthlac himself and Felix's biography, Guthlac was a wealthy individual, in fact a member of the Mercian royal family. At the age of fifteen Guthlac became a soldier, but nine years later he left the army and entered the monastery at Repton. Following two years of impeccable service, Guthlac, according to the *Vita sancti Guthlaci*, 'intended to make for the desert with particular diligence [and] devotion of spirit'.[8] This was explicitly an act of imitation: 'for when he was reading about the lives of the ancient solitary monks, then his heart was illuminated [and] burned with a passionate desire to seek the desert'.[9] Anglo-Saxon England did not have any hot, arid deserts like those inhabited by Antony and his Eastern followers, but it did have vast areas of wilderness that not only matched their level of isolation and danger but met the strict definition of a desert. These wild, uncivilized places, which we have already learned plenty about, were able substitutes for the homes of the Desert Fathers.

Guthlac's choice of hermitage was easily as hazardous as those of the solitaries that inspired him:

> There is in the midland part of Britain a very black fen [*palus*] of immense size, which starts at the banks of the River Granta, by no means far from the stronghold which is called Gronta [Cambridge]. It is a very long tract, [and] extends from the south right up to the North Sea: there are now swamps, now bogs, sometimes black, stagnant waters overhung with mist, crossed by the bends of tortuous rivers, and also many wooded islands.[10]

The area Guthlac decided upon is still known today as the Fens, a marshy area of eastern England that in places remains a desolate and thinly populated part of the country. Despite Felix's damning assessment, the Fens had considerable economic importance in the Anglo-Saxon period, and people did live there. In fact, people have inhabited Britain's fenlands since prehistoric times, when wooden walkways were raised across the treacherous marshes and wetlands, the earliest of which, the Sweet Track in Somerset, dates to about 4000 BC.[11] The Fens were also first drained in the Iron Age to make them more habitable, long before the Anglo-Saxons arrived.[12] In the Anglo-Saxon period, the Fens were used for hunting, fishing, fuel extraction and livestock grazing, and the late eleventh-century Domesday Book records fifty Fenland villages.[13] This is not to say that Felix was entirely mistaken in his desolate account of the area, since Anglo-Saxon marshlands were riddled with malaria and some areas were potentially deadly to people straying from the path, but the passage is certainly hyperbolic.

Felix's description of the Fens is in part a means to emphasize Guthlac's sanctity and ensure that he is reckoned the equal of the most elite hermits of the Eastern desert. However, his hyperbole is also symptomatic of the Anglo-Saxon obsession with the boundaries of wilderness and civilization. For the Fens were only sparsely populated: the fifty Fen villages of the Domesday Book were located across a staggering million acres of fen and saltmarsh separating Mercia from East Anglia.[14] Along with their potentially deadly nature, the Fens had no big towns or monasteries, the pinnacles of civilization, in Guthlac's day. Further afield, but nonetheless relevant to the folklore of fens, is a reference to a deadly monster in the *Letter of Alexander to Aristotle*: 'there came suddenly a certain wild-beast from the fen and the fastness [*of þæm fenne ⁊ of ðæm fæstene*]; the wild-beast's spine was all covered with pegs like a head-dress . . . and that wild-beast slew two of my thanes.'[15] It is telling that such a hideous monster – a crocodile – was believed to live in a fen. Despite the area's small population, Guthlac's chosen home was very much in the uncivilized wilderness, and in the strict Anglo-Saxon imaginative paradigm, Felix's description is fully justified.

As a final indication of the wild nature of the Fens, Felix calls them *inculta* (uncultivated), a loaded term that also means 'uncivilized' in a philosophical sense, and the Old English poem *Guthlac A* of the Exeter Book designates the area as a *mearclond* (borderland).[16] *Guthlac A* is nowhere near as forthcoming as Felix about the nature of the Fens, but both sources agree on his dangerous choice of abode within them. On an island called Crowland, Guthlac finds an ancient, heathen burial mound, described in the *Vita* as 'a barbarous tumulus heaped up with lumps of earth, which avaricious frequenters of the wilderness [*solitudinis*] once broke asunder for profit, excavating to acquire it'; the equivalent Old English passage reads simply that 'he began, alone, to live in a burial-mound home [*beorgseþel*]'.[17] *Tumulus* and the element *beorg* are terms used elsewhere for the heathen burial mounds inhabited by treasure-guarding dragons. Not content with the essential wilderness of the Fens, Guthlac goes further and chooses the most heathen, and thus the most perilous, place within them. Like Antony before him, Guthlac is in very dangerous territory.

As we have seen, among the fauna inhabiting such a wilderness had to be monsters. The only creatures plaguing the Fens, however, are demons.

> [An] island in the concealed [and] remote parts of the desert . . . many had tried to live there, but had rejected it because of the unknown monsters [*monstra*] of the desert and the terrors of diverse forms.[18]

> Often monsters [*brogan*] came there, terrifying and unknown, the hatred of the ancient fiend, strong in treacherous arts; they revealed their shapes to him [Guthlac], and there before had established many seats.[19]

Evidently, these demons are thought of as monsters: beyond the demonstrative vocabulary used (*monstra*, *brogan*) and satanic associations, by living in the most hostile wilderness the demons fit the all-important monster topography. Felix is explicit in highlighting the *monstra* as the reason for the island in the Fens remaining uninhabited and *inculta*. As the *Liber monstrorum* tells us, 'now the human race has multiplied and the lands of the earth have been filled, under the stars fewer monsters are brought forth':[20] civilized humans and monsters, demonic or otherwise, cannot live together. Authoritative reports of demons in the Eastern deserts from scripture and hagiography meant that the creatures fitted seamlessly into the Anglo-Saxon view of the world. It is even possible that the association between devils and the Fens has survived in the monstrous black dog of English folklore. The Shuck, as it is sometimes known, is associated with watery and marshy places in the East Anglian part of the Fens, and its name is thought to be derived from the Old English noun *scucca*, demon.[21]

Armed with Christian desert lore, Guthlac expresses no surprise when demons arrive to assault him. The first devilish trick played upon Guthlac is to make him fall into despair, an occupational hazard for hermits and one of the chief reasons that few monks were permitted to pursue the solitary life by their superiors.

> On a certain day he was engaged in his customary singing of Psalms, while the ancient enemy of humanity [a devil], like a roaring lion through the spaces of the vast sky, was modifying his power, meditating new arts in his mind. Thus, testing the strength of all his wicked force, with a cunning mind he fired with all his might, as if from a fully extended bow, a poisoned arrow of despair so that it stuck dead-centre in the mind of the soldier of Christ . . . he began to despair about what he had undertaken alone.[22]

> 'But on what shall you live, even though you own the land?' [ask the demons] 'No man will nourish you here with food; hunger and thirst will be hard enemies if you flee like a wild-beast alone from your homeland.'[23]

Felix gives a somewhat more florid description of the demons' opening tactic, but what is clear in both quotations is that they just want Guthlac to leave Crowland. Whereas demons pursue Antony to the Egyptian desert because he is vulnerable there, and they find his zealotry offensive, these Anglo-Saxon demons are in the Fens long before Guthlac. They show no interest in damning his immortal soul at this stage, which is supposed to be their mission away from Hell (as seen earlier in the quotation from *Christ and Satan*), instead they just want him out of the Fens and in his proper place. That is, like all monsters, they are protecting the boundary between man and monster. Later in *Guthlac A* the demons are more explicit about the nature of their dispute: 'you have vowed that it will come to pass that you will [win] a home from us.'[24] More than any other saint's life, the story of Guthlac is one of land ownership and boundaries.

The tumulus or *beorg* takes centre stage in this dispute. Both the *Vita* and *Guthlac A* make it clear that the wooded island with a burial mound, specifically, is where the demons live. As we have seen, the burial mound was seen as a particularly dangerous and haunted part of the Anglo-Saxon world. Further evidence for this superstition comes from the Old English charm 'Wið færstice' (Against a sudden stitch): 'loud they were, lo, loud, when they rode over the burial mound [*hlæw*], they were fierce when they rode over the land. Shield yourself now, so that you might escape from this evil.'[25] Although this is a charm against a transitory abdominal pain, the culprits are elves, creatures from the pagan pantheon often conflated with demons in popular lore, firing tiny arrows into their human victims like their counterparts in Christianity. Elves were also held responsible for the spread of malaria through similar means, and, as mentioned, the disease was rampant in the marshy conditions of the Fens, suggesting further the heinous and deadly nature of Guthlac's barrow. There is also a depiction of a monster sitting on a barrow on the much disputed and perplexing right-hand side of the Franks Casket.[26] Here a bipedal, beast-headed creature sits on a small mound among trees, identified as a barrow by a cryptic runic inscription: 'Here Hos sits on the sorrow-mound [*hærmberge*, the latter element a form of *beorg*]; she suffers distress as Ertae had imposed it upon her a wretched den (?wood) of sorrows and torments of mind.'[27] No one knows exactly who or what

The right side panel of Franks Casket, which shows the mysterious creature known as Hos on the left.

Hos is, but she is clearly some sort of monster associated with a woodland tumulus, and so must have some relation, however distant, to the barrow-dwelling demons of the Guthlac legend. Indeed, Guthlac's hermitage is described as a *beorg on bearwe* (burial mound in the woods)[28] in *Guthlac A*, possibly indicating a now lost tradition of lore surrounding woodland barrows. Perhaps Hos is a monster from pagan legend associated with burial mounds that easily translated into the demons of Christian myth living in a similar place. In a further parallel with the Guthlac story, Hos is approached by a soldier, mirroring Guthlac's military past and status as the *miles Christi* (soldier of Christ) who banishes demons from a barrow in the *Vita sancti Guthlaci*.[29]

Guthlac's chosen home is thus the monster dwelling par excellence within the monstrous environment of the Fens. Unlike the demons, Guthlac does not respect the boundary between man and monster, and they respond accordingly. In Felix's account, they try to turn Guthlac away from God through decidedly slippery means. With uncanny knowledge of the imitative nature of hermits, the demons try to persuade Guthlac to emulate the extreme fasting of other desert solitaries:

> Two devils [*zabuli*] in human form with wild faces showed themselves to him . . . 'We will educate you in the monastic lives of the ancient hermits. For Moses and Elijah and the Saviour of the human race himself first of all mounted the summits of fasting; those famous monks who lived in Egypt did away with the vices of human infirmity with the spear of fasting . . . a fast of seven days is a worthy correction'.[30]

This might at first glance seem a strange way of turning Guthlac from God. Hermits, after all, were famous for their abstinence, and it is said by Felix that Guthlac 'ate no other nourishment except a small bit of barley bread and a little cup of turbid water after sunset'.[31] However, St Jerome warned of the dangers of taking pride in one's fasting habits, and numerous authorities cautioned that excessive fasting would make it impossible to think of anything but food.[32] Knowing this, the demons hoped that tricking Guthlac into a week's fast would leave him too weak to carry out his devotions or even make him proud, and thus turn him away from God. For Felix, Guthlac's regime is severe enough already, and scholars have even estimated his daily calorie intake at a mere 700, equating to slow starvation.[33] Dietary mortification has even been suggested as the cause of Guthlac's encounters with demons, via hunger-induced hallucinations. For our purposes, however, it is most important to note that the demons are trying to make Guthlac a suitable denizen of the Fens. Christianity has no place in the heathen wilderness, and its incursion, as we have seen, turns it from wasteland to civilization. In trying to prevent Guthlac from prayer and contemplation through starvation or overweening pride, the demons are trying to preserve and defend the integrity of the wilderness like any self-respecting Anglo-Saxon monster.

The demons of *Guthlac A* are nowhere near so nuanced in their attempts to deal with the Guthlac problem. Eventually, even their Latin cousins in Felix's text decide that subtle spiritual persuasion will not transform Guthlac into a suitable neighbour, and opt for terror and thuggery:

> He discerned immediately the diverse forms of various monsters [*variorum monstrorum diversas figuras*] intruding into his home from every direction. Thus a savage, roaring lion threatened to gnaw him with its bloody teeth; truly, a bellowing bull dug up the ground with its hooves and stuck its blood-stained horn in the earth . . . a snake, also, stretching its scaly neck, showing the sign of its malevolent poison . . . the grunting of the wild boar, the howling of the wolf [*lupus ululatum*], the whinnying of the horse, the bellowing of the stag, the hissing of the serpent, the lowing of the cow, the croaking of the raven made a cacophony of horrible voices to disturb the true soldier of the True God.[34]

Felix's demons are capable of shape-shifting and taking on the appearance of man and beast alike. This is a capability beyond the monsters we have hitherto discussed, but in changing their appearance the demons display a characteristically monstrous subversion of God's order. Even in their natural state, however, these demons are a potent force for disorder and confounding:

> For they were wild in their aspect, terrible in form, with large heads, long necks, lean faces, foul expressions, squalid beards, bristly ears, savage brows, grim eyes, fetid mouths, the teeth of horses, gullets vomiting flames, crooked throats, broad lips, horrible voices, burned hair, plump cheeks, pigeon chests, mangy loins, knotted knees, bent

> legs, swollen ankles, feet facing away from each other, gaping mouths, raucous shouts.[35]

Like the Satan of the Leofric Missal and the monsters of *Wonders of the East*, Felix's demons are hybrids that confound accepted norms regarding the appearance and nature of God's Creation. Even when confined to their true essence, the demons are still liminal creatures living in the distinctions drawn between different kinds of beast. That they would take on the familiar forms of a bull, wolf and snake rather than their repulsive natural form reminds us again that monsters were part of a terrifying and aggressive natural world. Their true appearance perhaps reflects the demons' ability to shift between forms and imitate other creatures. More than the map monsters, these demons posed an imminent threat, living in the wildernesses of Anglo-Saxon England rather than the other far edge of the world.

Just as they exist between categories, so too the demons live between worlds. As *Guthlac A* reminds us, these fen-devils are still essentially beasts of Hell, permitted a brief rest from being punished in the abyss:

> [Guthlac] broke the burial-mounds [*beorgas*] in the wilderness, where they, wretched enemies, were dwelling [and] before were permitted to enjoy a respite after torments at times, when they came weary from their wanderings to rest for spaces of time, enjoy the quietness.[36]

The demons move between two worlds just as deftly as they slither between definitions of known beasts and people, and so cannot be said to be monsters of one at the exclusion of the other. And it is this very journey between two worlds on which they attempt to take Guthlac. Although the demonic tactics of frightening and tempting the hermit have plenty of hagiographical precedent, the most famous incident in Guthlac's life appears largely original. Despairing at Guthlac's piety and stubborn refusal to head back across the boundary of civilization, the demons in both versions take the saint into Hell itself:

> They began to carry him through the cloud-capped places of the frozen skies to the grating sound of their horrid wings. When he had arrived at the steep summits of the sky (horrendous to say!) behold, the tracts of the northern skies were seen to grow dark with gloomy fog and black clouds . . . [then] they led Guthlac, the aforementioned servant of Christ, to the abominable gullet of Tartarus [Hell] . . . 'The fiery clefts of Erebus open for you with gaping doors; now the entrails of the [River] Styx want to swallow you and the hot chasms of Acheron gape open for you with horrible throats.'[37]

> Swollen with rage at heart [*bolgenmode*], they, the fierce wretches, brought him, the soldier of glory, the holy person who may partake of the Eucharist, to the gate of hell, where sinful doomed souls after death first set about seeking entrance into that dire house, down under the headlands in the deep abyss . . . 'Now we will repay you a reward for each moral stain, where it will be most evil to you, in the grimmest torment of the soul.'[38]

Guthlac tells the demons that he is content with damnation if such is God's will, and is saved at the eleventh hour by St Bartholomew, sent from heaven by God himself. It is interesting to consider the episode in light of the dragon's possible role as guardian of the pagan otherworld. In the previous chapter, we considered the possibility that the myth of the dragon developed as a means to prevent people from entering barrows and so accessing the land of the dead through it. In the Guthlac legend, intriguingly, the saint's infiltration of a barrow leads to him being taken by supernatural forces to the next world. Just as Hos and the elves haunting barrows possibly became Christian demons after the conversion, it is not impossible that Guthlac's trip to the underworld via a burial mound is a Christianized echo of a pagan folk belief.

The visit to Hell marks the climactic finale of the demonic torment in *Guthlac A*, and although Guthlac has a few more devilish visits to overcome in Felix's version before the demons leave Crowland, the outcome is eventually the same. In both texts, Guthlac's victory over the demons sees a wholesale transformation of the dismal Fens:

> The grace of his remarkable charity overflowed to all, so that even the birds of the uncultivated desert [*incultae solitudinis*] and the wandering fishes of the filthy swamps would swiftly come flying and swimming to his voice as if to a shepherd . . . Indeed, not only did the animals of the earth and sky obey his commands but, likewise, even the air and water themselves obeyed the true servant of the True God.[39]

> The many forms, the offspring of the tree-haunting birds, blessed him with strong voices, proclaimed the return of the blessed one with signs. He often held food for them, when they hungrily flew around his hand, greedily rapacious, rejoiced in his help. Thus that gentle heart, separated from the joys of mankind, served the Lord: he found joy in wild creatures since he despised this world. The field of victory was peaceful, and the dwelling new, the voices of birds were beautiful, the field blossomed; cuckoos announced the year. Guthlac, blessed and courageous, was allowed to possess the land. The green place stood in God's protection.[40]

The departure of the devils, achieved through Guthlac's piety, has transformed the Fens into little short of an earthly paradise, a superlative statement in a culture that saw nature as essentially hostile and deadly. For our purposes, however, it is most important to note that Guthlac's victory over the demons has turned an uncivilized wilderness to ordered civilization. As the *Liber monstrorum* says, men and monsters cannot coexist, and the latter must flee to more distant wild places as civilization expands and in so doing moves the boundary between the two places. The permanence of this transformation is borne out by the rest of the Guthlac legend: the island with the barrow became the site of an important monastery, maintaining the civilized status of a once heathen wilderness, which still exists today, as Crowland Abbey in Lincolnshire.

A final point to note about Guthlac and the demons is the importance of the saint's military past. Both texts speak of him as a soldier of God, and the encounters with the demons are explicitly conceived as a heroic battle. In effect, Guthlac has conquered the Fens, and Felix especially is keen for his readers to note the link between the capture of a demon's home and the Anglo-Saxons' divine mandate to spread civilization and Christianity throughout the British Isles. In a demonic visitation following the trip to Hell, omitted in *Guthlac A*, Felix describes how the demons took on the appearance of a familiar enemy:

> It seemed to him that he heard the shouts of a tumultuous mob. Then, quicker than speech, he was awoken from light sleep. He departed outside from the cell in which he was sitting and, upright, with ears pricked, he discerned the words that the multitude were speaking and understood that a British throng was advancing on his home . . . they intercepted him, too, and began to lift him in the air on the sharpened ends of their spears. Then at length the man of God, perceiving plainly the thousand forms

> and thousand crafts of this invidious enemy, as if prophetically sang the first verse of the 67th Psalm . . . when they heard this, at the same moment, quicker than speech all the crowds of the demons disappeared from his face like smoke.[41]

This passage makes Felix's text explicitly a narrative of nation-building. It seems a pale comparison to the other threats and demonic temptations: if visiting Hell, or seeing the demons in their own form and that of wild beasts, has failed to scare him off, why would Guthlac, a military veteran, fear an army of native Britons? The chapter is incongruous, unless it is included to increase the metaphorical import of Guthlac's legend beyond spiritual battles against temptation to the protection and expansion of Anglo-Saxon England's territorial boundaries. Against the British-speaking demons, God is clearly on the side of the pious Mercian soldier: we need not belabour the parallels to Mercia's continuing struggles against the Welsh who lived beyond Offa's Dyke to the west. In Felix's view, overcoming the Britons is approved by God and will transform their uncivilized home into an ordered, God-favoured land of plenty, where even nature obeys its Anglo-Saxon conquerors.

Cuthbert of Lindisfarne

The other most widely celebrated eremitic saint in Anglo-Saxon England was Cuthbert of Lindisfarne (*c.* 634–687). Cuthbert, too, was a demon-fighter but spent a comparatively short period as a hermit and is better remembered for his tenure as bishop of Lindisfarne and the miracles he performed while ministering to the poor and needy. Bede's account of Cuthbert's time as an eremite within the longer story of the saint's life was an influence on Felix's *Vita sancti Guthlaci*.[42] However, although Cuthbert and his *vitae* pre-dated Guthlac, the latter's recorded life is far richer in demons and more pertinent to a book about monsters. Cuthbert's life was first written by an anonymous monk of Lindisfarne in around 699, with Bede's prose version coming slightly later, in around 721, and using the former as its source.[43] Bede also wrote a 'Metrical Life' of Cuthbert and dedicated five chapters of his *Historia ecclesiastica* to the erstwhile Bishop of Lindisfarne. Cuthbert was even more widely venerated than Guthlac, appearing in a greater number of liturgies and service books and having his holy remains reinterred at Durham Cathedral. Between the so-called Anonymous Life, or *Vita sancti Cuthberti*, and Bede's 'Prose Life' of Cuthbert, there are nearly fifty extant copies of the texts, a handful of which are Anglo-Saxon.[44] These versions of Cuthbert's *vita* usually appear alongside the passions and lives of other saints.

Cuthbert followed a far more conventional route to canonization. Unlike Guthlac, he was sent at an early age to study in a monastery, and he was a monk for many years before becoming a hermit and, later, a bishop. After living communally with other monks on Lindisfarne (or Holy Island), off the northeast English coast in Northumberland, Cuthbert decided that the solitary life of the desert would suit him better. The anonymous author and Bede relate how:

> . . . after more years, desiring a solitary life, he made for the island which is called Farne, which is in the middle of the sea and surrounded by waves, where previously no one could endure alone for any length of time owing to the numerous apparitions caused by demons [*uarius demonum fantasias*].[45]

> There is an island placed in the middle of the sea which is called Farne . . . it is some miles away to the south-east of this semi-island [Lindisfarne] . . . no colonist had been

> able to live there alone easily before Cuthbert, the servant of the Lord, namely owing to the apparitions of demons [*phantasias demonum*].[46]

The similarities with the *Vita sancti Guthlaci* are immediately apparent, for Felix repeats almost verbatim Bede's description of devils preventing anyone from dwelling on Farne (referring to Inner Farne, an island a short distance southeast of Lindisfarne) before Cuthbert. Like Guthlac, upon hearing of an island whose resident demons have made it uninhabitable for men, Cuthbert goes alone to fight them. The demons being associated with the place rather than the saint is again a characteristically Anglo-Saxon view of the creatures and an emphatic sign of their monstrosity. Like their cousins in the Fens, Farne's demons appear to respect the boundary between civilization and wilderness and have not attempted to occupy the territory of Christian men on Lindisfarne. It is fascinating to note that Farne, where the demons live, is just a stone's throw from Lindisfarne, on which a famous monastery has existed since St Aidan founded it in 634. On the one hand, this is a reminder of the eremitic origins of monasteries, which were conceived as larger-scale communal hermitages built as holy places for devotional activities in the midst of the evil outside world, and so were frequently built in inhospitable places far from secular men and women to avoid distraction. On the other hand, and most relevant to our discussion, this is an ominous indication of how close to civilization monsters – in this case, demons – lived. While Lindisfarne was sacred ground by merit of its monastery, the smaller neighbouring island of Inner Farne was unconsecrated and untilled land. Between them, Lindisfarne and Farne are a microcosm of the Anglo-Saxon world-view.

The account of Cuthbert's battles with the demons is disappointingly short in both texts:

> With intrepid mind he chased them away and, quarrying down almost a cubit of a man into the earth through very hard and stony rock, he made a living space.[47]

> But when the soldier of Christ entered, armed with the 'helmet of salvation, the shield of faith, and the sword of the spirit, which is the Word of God, all the fiery arrows of the most wretched one' were extinguished, and the most wretched enemy himself was chased far away with all the host of his accomplices.[48]

Both lives of Cuthbert have bigger fish to fry with the saint's myriad other miracles and good deeds, and so here ends the infestation of demons, with no pigeon-chests, mangy loins or day trips to Hell recorded. One item of interest in the accounts is Bede's mention of 'the most wretched enemy himself' being banished along with 'all the host of his accomplices' by Cuthbert, which suggests a different tradition regarding Satan's ability to leave Hell from that expressed in the Guthlac legend and the poems and illustrations of the Junius manuscript.

Like Guthlac, albeit with apparently far more ease, Cuthbert defeats the demons living on Farne. Thenceforth, the island becomes a civilized, holy centre of learning. As at Crowland, the newly purged Farne becomes an earthly paradise: fresh water miraculously appears at Cuthbert's command, the local birds obey his request that they leave his crops alone, and the sea calms according to his needs. Cuthbert's agricultural enterprises enact a Latin pun:

> On a certain day on his island he was digging and ploughing the earth, for at first, for two or three years before he stayed barricaded within closed doors, he laboured every day and gained nourishment by the work of his hands.[49]

> According to the example of the fathers, he thought it more apt to live by the labour of his own hands. Thus he asked for instruments with which to work the land to be brought to him, and wheat to plant.[50]

Cuthbert's success as a farmer is a demonstrative sign that Farne has turned from wilderness to civilization with his arrival and the demons' corresponding departure. The land is now literally cultivated, recalling the Latin term for uncivilized, *incultus*, whose basic meaning is 'uncultivated' in an agricultural sense. Cuthbert even goes one step further in civilizing the island by building himself a hermitage:

> He also built a wonderful wall another cubit above [the pit that he dug] by collecting together earth mixed with stones of such incredible bulk as no one would believe except those who knew so much of the goodness of God was in him. There he made little dwellings.[51]

> This soldier of Christ, as soon as he had defeated the battle-line of tyrants and become monarch of the land he had come to, constructed a city apt for his dominion, and in this erected houses equally suited to this city . . . some of these [stones] were so large that it would have seemed barely possible for four men to have lifted them, but he was discovered to have been helped by angelic aid to carry them there from another place and put them in the wall.[52]

As previously mentioned, building in stone was the preserve of elite sites, and wealthy churches in particular. Stone was a symbol of civilization's permanence against the surrounding wilderness, and in the Junius manuscript heaven is a marvellous stone city. In Bede's terminology, Cuthbert, a soldier of Christ like Felix's Guthlac, resembles an invading army, fighting the native inhabitants and adapting the conquered land to his own use and convenience. Building in stone – and stone, moreover, that has been found lying unused in the new territory itself – is the surest sign that wilderness has been transformed into civilization, a key indicator of Cuthbert's sanctity.

This brief section of the *Lives* of Cuthbert, then, repeats or, more accurately, anticipates in miniature, the life and deeds of Guthlac: a saint hears of a wilderness so evil that only demons live in it and where Christian men cannot live, he does battle with them, and his victory transforms the area into civilization. Despite the religious context, this is also a basic heroic narrative and one we will see again in the later chapters on Beowulf's fights with Grendel and Grendel's mother.

Interview with the Demon

The demons against which Cuthbert and Guthlac battle are akin to the monsters of *The Wonders of the East* in their movements and reactions to people. Though no doubt unpleasant and filled with malice for humanity, they live in their wilderness homes away from people until someone crosses the boundary separating them from civilization, at which point they attempt to scare the interloper off in order to protect the integrity of the wilderness they must inhabit. However, in other traditions, demons on earth are not just there to be pseudo-green warriors protecting the wilderness from the incursion of civilization. As we saw in *Christ and Satan*, 'some [demons] must roam throughout the land of men and often stir up strife in the families of men throughout middle earth.' To cause such trouble, demons naturally have to seek civilization, though they may base themselves in the wilderness.

Juliana is an Old English poem with the unusual distinction of having a named author, Cynewulf, who is also known to have written the poems *Christ* II, *Elene* and *The Fates of the Apostles*, which he signed with a runic inscription. Like *Guthlac A*, *Juliana* is found in the Exeter Book. The poem tells the story of the titular martyr, Juliana of Nicodemia, who was imprisoned for refusing to marry a pagan and suffered a horrible death. While she is in prison, a demon comes to tempt her to go ahead with the marriage and save her skin. Far from being tempted, Juliana instead restrains and interrogates the demon with divine assistance. Important to our discussion is the fact that the demon gives an account of its doings out of Hell. After claiming responsibility for Christ's execution and the deaths of various martyrs by influencing such illustrious villains as Herod, Pontius Pilate and Nero, the demon reveals its modus operandi:

> Listen: my father, the king of the inhabitants of hell, sent me on this journey here to you from the narrow home ... he sends us so that we change the heart of the pious ones through error to turn away from salvation ... If I meet any noble-spirited warrior of the Lord courageous against the violence of arrows, [and] he will not swerve from the battle, but he, wise of mind, heaves up a board, the holy shield, the ghostly armour, nor will he wander from God, but he, courageous in prayer, stands fast in his tracks, I must depart far from there dejected, deprived of pleasures, in the grip of the fire ... [Then] I, sorrowful, must seek another less brave in the phalanx, a cowardly soldier that I may incite with my froth, hinder at the battle ... then through the shooting of arrows I first send bitter thoughts into his mind, through various desires of the heart, so that he himself thinks it better to commit sins, the desires of the flesh, than love of God.[53]

From this testimony, it is clear that part of the role of demons is to probe the boundaries they protect in the Guthlac and Cuthbert stories. Cynewulf makes it clear that they are actively looking to move that boundary further into civilization. For, like wolves to a sheepfold, the demons travel from Hell or the wilderness into the civilized world to seek victims, ideally 'pious ones', who by definition live in the most cultivated locales. Though their chief aim is to win the victim's soul for Hell, by perverting people to moral turpitude the demons simultaneously alter the character of the victim's home, making it a suitable environment for themselves to inhabit. Some of the sins they encourage in the weak-willed will be committed against others, in turn reducing their resolve and making the demons' task all the simpler, as the interrogated demon reveals: 'some I have incited with teachings, brought them to dispute, so that, drunk with beer, they suddenly renew old grudges.'[54] The chief boundary between people and monsters is where civilized men live, and demons are actively engaged in looking for weaknesses at this ideological threshold. By turning people from the 'love of God' to 'the desires of the flesh', therefore, demons change the Christian, civilized world into a heathen wilderness, suitable even for the demons themselves. Demons thus posed a very serious threat to the fabric of the Anglo-Saxon world.

ALL IN ALL, DEMONS are far more dangerous to man than perhaps any other monster in this book. For though they are based in the wilderness, there can be little doubt that they will move into the civilized territories they sully by tempting foolish people into moral transgression. The message of *Juliana* is clear, and dire: to turn civilization to wilderness, the demons have but to target those lacking the piety to resist them, and a single individual in an otherwise civilized place is all it takes to start the process. Like Guthlac and Cuthbert, the 'soldiers of Christ', and the 'noble-spirited warrior of the Lord' in *Juliana*, each Christian Anglo-Saxon must gird their loins and prepare to fight off the temptations of demons, for failure to do so will spell disaster for the country at large as it is slowly but surely turned into a pagan wilderness, sinner by sinner. This adds another element to the conquest narratives of Felix and Bede, for both texts essentially align demon-fighting with colonial expansion. Evidently, Satan's emissaries share mankind's colonial ambitions, but moving in the opposite direction. From *Juliana* and its bellicose terminology it is clear that defending oneself against demons is a matter of national security.

Though there is no threat of people themselves turning into demons, as the *Juliana* passage demonstrates the demons are also testing the humanity of denizens of the civilized world. For the Anglo-Saxons, as we have seen, it was possible to lose one's humanity by committing certain deeds and to become more monster than man. Committing sins, into which one is insidiously tempted by demons, could easily result in the wrongdoer losing their humanity. It is clear from Guthlac's temptations that demons are happy to share a home with unpious people who succumb to the monstrous sin of pride and place the desires of the flesh above spiritual duties. If sufficient numbers give in to the temptation of demons, men will become monsters and live alongside demons in a nationwide wilderness: perhaps Felix's 'very black fen of immense size' is less topographical description than dire warning of the future facing Anglo-Saxon England unless Guthlac's example is followed.

V
THE DEVIL AND THE DEEP BLUE SEA

Many were the monster-infested wastelands of Anglo-Saxon England, but in terms of danger to people and apparent misanthropy, one place stands head and shoulders above all: the sea. As an island, Great Britain is surrounded by saltwater, which was widely feared and mythologized. In this chapter we will sail the turbulent seas of Anglo-Saxon England and meet its chief, very real, monster: the whale.

The Ultimate Wilderness

> [Britain] is defended by a large and, if I might so call it, impassable ring of sea in every place.[1]

For Great Britain and Ireland, being relatively small islands, the exploitation of the sea through fishing and as a medium of travel and transport forms an important part of their economies and ability to feed their populations. This dependence dates back at least to the Bronze Age. The Dover Bronze Age boat, which made its maiden voyage around 1550 BC, is the world's oldest-known seagoing vessel. For thousands of years before the invention of flight, the only means of travelling to and from continental Europe and beyond was by sea, on which trade therefore depended. As Gildas suggests in the quotation above, the wide and tempestuous sea also provided an important natural defence against invaders, and it remained a formidable barrier until military technology provided new avenues for attack and invasion in the twentieth century.

But while the sea had economic and defensive importance, it was also viewed with sheer horror. Humans are mammals evolved for living on land, not water, and people were at their most vulnerable when venturing away from the relative safety of the land into the immense, volatile seas. The sea's annual body count remains vast even today, despite our superior technology and expertise, and so we can but wonder how many people were claimed by the deep in the first millennium AD. The awesome power of the sea has thus equally terrified and fascinated mankind across recorded history. Pliny the Elder perhaps best captures this paradox in the *Historia naturalis* when discussing the use of the flax plant for sails. 'What greater miracle is there than a plant that brings Egypt so close to Italy!' he marvels, before castigating the inventor of the sail in no uncertain terms: 'no execration is sufficient for the inventor . . . who was not satisfied that men must die on land, unless they perished without burial rites.'[2]

The healthy fear of sailing expressed by Pliny was even more intense among those living in northern Europe. *The Seafarer*, an Old English poem that survives in the Exeter Book and in which an old sailor reflects on his experiences, memorably describes the terrors of sailing a ship:

> I can utter a true lay about myself, relate journeys, how I often suffered harsh times in days of tribulation, have experienced bitter sorrows of the heart, experienced many sorrowful dwellings in a ship, the terrible rolling of waves; there the narrow night watch has often got me at the prow of a ship, when it tosses by the cliffs. My feet were oppressed with cold, bound with frost, with cold fetters, sorrows

> lamented hot around the heart; hunger tore within the mind of the sea-weary one [*merewerges mod*].[3]

Although *The Seafarer* is best read in the context of the metaphorical Christian sea outlined below, the first part of the poem draws its effectiveness from a vivid account of the real miseries of life on the ocean. In *Andreas*, preserved among homilies and other Old English poems including Cynewulf's *Elene* in the late tenth-century Vercelli Book, St Andrew is only able to cross a tumultuous sea because his ship's captain is none other than God himself, disguised as a man:

> The whale-sea [*hwælmere*] became disturbed, moved violently. The garfish danced and glided through the sea, and the grey gull roamed, eager to prey on the dead. The sun [*wedercandel*, lit. 'weather candle'] darkened, the winds strengthened, the waves crashed, the currents stirred, the ropes creaked, the sail became wet. The water-terror [*wæteregsa*] rose up with the strength of troops. The thanes became frightened at heart.[4]

The seafaring section of *Andreas* is one that belongs to the allegorical tradition, discussed below, and similarly derives its narrative power from describing the real horrors of the physical sea. Both *Andreas* and *The Seafarer* evidence a keen awareness of the dangers of sailing and the helplessness and plight of sailors crossing a stormy sea. The garfish and gull of *Andreas*, waiting hungrily for the corpses of drowned sailors, are presented as equivalents to the land-based Beasts of Battle, suggesting that seafaring was seen as a life-or-death conflict between man and water.

The sea is associated with chaos in many world religions. Ancient Mesopotamia's Tiamat, the mother of dragons, was also the goddess of the sea and often depicted as a sea monster. Tiamat also mothered other deities via her marriage with the god of fresh water, Abzu, and these unruly children later killed her and made the earth and heavens from her dismembered body. Tiamat represented primordial chaos, and her grisly death and mutilation equate to the creation of order from chaos. We see a similar pattern in Genesis:

> And the earth was void and empty, and darkness was upon the face of the deep; and the spirit of God moved over the waters . . . And God made a firmament, and divided the waters that were under the firmament, from those that were above the firmament, and it was so. (1:2, 7)

In Hebrew and Christian cosmology, God creates the world by imposing order on the primordial chaos of the sea, which is logically older than Creation itself.[5] Even heaven is wrought from this astonishingly powerful element, which must have been a comforting thought for mariners praying for calm seas before a voyage.

But despite divine intervention, for Christians the sea remained a savage and hostile place. The sea in Christianity was the realm of the Devil, based upon another biblical passage: 'he will turn again, and have mercy on us: he will put away our iniquities: and he will cast all our sins into the bottom of the sea' (Micah 7:19). This passage casts the sea as Hell, which the Devil himself ruled over, and the term *abyssus* (the deep) was used interchangeably for Hell and the depths of the sea. The Book of Revelation tells of how, during the last battle between Heaven and Hell at the Apocalypse, a demonic monster will rise up from the sea: 'and I saw a beast coming up out the sea, having seven heads and ten horns' (13:1). For Gregory the Great, the pope who ordered the conversion of the Anglo-Saxons and is one of the nation's most widely read sources, the sea is *aeternae mortis profunda* (the depths of everlasting death).[6]

A broader Christian tradition cast the sea as the sinful, postlapsarian world. Foundational Christian thinkers such as Gregory the Great, in his *Moralia in Iob* (Commentary on Job, *c.* 578–95), used the image of a small boat crossing a tumultuous sea as a metaphor for mankind's perilous voyage through the mortal world: 'the ship of our mind is lightly driven here and there, in that we are mindful of the height of Paradise with the remembrance of a perfume, and endure the inconvenient waves of temptation coming from the flesh.'[7] Temptation, as we have previously discussed, is provoked by the Devil via his emissaries, and is here equated with crashing waves threatening to sink a boat. A boat that sinks, buffeted by waves, will enter the *abyssus*, just as someone who succumbs to temptation and sin will be sent to Hell. The currency of this image in Anglo-Saxon England is evident in *The Seafarer* and many other Old English texts, such as the translation of Augustine's *Soliloquies* associated with Alfred the Great:

> [Faith, hope and love] are the three anchors that hold fast the ship of the mind in the midst of the danger of the waves. The mind however has great consolation in that it believes and well-knows that the troubles of this world are not eternal. Just as the ship's lord, when the vessel moves most unsteadily at anchor and the sea is most tempestuous, then knows of the truth that peaceful weather approaches.[8]

Beyond being a real physical threat to anyone intrepid enough to venture out on its waters, the sea was philosophically the home of the Devil, a threat to both body and soul. Only the civilizing power of piety could save such puny vessels from sinking.

That the Anglo-Saxons viewed the sea also as a wilderness is clear from Old English poetry. In their migration myth, the Anglo-Saxons linked their journey from continental Europe to Britannia with the Israelites leaving Egypt to reach the Promised Land.[9] This gave them divine sanction for colonizing England, where they abandoned their pagan beliefs in favour of Christianity. In this myth, the Israelites' crossing of the desert out of Egypt is echoed by the movement of the Anglo-Saxons across the North Sea to their own promised land. In the Old English *Exodus*, which survives in the Junius manuscript, incongruous seafaring imagery is used to describe Moses leading his people across the desert. The pillar of cloud (Exodus 13:21) is the *segle* (sail) of a boat, and the Israelites are 'seamen [*sæmen*] [who] travelled, following the flood-way [*flodwege*]', metaphorically sailing across the desert, protected by God, who is described as the *flodwearde* (flood-guardian) and *mereflodes weard* (guardian of the sea-flood).[10] The desert has become the sea. Appropriately enough, both the sea – a desert of northern Europe – and the Egyptian desert were held by Christian tradition to be full of demons.

Given their uncivilized nature and hostility to people, designating the sea and desert as home to demons and other monsters made perfect sense to the Anglo-Saxons. Early on in *Beowulf*, the titular hero describes a swimming race with his friend Breca that took place at sea. Beowulf recalls how they both went out armed and in full chainmail, knowing that they would inevitably be attacked by monsters in this wilderness. Soon, *merefixa* (sea fishes) attack him, and a *feondscaða* (dire enemy) drags him to the bottom of the sea.[11] Beowulf, fortunately, slays this *mihtig meredeor* (mighty wild beast of the sea)[12] before it can eat him, and manages to kill a total of nine sea monsters. The sea beasts here behave like all Anglo-Saxon monsters: they live far from man and attempt to preserve the boundary between civilization and wilderness by killing interlopers. Like some of the monsters in *The Wonders of the East*, they even try to eradicate any trace of Beowulf by devouring him. Another indication of the sea's status as a wilderness inhabited by monsters comes after Beowulf's final battle: '[the Geats] also shoved the dragon, the *wyrm*, over the steep cliff, allowed the wave to seize it, the sea [*flod*] to devour the guardian of the treasures'.[13] Beowulf civilizes the barrow by slaying the dragon and giving its treasure hoard to his people, and the monster no longer has its proper place there. The sea remains a wilderness and is hence a most suitable grave for the unfortunate *wyrm*.

One might suppose that, unlike other wildernesses, the sea would have no heathen associations. However, on closer consideration, one group of heathens in fact came from the saltwater wastes to attack the civilized places of Anglo-Saxon England. The *Anglo-Saxon Chronicle* records that in 793, just after dragons flew over Northumbria, 'the harrowing of heathen men wretchedly destroyed God's church on Lindisfarne through plunder and slaughter.'[14] That is, pagans came from the wilderness of the sea to the Christian world of Lindisfarne and laid waste to it. Gildas's faith in the 'impassable ring' of the sea was misplaced: the Vikings who attacked Lindisfarne used it to reach civilization and desecrate it. The Viking Age continued roughly until the death of Harald Hardrada in September 1066, with occasional periods of increased terror as different Viking nations and rogue families launched fresh attacks. Early medieval Christians saw all paganism as devil worship, as in Gregory the Great's famous letter to Melitus on the recycling of heathen temples, quoted by Bede: 'it is necessary that they [pagan temples] be corrected from the worship of demons [*cultu daemonum*] to the service of the True God.'[15] Since Satan, the god of heathens, lived in the sea, it is no wonder that the Vikings were so adept at crossing it.

The equation of the sea with the desert is an established trope in Insular hagiography, too. Cuthbert's hermitage, as we saw in the previous chapter, is an island in the sea, and equates to the desert that Antony the Great and others made their home. Locating hermitages on sea islands is most common in Ireland, for example at Skellig Michael at the southwest tip of the country, where a group of hermits lived in tiny cells looking out over the immense ocean. Like Cuthbert, other Anglo-Saxon hermits lived in the sea-desert, such as Balthere of Tyninghame, who according to Alcuin dwelled in a cave on Bass Rock, in the Firth of Forth, 'a place completely encircled by the ocean waves / hemmed by terrible crags and steep cliffs'.[16] Perhaps the example of hermits living at sea influenced the holy men who lived alone on tiny islands in the seasonally flooded Somerset Levels.[17] It is easy to see how the sea, uninhabited by men and full of demons and other monsters, took on the role of the Egyptian desert for British and Irish hermits.[18]

British Whales

It is clear that, for the Anglo-Saxons, anything making its home in the sea must be truly awful. One of this monstrous brood in particular straddled both the physically harmful and philosophically satanic aspects of the sea: the whale. We will get on to how and why these giant aquatic mammals were thought of as monsters – even the kings of sea monsters – but first we must examine the real whales encountered around the British Isles.

The seas surrounding Britain and Ireland are home to a surprising variety of cetaceans, the biological group that includes whales, dolphins and porpoises. Native species range from the common minke whale (*Balaenoptera acutorostrata*), which is only around 8 metres in length and 10 tonnes in weight, to the fin whale (*Balaenoptera physalus*), the second-largest whale in the world, which can reach 26 metres and 74 tonnes. Sperm whales (*Physeter macrocephalus*), made notorious by Herman Melville's *Moby-Dick*, are somewhat less common but do occur around Britain and Ireland and can grow to 18 metres and 57 tonnes. Humpback whales (*Megaptera novaeangliae*), which can reach 16 metres and 30 tonnes, and even blue whales (*Balaenoptera musculus*), the largest animal that has ever existed at nearly 30 metres and 173 tonnes, are occasional visitors. Although the larger species of whale, in particular, are usually confined to deeper waters, strandings are fairly common to this day, and humpback whales have even turned up in the River Thames. A glimpse, let alone a stranding, of such a whale would no doubt live long in the folk memory and confirm that the sea was home to monsters.

Though whales, according to marine biologists, are mostly harmless to humans, their sheer size makes them a serious threat to vessels. The largest Anglo-Saxon ships measured up to 27 metres in length, but most were far smaller, and all were flimsy in comparison to the bulk of a whale.[19] This made them vulnerable to the accidental aggression of cetaceans. A clumsy whale may come up for breath and unintentionally capsize a ship. Some whales have been recorded breaching (leaping playfully out of the water) directly onto vessels. Although such behaviour is hardly a deliberate act of violence, to the Anglo-Saxons, who saw nature as inherently hostile and the sea as a wilderness full of deadly monsters, any damage to a boat caused by a whale would be seen as a deliberate attempt to kill the sailors. Some inquisitive species and individuals will approach and interact with boats, which could likewise be mistaken for aggression or threatening behaviour. Indicatively, Beowulf and Breca head out to their swimming contest armed with swords in order to be protected specifically *wið hronfixas* (against whale-fishes).[20]

Though usually only incidentally dangerous to people, whales, like all animals, will protect themselves when attacked. For this reason, and owing to the sheer size of the quarry, whale hunting was a very dangerous activity. Although there is only scant evidence for Anglo-Saxon whale hunting, it took place elsewhere in Europe in the same period, and the practice is mentioned in Ælfric's *Colloquy*.[21] Asked if he would like to catch a whale, the fisherman replies,

> No . . . because it is a dangerous thing to catch a whale, [and] it is safer for me to travel in a river with my ship than to travel with many ships to hunt whales . . . it is more pleasant for me to catch fish than it would be for me to kill that

> fish which could drown or kill me and also my companions with one blow.[22]

We should remember, as we did when quoting the *Colloquy* for evidence of wolf–livestock predation, that the text is by no means a reliable account of whale hunting, but since it is a school text intended to help students learn Latin, it is likely that Ælfric would have included only subjects or activities familiar to the audience. The *Colloquy*, therefore, demonstrates what are likely to be common attitudes towards whales: they are to be feared based on their size and strength, and kill people by design rather than accident. Certainly, some species are more dangerous than others. Sperm whales, for example, have been recorded ramming whaling ships when attacked. In 1820, one sperm whale in the Pacific deliberately struck the whale ship *Essex* with its great head, sinking the vessel altogether. This incident inspired Melville's *Moby-Dick*, but such attacks are rare. Clearly, however, many whales are of a sufficient size to prove deadly if provoked, and their great bulk in comparison to Anglo-Saxon boats, and the availability of less dangerous resources, is probably the reason whale hunting does not seem to have been a very common activity. Whalebone was a highly valued material, but largely the product of beached whales being butchered, and several whale skeletons from the Anglo-Saxon period have been excavated, criss-crossed with cut marks from the knives of scavengers.[23]

Being far bigger (in weight at least) than any Anglo-Saxon ship, deemed aggressive and dangerous to man, and living in the most misanthropic wilderness of all, it is little wonder that whales wound up being defined as monsters. Before we examine the whale's idiosyncratic monstrosity, we can end with a compound noun linking the creatures with other monsters we have already met. In the Old English poem known as *The Whale*, a fragment of a longer text about the natural world known as the *Physiologus*, preserved in the Exeter Book, the beast is called a *mereweard* (guardian of the sea).[24] The element *weard* is also used to describe the relationship between wolves and dragons and their habitat, in the words *mearcweardas* and *hordweard*, respectively. Like these other monsters of Anglo-Saxon England, whales literally guard their home against human trespassers, as in the case of Beowulf's swimming race, maintaining its status as wilderness as opposed to the civilization a wandering Christian represents.

Whales as Monsters

> The fish beat up the sea on to the mountainous cliff. The king of terror became sad when he swam on to the shingle. Whale's bone.[25]

In the inscription above, a quasi-riddle explaining the origin of the material used for the Franks Casket, the monstrous qualities of the whale are implicit. As the largest beast in the ocean, the whale is logically 'the king of terror': a huge, aggressive creature that threatens any interloper into its kingdom. In Old English poetry, there is similarly no doubt as to who rules the monstrous wasteland of the sea: *The Seafarer* calls the sea *hwælweg* (path of the whale) and *hwæles eþel* (whale's homeland), a formula repeated precisely in the poems *Andreas* and *The Death of King Edgar*.[26] Elsewhere, the sea is simply associated with its monster king. In Riddle 2 of the Exeter Book, describing a storm at sea, the saltwater is called *hwælmere* (whale-sea), a term repeated in *Andreas*.[27] Another Old English word for whale, *hran*, appears in similar compounds: *hronmere* (whale-sea) in the *Metres of Boethius*; *hranrade* (whale-road) in *Andreas*; *hronrade* (whale-road) in both *Beowulf* and *Andreas*.[28] Beowulf is buried at a place named *Hronesnæsse* (whale's headland), presumably a cliff from which whales have been spotted in the past.[29] The whale unequivocally ruled the sea as its chief monster in Anglo-Saxon thought.

The Franks Casket inscription also concerns boundaries. The whale, emphatically described as the *mereweard* in *The Whale*, guards its watery wilderness by attacking men and ships that cross it. But more than any other monster, the whale is inextricably linked with its environment. The Franks Casket reveals that it was carved from the bone of a stranded whale: 'the king of terror became sad when he swam on to the shingle.' In other words, when this particular monster leaves the wilderness, it dies. Wolves, dragons and demons can all make temporary forays from their wilderness homes, but not this gigantic foe. It does not specifically take a civilized place to kill a whale, but this simply makes the whale yet more contemptible, for so monstrous is the whale that it cannot survive anywhere but the most dangerous wilderness of all. Ælfric's *Colloquy* notes that whales do not live in the far more tranquil fresh water, another indication of their monstrosity: 'it is safer for me to travel in a river with my ship than to travel with many ships to hunt whales.'[30] Just as the whale cannot survive outside its natural element, so too man cannot survive in the *hwæles eþel* without a ship and plenty of luck. This mutual opposition between the land of men and the land of monsters is central to the Anglo-Saxon world-view, but unlike the forest, fen and barrows where the land monsters live, this state cannot be changed: since nothing can be grown on the sea, it will always be literally *incultus*, uncultivated.

Like the other monsters we have studied, the whale not only is defined by its environment but, in turn, defines it. The whale's inextricable link to its habitat is evident in the kennings for the sea quoted above: compounds such as *hranrade* only mean 'sea' because whales are mentioned. Moreover, some sources even suggest that the whale contributes to the physically horrible nature of the sea itself. Isidore of Seville links the etymology of the whale's Latin name to its physical abilities: 'whales [*ballenae*] are beasts of immense size, so-called from emitting and spraying water, for they throw waves higher than other sea-beasts. In Greek Βάλλειν means "emit".'[31] Beyond waves, the mere presence of the gigantic, deadly monster in the sea made its watery wilderness all the more dangerous and unwelcoming to man. After all, the whale is the *mereweard*.

A final point to note about the Franks Casket inscription is the apparent unfamiliarity of the material. As previously mentioned, there is little evidence for Anglo-Saxon whale hunting, and though beached whales were plundered for their flesh and bones, the casket still goes to some lengths to explain the material from which it is made. Whalebone was not unheard of as a material, but one cannot imagine that a similar inscription would be necessary for a box made of cow's bone, for example. Moreover, the fact that the material is specifically identified indicates that its origin adds value to the final artefact.[32] The casket is a high-status item, produced for a well-read and wealthy ecclesiastical community, and the choice of material for its construction demonstrates the value placed on whalebone in the period.[33] Using a riddle to describe the beaching of the 'king of terror' evidences the awe and fear in which this monster was held. The casket was made from the bone of a dead monster, and as such the material's origin is both worth recording and a thing at which to wonder.

In our discussion of the *Letter of Alexander to Aristotle*, we made a note of the word used for the ferocious hippopotamuses that kill many of Alexander's most valued men. That term, *nicor*, is a general noun for water monsters, and also appears in glosses to translate 'hippopotamus', which to the Anglo-Saxons was simply a water-dwelling monster that lived on the other side of the world. During his perilous swimming contest, Beowulf encounters many such beasts: 'among the waves I slew sea-monsters [*niceras*] at night'; 'I slew nine sea-monsters [*niceras*] with my sword.'[34] It is most likely that the *nicor* described here is a whale: Beowulf explicitly says that he carries his sword *wið hronfixas*, and from other poetic sources we have seen that the whale was deemed the most dangerous inhabitant of the sea. *Nicor* is used again to describe the other monsters living in Grendel's mere, where Grendel flees after Beowulf fatally rips off his arm: *nicera mere*, the sea-monsters' mere.[35] Although Grendel's mere appears to be inland, *mere* is an ambiguous term that could mean either the sea or a pool of water, and it is elsewhere called explicitly *brim*, 'the sea'.[36] It is also home to other sea creatures, including a *sellice sædracan* (strange sea-dragon),[37] and so is logically accessible to saltwater monsters such as whales. *Nicor* is a catch-all term for water monsters, but its employment to describe creatures dwelling in the sea must surely refer to whales, the largest and most dangerous of saltwater monsters.

The Whale and the Devil

Another occurrence of *nicor* brings with it an even more terrifying context for the whale. Blickling Homily XVII gives a memorable description of Hell as seen by St Paul in the apocryphal, but exceedingly popular, *Visio sancti Pauli* (Apocalypse of Paul). Among the demons tormenting the unfortunate sinners, Paul sees some that are of particular relevance to our current discussion: 'devils in the likeness of water-monsters [*nicras*] were gripping [the damned souls] like greedy wolves.' We have already noted the association of the sea with the Devil, and the bottom of the sea with Hell itself in the noun *abyssus*, but the homily's vocabulary here indicates that aquatic monsters like whales were also associated with the Devil and all his minions.

This is far from a unique reference, specific vocabulary aside, but part of a larger tradition that links the whale directly with the Devil. In Christian thought, exemplified here by Augustine, the whale that swallowed Jonah was interpreted as Hell.

> The prophet Jonah, not so much by discourse as by his own suffering, prophesied Christ's death and resurrection more clearly than if he had shouted with his voice. For why was

> he removed to the whale's belly [*uentre beluino*] and returned on the third day, unless he might signify that Christ should return from the depth of hell on the third day?[38]

Likewise, Isidore says in *Etymologiae* that a 'sea-monster [*cetus*] received Jonah, the belly of which was so large that it appeared the likeness of Hell, as the prophet says: "he heard me from the belly of hell" [Jonah 2:3]'.[39] The whale's traditional infernal connotations led to a more specific description in the *Physiologus*. The *Physiologus* is a forerunner of the medieval bestiary, which seeks to find evidence of the Word of God in the natural world. Originally a Greek text written in around the second century AD, the *Physiologus* was translated into Latin around the year 400. The *Physiologus* was so popular in Anglo-Saxon England that three fragmentary Old English poems in the Exeter Book translate sections of it, including *The Whale*, which gives an interesting account of the behaviour of the 'king of terror':

> He is often encountered unwillingly, savage and fierce of spirit to sailors, by all men; to him, the floater on the ancient streams, the name Fastitocalon is given. His colour is like a rough stone, such as wanders by the shallow water's edge, surrounded by sand dunes, mostly reed beds, so that seafarers believe that they are gazing on an island with their eyes, and then fasten their high-prowed ships to that not-land [*unlonde*] with anchor ropes, settle their sea-horses [ships] at the water's end, and then go up to that island bold of spirit . . . When the one deceitful in cunning feels that the sailors are fast-abiding on him, making a dwelling place and desiring [good] weather, then suddenly down into the salty way the spirit of the ocean dives with his victims, seeks the ground [seabed], and then in the death-hall drowns the ships with their sailors. Such is the custom of evil spirits, the way of devils . . . with them [damned

> sinners] he [Satan] goes, covered with a helm of invisibility, void of goodness, seeking hell, the bottomless surge beneath the misty darkness, just like the great whale who sinks seafaring men and ships.[40]

This particular whale poses a different threat to the other cetaceans we have been discussing: treachery. The monster's great size is part of an elaborate ruse to make it look like an island, rather than overpower boats as real whales would occasionally have done. It is, though, another anti-human string to the monster's bow, and, in popular thought, pretending to be an island and smashing ships to pieces need not have been deemed mutually exclusive. The whale-as-false-island trope is also to be found in an eighth-century Irish text, the *Navigatio sancti Brendani abbatis* (Voyage of St Brendan the Abbot). Although no manuscripts of the text from Anglo-Saxon England survive, it is generally assumed that it would have circulated as an oral legend if not in manuscript form.[41] Travelling with his monastic companions in search of a mysterious island, Brendan's ship alights one day on land that turns out to be a whale, and the men narrowly escape before it dives:

> Last night God revealed to me the meaning of this wonder in a vision. It was no island that we landed on, but that animal which is the greatest of all creatures that swim in the sea. It is called Jasconius.[42]

The presence of the tradition in two discrete texts from Ireland and Anglo-Saxon England suggests wide familiarity with this aspect of early medieval whale biology. It is highly unlikely that a ship ever managed to get dragged below the waves after landing on a surfacing whale, but it is not hard to see why the vast barnacle-encrusted back of one of these behemoths inspired sailors' tall tales, which later became Christian allegory.

The Whale attributes one more fiendish trick to the creature, again involving deceit:

> He has another nature, the proud water-rusher, yet more wondrous. When hunger afflicts him on the sea and when the monster [*aglæcan*] wishes to eat, then the guardian of the sea [*mereweard*] opens his mouth, the wide lips; a pleasant stench comes from his innards, so that other kinds of sea-fish become deceived, the vigorous swimmers swim to where the sweet stench comes from. Then the unwary troop goes in, until the wide jaws are filled; then suddenly the grim jaws crash around the spoils . . . [likewise] the evil one opens hell after death to those who, ill-advised, vainly advance the pleasures of the body over the soul's direction . . . then he crashes the grim jaws, the gates of hell, quickly together, in slaughter; those that come in there have neither return nor departure, any more than the swimming fishes may return from the grasp of the whale.[43]

The whale, in these satanic contexts, operates in line with Isidore's theory of monsters: 'they are seen to portend and exhibit, show [*monstrare*] and predict things in the future.'[44] The whale is a monster not merely owing to its enormous size, wilderness home and aggression towards men, but for demonstrating something of God's plan. Although not every monster known to the Anglo-Saxons conforms to Isidore's definition, the whale's additional associations with the Devil and his cohort and apparent use of trickery increase its monstrosity within the culture's prevailing sense of what made a monster. Being large is one thing, but being large and extremely sly makes the whale a truly dreadful proposition.

A final demonic aspect of the Anglo-Saxon whale is its association with a specific biblical monster. Leviathan is a demon in the Old Testament, sometimes described as a sea serpent, that is commonly associated with whales: 'in that day the Lord with his hard, and great, and strong sword shall visit Leviathan the bar serpent, and Leviathan the crooked serpent, and shall slay the whale that is in the sea' (Isaiah 27:1). Being a sea monster, it is only natural for Leviathan to be visualized as the largest thing in the sea. The fullest description of Leviathan comes in the Book of Job:

> When a sword shall lay at him, it shall not be able to hold, nor a spear, nor a breastplate. For he shall esteem iron as straw, and brass as rotten wood . . . As stubble will he esteem the hammer, and he will laugh him to scorn who shaketh the spear . . . There is no power upon earth that can be compared with him who was made to fear no one. (41:17–18, 20, 24)[45]

The sheer size of Leviathan and its apparent imperviousness to human weapons are both whale-like characteristics. As well as the Book of Job, the Anglo-Saxons had further information on Leviathan from Gregory the Great's *Moralia in Iob*. Gregory is convinced that the Leviathan is a whale: 'in this abyss of waters, that is, in this immensity of the human race, therein this whale [*cetus*] was moving forth with open mouth, eager for the death of all, swallowing up the life of almost all.'[46] Further evidence of this conceit comes in the bewilderingly arcane prose text *Solomon and Saturn* II. In one particularly absurd exchange, Saturn asks Solomon about the forms that the *Pater Noster* and Satan take on when they fight one another, imagining the sacred words uttered fighting off the Devil. The eighth form of the *Pater Noster* is said to be *on ðæs hwæls onlicnesse ðe leuiathan hatte* (in the likeness of that whale which is called Leviathan).[47]

The Leviathan described by Gregory has some important links to the whale in the Old English version of the *Physiologus*. Like the latter, Leviathan is markedly deceitful, as Gregory tells us:

> This Leviathan tempts the mind of religious men in one way, and those devoted to the world in another. For he openly offers to the wicked the evil things that they desire, whereas he secretly lays traps for the good, and attacks them under a display of sanctity.[48]

The Old English whale likewise deceives sailors by pretending to be an island safe for resting upon, before destroying them. Its emission of a sweet scent to lure fish into its great jaws is a similar ploy but has an even closer parallel in Leviathan's infernal wiles. Regarding Job 41:10 ('out of his mouth go forth lamps, like torches of lighted fire'),[49] Gregory notes that

> When a torch is kindled, it has a pleasant odour but a dim light. Thus the preachers of the Antichrist, who assume an appearance of sanctity for themselves but do works of iniquity, give off a pleasant scent, as it were, but the light they emit is dark.[50]

Gregory's Leviathan and the Old English whale are also linked by their monstrous pride. Regarding the detail that Leviathan's strength is in his neck (Job 41:13),[51] Gregory asks: 'for what is signified by the neck of this Leviathan except the enlarging of his pride, with which he rises up against God, when with feigned sanctity he is also exalted with the arrogance of power?'[52] Elsewhere in Job, Leviathan is called 'king over all the children of pride' (41:25).[53] The expression *wæterþisa wlonc* (proud water-rusher) used in *The Whale* echoes the defining pride of Leviathan. Whales are also associated with the sin by Aldhelm, who warns his readers against succumbing to the *superbiae balenus* (whale of pride).[54]

Like the whale of *Physiologus*, Gregory also identified Leviathan as a form of the Devil. His deceitful behaviour recalls the Devil's snares and tricks intended to damn unwary humans, and Gregory explicitly names Leviathan as Satan himself. 'The elect spirits of the angels now oppress this Leviathan enclosed in the pit of the abyss,'[55] he notes, citing Revelation 20:2 as corroboration: 'he laid hold on the dragon, the old serpent, which is the devil and Satan, and bound him for a thousand years.' This has a rather neat link with the soul-as-boat image, as Leviathan, whales and the Devil are responsible for 'the inconvenient waves of temptation': 'he shall make the deep sea to boil like a pot' (Job 41:21).[56] The whale's hellish connotations are only increased when we remember that pride is not merely the sin of Leviathan but the crime that made Satan rebel against God. All things considered, it is most likely that the *nicras* in the Hell of Blickling Homily XVII are whales.

THE WHALE, THEN, WAS indubitably a monster in Anglo-Saxon culture. It lived in the ultimate wilderness, the sea, which it was unable to leave, protecting its home's integrity by attacking all intruders through brute force and deceit. The king of terror's associations with the Devil and Leviathan confirm its evil, monstrous nature. Like demons, its infernal land-dwelling colleagues from the previous chapter, the whale is not a creature into which one can transform by committing certain crimes or breaking cultural taboos. It is unique among the native Anglo-Saxon monsters, however, in its inability to cross boundaries: the only physical *mearcstapan* (boundary-walkers) in the accounts of the whale are people brave or foolish enough to sail the seas. In our final two chapters, however, we will meet *mearcstapan* that move between wilderness and civilization, human and monster, with terrifying ease: Grendel and his mother.

VI
MEARCSTAPAN, PART ONE: THE GRENDELKIN

We come now to perhaps the most famous monsters in the whole of English literature: Grendel and his mother, known collectively as the Grendelkin. Like Beowulf we will attempt to pin down the Grendelkin in this chapter and, while trying to avoid murdering them, examine what makes them monsters, what motivates their rapacious evil and, most pertinently, what they really are.

The Text of *Beowulf*

As mentioned earlier, *Beowulf* is found only in a single manuscript, the Nowell Codex, part of the volume Cotton MS Vitellius A XV. *Beowulf*'s neighbours in the manuscript include the *Passion of St Christopher*, *The Wonders of the East* and the *Letter of Alexander to Aristotle*. As discussed in the first chapter, the Nowell Codex manuscript dates to the late tenth or early eleventh century.[1] It contains five Old English texts, with *Judith* (an Old English retelling of the slaying of Holofernes) the other item. *Beowulf* comes after the *Letter* and is followed by *Judith*, the final item in the manuscript. Two scribes, known unimaginatively as Scribe A and Scribe B, wrote down all five texts. Scribe A wrote most of the manuscript, while Scribe B wrote roughly the final two-fifths of *Beowulf* and the entirety of *Judith*.[2]

Although the text as preserved in the Nowell Codex was written down around the end of the first millennium, it is indubitably far older. We know from palaeography that it was copied from another exemplar, meaning that *Beowulf* was once better represented in Anglo-Saxon libraries; but, based on the historical period and location of the events in the poem, it is likely that *Beowulf* was originally an oral tale passed by word of mouth, possibly among the earliest pagan settlers in England, before it was eventually committed to manuscript. The dating of the composition of the version we know today is a matter of fierce debate. Suggested dates range from the late seventh to early eleventh century, but most commentators generally agree upon an eighth- to early ninth-century origin. Many scholars have forged careers arguing for one date or another, but we can leave the debate here.[3] With only a single manuscript of the poem, it is impossible to pinpoint precisely when *Beowulf* took its only known form, and we need only be mindful that *Beowulf* was a tale told long before it was committed to the Nowell Codex.

During the period between the first, oral tellings of *Beowulf* and the Nowell Codex version being copied by its two scribes, England was converted to Christianity. Although, as we have noted, this was far from a simple or instantaneous process, the vast majority of Anglo-Saxon England practised Christianity by the end of the first millennium, and the scriptoriums that produced the manuscript versions of *Beowulf* were at either monasteries or cathedrals. We therefore have an originally pagan tale about a pagan period of history, retold and interpreted by Christians. Much early scholarship on the poem focused on identifying the pagan aspects of the poem and lamenting the Christian 'additions' to it. However, besides the fact that we know next to nothing about Anglo-Saxon paganism, we also do not know when in the tale's history it took its present form – whether that pre-dated its committal to a manuscript or whether any of the Christians who decided to write it down made any wholesale changes. Though the core tale of a man slaying monsters has links to Old Norse literature, in particular *Grettis saga* (Grettir's Saga) and *Hrólfs saga kraka* (Saga of King Hrolf Kraki), these texts were copied down far later and, again, we know not what, if anything, was added to or taken away from their original versions by later authors. J.R.R. Tolkien explained the problem with focusing only on the 'pagan' elements using a rather neat allegory in his famous 1936 lecture '*Beowulf*: The Monsters and the Critics':

> A man inherited a field in which was an accumulation of old stone, part of an older hall. Of the old stone some had already been used in building the house in which he actually lived, not far from the old house of his fathers. Of the rest he took some and built a tower. But his friends coming perceived at once (without troubling to climb the steps) that these stones had formerly belonged to a more ancient building. So they pushed the tower over, with no little labour, in order to look for hidden carvings and inscriptions, or to discover whence the man's distant forefathers had obtained their building material. Some suspecting a deposit of coal under the soil began to dig for it, and forgot even the stones. They all said: 'This tower is most interesting.' But they also said (after pushing it over): 'What a muddle it is in!' And even the man's own descendants, who might have been expected to consider what he had been about, were heard to murmur: 'He is such an odd fellow! Imagine his using these old stones just to build a nonsensical tower! Why did not he restore the old house? He had no sense of proportion.' But from the top of that tower the man had been able to look out upon the sea.[4]

The only contemporary links to the text we have, which we will be discussing across this chapter and the next, are from Old English literature, and so we will not be fruitlessly speculating on what was 'original' and what was 'added': *Beowulf* as we know it is a product of Anglo-Saxon culture, written by Christians. Instead, we will simply bask in the glory of a masterpiece in its only known form and examine how it fits our understanding of Anglo-Saxon monsters.

The World of *Beowulf*

In briefest terms, *Beowulf* is the story of a Geat warrior who travels to Denmark to rid King Hroðgar of a monster, named Grendel, who has been launching murderous raids on his great hall, Heorot, ever since it was first erected. After killing Grendel in single combat, it transpires that Grendel has a mother, who kills another Dane in revenge for her son's death. Beowulf next kills her in her watery lair – again in single combat – and returns to his home a hero. Some years later, Beowulf is king of Geatland, and his peaceful fifty-year rule is disrupted when the dragon we met in Chapter Three is roused after losing a small piece of treasure. Learning of the terrible revenge the dragon has taken on his land and people, Beowulf fights it in single combat (aided at the eleventh hour by a trusty retainer, Wiglaf). Despite his great age, Beowulf is victorious, albeit mortally wounded. He dies of his injuries, to the understandable despair of his people.

Beowulf is a poem of place. Despite its English provenance, the action all occurs in sixth-century Denmark and Sweden, the ancestral Germanic homes of the Anglo-Saxons. Within the fictionalized version of these countries, the land is divided up into civilized and uncivilized places, with characteristically Anglo-Saxon flair.[5] In fact, this technique of contrast and mutual definition makes *Beowulf* a version of Anglo-Saxon England in microcosm. First of all, we are introduced to Heorot, the centre of civilization, in the early part of the poem.

> Then Hroðgar [a Danish king] was given military success, the worldly honour of war, so that his retainers eagerly obeyed him, young warriors that grew to a great band of men. It came into his mind that he would order men to build a palace, a great mead hall, that men should hear of forever, and within there to share all such as God gave him with young and old . . . then, I have widely heard, work was ordered from many people throughout this middle-earth, to decorate the people's place [*folcstede*]. It came to pass in a space of time, swiftly according to men, that it was all ready, the greatest of palaces; he whose words had wide power gave it the name Heorot ['hart']. He did not fail his vow: he dealt rings, treasure at feast. The hall towered up, high and horn-beamed.[6]

Hroðgar's natural instinct after his successes is to build a mighty hall. As we saw in the chapter on dragons, the hall was the literal and symbolic centre of Anglo-Saxon society. As well as commemorating the peace and prosperity that his military prowess has won, Hroðgar intends to use Heorot to share out treasure among his men as reward for their service and loyalty. This treasure in and of itself symbolized the ties of loyalty that bound men in fellowship, ensuring peace and cooperation. Simultaneously, Heorot is the place where the community meets to eat and drink together, and we later learn that men sleep in it. It is indicative of the mead hall's centrality to the community that the poet calls Heorot *folcstede* (the people's place). From Heorot, Hroðgar rules his kingdom, keeping the peace and defending the realm.

The great size of Heorot is not a piece of poetic hyperbole: Thetford Great Hall in Norfolk, for example, was almost 35 metres long.[7] Heorot, the most splendid hall ever seen and symbol of a successful, peaceful society, represents the triumph of order over chaos. Hroðgar's building of Heorot, moreover, mirrors the very act of Creation, as many critics have noted.[8] For the philosopher and historian Mircea Eliade, 'settlement is the repetition of a primordial act: the transformation of chaos into cosmos by the divine act of Creation.'[9] This link is compounded by the court poet singing a song about God's Creation to celebrate Heorot's construction. Hroðgar is, anachronistically, a Christian, and acknowledges that his wealth and success come from God. Heorot, like all civilized places, is thus also a centre of Christianity.

To make any hall, trees, an important component of one of the most feared forms of wilderness, were transformed through mankind's genius into a statement of sophisticated, civilized creation. The hall to the Anglo-Saxons represented the zenith of man's triumph over nature, and halls stood as conspicuous physical metaphors for this impressive achievement. The situation of the hall, and its flexibility as a metaphor, is perhaps best captured by Bede:

> The present life of men on earth, in comparison to that time which is unknown to us, seems to me as when you are sitting at a feast with your generals and attendants in winter time, the fire kindled in the hearth in the middle, and all within is warm, while outside the tempests of wintry rain and snow are raging; a sparrow flies swiftly through the hall, proceeding through one entrance and soon leaving through the other. For the time that it is inside, it is not touched by the tempests of winter, but after the smallest period of serenity has passed, it glides away from your eyes, soon returning from winter to winter once more. Thus this life of men appears for a little while; but of what comes afterwards, of what came before, we are utterly ignorant.[10]

Bede's sparrow image still speaks to us powerfully, over a millennium later, about the transience and uncertainty of life. For our purposes, it is germane to note the stark contrast between the warmth and light within and the unknown, dark and hostile natural world without, for this disparity is a key component of *Beowulf*.

Directly opposed to Heorot in literal and metaphorical terms is the mere, home to the monster Grendel and his mother. The following description is Hroðgar's account of where Beowulf must travel to fight Grendel's mother.

> They [the Grendelkin] occupy a secret land, wolf-slopes [*wulfhleoþu*], windy cliffs, the terrible fen-path, where the mountain-stream goes down beneath the cliffs' mists, the flood under the ground. It is not far in the measure of miles from here that the mere stands; the frost-covered groves hang over it, the fast-rooted wood overshadows the water. There each night one might see fire on the water, a fearful wonder. No one wise of the sons of men lives that knows the bottom [of the mere]; though the heath-stepper [*hæð-stapa*, a stag] is fatigued by dogs, the hart [*heorot*] with strong horns, seeks the wood, put to flight from afar, he will sooner give up his life, his vital organs on the bank, before he will hide his head in there. That is not a pleasant place! From there the surging waves rise up dark towards the clouds, when stirred by wind, a hateful tempest, until the sky becomes gloomy, the heavens weep.[11]

The mere inhabited by Grendel and his mother is the Anglo-Saxon wilderness par excellence. Beyond the fact that monsters live there, we see in Hroðgar's description many of the topographical signifiers of wilderness that we have been discussing over the course of this book. The mere is out in the fens, the same environment as that in which demons torment St Guthlac. It is home to wolves, after which a landmark is named, creatures of satanic association that live only in the wilderness and have a close affinity with criminals and exiles. Surrounding the mere is a thick wood, one of the characteristic signs of wilderness, with a darkening canopy. The most misanthropic and deadly element of all, water, sits at its epicentre and behaves in a manner more befitting the deep sea; in fact, *mere* could also mean 'sea', and the water it contains is later explicitly called *brim* (the sea).[12] We also see the very worst of the chaotic, hostile nature against which the warmth and light of the hall are contrasted: roaring winds, steep and precarious cliffs, rain and darkness. Moreover, the natural elements in the mere behave in a most uncanny manner, with fire appearing on the water and the water darkening the sky.

Two further aspects of the mere may not on first glance seem obvious but mark it emphatically as a wilderness. First, beyond its location in fenland, the mere has a more specific demonic association. Scholars have long noted the similarities between Grendel's mere and the Hell of Blickling Homily XVII:[13]

> As St Paul was looking towards the northern part of this middle-earth, where all waters flow down, and there he saw over the water a certain hoary stone, and to the north of the stone exceedingly frosty trees had grown, and there were dark mists, and under that stone was a dwelling-place of water-monsters [*niccra*, from *nicor*] and *weargs*, and he saw that on the cliff in those icy trees were hung many black souls, bound by their hands . . . and the water was black beneath that cliff, and between the cliff and the water there were about 12 miles.

In brief, this vision of Hell has in common with Grendel's mere the frosty trees overhanging the pool, water whose bottom is beyond the perception of man, cliffs, shadows, wolves and *niccra* (the mere is elsewhere called *nicera mere*, 'the sea-monsters' mere').[14] The mere is quite clearly intended to conjure up an image of Hell for the reader: both *Beowulf* and Blickling Homily XVII likely draw on a common stock of infernal imagery.

Second, the mere has a further resemblance to sites sacred to pagans. Sacred groves and pools were part of the pagan religious landscape, at least as understood by Christian writers.[15] Pope Gregory III, for example, warned against 'prophecies in groves or by fountains', and both Alcuin of York and the Anglo-Saxon missionary St Boniface wrote of pagans on the Continent who worshipped trees and water.[16] To a learned reader, the mere would have been associated with paganism, too, by its appearance. That heathenism was equated to devil worship by Christian writers makes this heathen identification doubly important.

We have two final points, for the time being, to note about Hroðgar's description of the mere. Despite its standing as the supreme statement of wilderness, the mere is 'not far in the measure of miles from [Heorot]', which indicates Heorot's troubling but not uncommon position. Like real instances of Anglo-Saxon civilized spaces, such as monasteries, cities and other great halls, it is surrounded by hostile nature and wilderness that seek to overcome it. The mere's direct opposition to Heorot is manifest in the detail of the reluctant hart.[17] The animal is the symbol of Hroðgar's kingship, which has an analogue in the stag-topped sceptre from the royal burial at Sutton Hoo, and the same noun, *heorot*, is used for both the animal and the great hall in *Beowulf*. This deer, then, represents Hroðgar and his men and their attendant civilized values, which stand in direct contrast to the Grendelkin and their wilderness. As a symbol of civilization, the stag would rather die than risk absorption into the uncivilized horror of the mere.

The land of Denmark is split between two polarized places, Heorot and the mere. An Anglo-Saxon reader would by no means be surprised to learn that monsters lived in the mere, which is characterized by almost every defining feature of the wilderness. Despite its proximity to Heorot, the mere could be tolerated so long as its resident monsters stayed there, and the humans in the civilized space of Heorot. The horror of *Beowulf*, however, to an Anglo-Saxon audience, is that the rightful inhabitants of the uncivilized mere do not stay where they are supposed to.

Grendel the Monster

> *þyrs sceal on fenne gewunian / ana innan lande.*[18]
> The giant must live in the fen, alone within the land.

Grendel is a large humanoid monster who has attacked Heorot every night for the twelve years since its completion, damaging the building and slaughtering the Danes huddled within it. Like all monsters, he is firmly linked to a specific environment, which his behaviour both defines and is defined by. From the beginning of his bloody entrance into the poem, Grendel is associated with the wilderness: 'the grim spirit was called Grendel, the notorious boundary-walker [*mære mearcstapa*], he who ruled the moors, the fen and fastness, the homeland of the monster race [*fifelcynnes eard*].'[19] The places Grendel rules are placed in apposition with the phrase *fifelcynnes eard*, lest we needed another reminder that wilderness and monster lairs are one and the same. This marks the first mention not only of Grendel by name, but the Danish wilderness, making an instant, forceful contrast between the monster and his home on the one hand and Hroðgar and Heorot on the other, just as Grendel's first mention as an *ellengæst* (bold spirit)[20] comes directly after the description of Heorot's creation.

Beowulf is unequivocal about the status of this wilderness: it is *fifelcynnes eard*, with Grendel as its horrifying ruler. The association of monster and wilderness is sustained throughout the poem: 'the dark death-shadow [*deorc deaþscua*] . . . who ruled the misty moors in perpetual night.'[21] Even Beowulf himself, who initially knows Grendel only by repute, is aware of his association with the wilderness, and prophesies that if he loses the fight, the monster will devour him in his *morhopu* (moor-retreat).[22] The vocabulary here makes it demonstratively clear that Grendel's proper place is in the wilderness, and other compounds elsewhere refer to the comfort and protection his home turf gives him: *fenhopu* (fen retreat), *fenfreoðu* (fen refuge).[23]

When Grendel is fatally wounded he flees back to his wilderness, and, as he enters, the mere reacts physically to his moribund state: 'he took his dying steps in the sea-monsters' mere [*nicera mere*], doomed and put to flight. There the sea [*brim*] was surging with blood, a terrible swirling of waves, all stirred-up with hot gore, it bubbled with sword-blood.'[24] Similarly, when Beowulf decapitates Grendel's corpse after defeating Grendel's mother, 'at once the wise men, those that gazed with Hroðgar on the water, saw that the surging waves were all stirred-up, the sea stained with blood.'[25] So closely aligned with the mere is Grendel that his death and mutilation produce a corresponding physical response, in a reversal of the glorious changes Guthlac's victory over the demons brings to Crowland. In an echo of the gnomic saying quoted above (from *Maxims II*), Grendel is called a *þyrse* (giant).[26] However, this particular *þyrs* does not stay in his fen home, and therein lies the problem at the start of the poem.

Grendel's reign of terror comes to a grisly end on the night Beowulf arrives at Heorot. Lying awake while other men sleep in the great hall, Beowulf is ready when the monster attempts to kill and eat him, and succeeds in ripping Grendel's arm clean off. Grendel manages to escape, but succumbs to this dismemberment in the mere. Grendel's journey to Heorot on that fateful night again stresses the importance of place:

> Then he came from the moor under the misty slopes,
> Grendel walked, bearing God's anger; the wicked ravager
> of mankind intended to ensnare someone in that illustrious

> hall. He moved under the heavens to the point where he most readily knew the wine-hall, the gold-hall of men, decorated with ornaments, to be . . . at once the door, fast with fire-forged bars, sprung open after he touched it with his hands; intending evil he tore it open, the mouth of the hall, when he was swollen with rage [*gebolgen*].[27]

The starting point of Grendel's journey is emphasized to remind the reader of Grendel's essential monstrosity, and when he moves into the civilized space of Heorot, the result is immediate and violent, as he tears the firmly fixed door from its hinges in crossing a literal and symbolic threshold. Able to move freely between civilization and wilderness, Grendel is a *mearcstapa*. Grendel brings with him the values and associations of the mere in the wilderness, and lays waste to Heorot in anthropophagic fury. That is, like the wolf, dragon and demon we discussed earlier, Grendel tries to change civilization into wilderness. Earlier in the poem, after Grendel's raids are detailed, the poet says that '[Grendel] reigned and strove against righteousness, alone against all, until the best of houses stood idle.'[28] Until the coming of Beowulf, Grendel's nightly atrocities have successfully turned order back to chaos. This symbolic act reverses the allegorical Creation narrative we discussed earlier. In fact, Beowulf describes Heorot as *idel ond unnyt* (idle and useless), a phrase specifically employed in *Genesis A*'s description of the primordial chaos that existed before Creation.[29]

Another sign of Grendel's success in this characteristically monstrous venture is the reaction of some of Hroðgar's men: 'sometimes at heathen temples [*hærgtrafum*] they offered homage to idols, prayed with words that the slayer of souls [the Devil] might offer them help against the nation's calamities. Such was their custom, the hope of heathens [*hæþenra*].'[30] To Christian Anglo-Saxons, heathenism naturally equated to worshipping the Devil, as in the late seventh-century law code of King Wihtred, which prescribes punishments for sacrificing to devils.[31] As we have seen, the heathen (and thus satanic) nature of the wilderness is one of its defining features. Like the mere itself, Grendel is also associated with both heathenism and the Devil. The poet twice calls Grendel a *hæþen* (heathen),[32] and he is described by a whole litany of satanic vocabulary: *feond on helle* (enemy in hell);[33] *feond mancynnes* (enemy of mankind),[34] which is used twice for demons and once for Satan in *Juliana*;[35] *godes ondsaca* (God's adversary), the latter noun used for demons in *Guthlac A*;[36] *ealdgewinna* (ancient adversary);[37] *deofla* (devils),[38] along with his mother; *helle gast* (hell spirit), a term used twice in *Juliana* to describe the Devil.[39] Grendel's reign of man-eating terror has caused the Danes to forsake Christianity and resort to heathenism, more befitting the monster's wilderness.

Some scholars ascribe Grendel's attacks to the Danes' heathenism at this part of the poem. However, a close reading of the text makes it clear this devotional lapse is a response to Grendel's attacks, and that previously the Danes were Christian. Moreover, Heorot is explicitly attacked by Grendel because it is a Christian place. To celebrate the building of Heorot, an oral poet sings a song in praise of God, and this irks the demonic monster:

> Then the bold spirit suffered painfully for a time, he who dwelt in the shadows, when he heard joy loud in the hall each day; there the harp sounded, the clear song of the *scop*. He that knew how to recount the creation of men from long ago said that The Almighty [*se ælmihtiga*] made the earth, a splendidly beautiful place surrounded by water, triumphant he fixed the sun and the moon, to give light to the land-dwellers, and decorated the corners of the earth with branches and leaves. He also created life for every kind of being that lives and moves about.[40]

It is hearing the festivities and the praise of God that angers Grendel and provokes him to launch his horrific attack on Heorot. In this, Grendel's behaviour recalls the reaction of the demons of the fens who attack Guthlac in the *Vita sancti Guthlaci* after hearing him singing devotional songs: 'he was engaged in his customary singing of Psalms . . . thus, testing the strength of all his wicked force, with a cunning mind [the Devil] fired with all his might, as if from a fully extended bow, a poisoned arrow of despair.'[41] Like all monsters, Grendel hates mankind and Christianity, both of which are essential components of civilization in the Anglo-Saxon mind, and responds in kind to this beacon of civilization within a wider wilderness.

Misanthropic, wilderness-dwelling and associated with the Devil and other monsters, Grendel and thus his crimes against the men of Heorot are certainly worthy of this contextual billing: 'he quickly seized as his first deed a sleeping man, tore unrestrainedly, bit the bone-enclosures [that is, the flesh], drank the blood from the veins, swallowed sinful gobbets; soon he had consumed all of the dead man, feet and hands.'[42] The poet effectively details Grendel's gleeful gluttony and pleasure in his feast. The description perfectly captures the horror of being eaten – one of the primordial fears of mankind, which early in human history found itself part of the diets of large carnivores. The reference to Grendel's eyes emitting light ('from his eyes appeared a flame most like a hideous light')[43] likewise recalls the terror of seeing eye-shine from unseen animals lurking near a fire at night, another symptom of the deep-seated human fear of man-eaters. The detail of Grendel's vampiric refreshment further has a specific context in Anglo-Saxon texts.[44] *Genesis A* renders God's command to Noah in Genesis 9:4 ('flesh with blood you shall not eat') as the more emotive 'never, defiled by sin, shamefully consume your feast with blood, soul's gore [*sawldreore*]'.[45] Anglo-Saxon texts contain many prohibitions against drinking blood, complementing a wealth of biblical orders, meaning that Grendel shamelessly violates a serious cultural taboo. As an extra evil fillip, Grendel is said to delight in his murderous deeds: before the feeding frenzy mentioned above, *his mod ahlog* (his mind laughed).[46]

Grendel's size is a final indication of his monstrosity. Beowulf refers to him as a giant (*þyrse*), but there are other indications of his bulk in the poem. On his maiden raid on Heorot, having grown intolerably furious at the *scop*'s song of Creation, Grendel 'carried away thirty thanes at rest'.[47] Until Beowulf saves them, the Danes are utterly helpless and, despite superior numbers, cannot slay Grendel. To give a clearer idea of Grendel's size, we can consult later events. After killing Grendel's vengeful mother at the mere, Beowulf finds Grendel's bloodied corpse and decapitates it, in order to bring home a gruesome trophy. Meeting his companions waiting beside the mere, Beowulf chucks them Grendel's head to transport back to Heorot: 'four of them [Geat soldiers] with difficulty had to carry Grendel's head to the gold-hall on a spear.'[48] Grendel's severed arm, also presumably enormous, is an object of wonder to the Danes:

> At the front of each [finger], each of the hard nails was most like steel, the heathen warrior's horrible, monstrous talons. Everyone said that no hard weapons of prime goodness would strike him that would destroy the monster's [*ahlæcan*] bloodied battle-hand.[49]

Grendel's skin is tough, and his great hands are armed with talons as hard as steel: his monstrous, oversized body matches his horrible, monstrous nature.

Beowulf describes Grendel as both a huge, physical being and a demonic spirit interchangeably, without resolving the apparent paradox. In truth, he partakes of both natures simultaneously, hence the *mearcstapa* moniker: Grendel moves from spirit to flesh, wilderness to civilization, apparently at will. But he is, essentially, a monster: a heathen and satanic creature that lives in the uncivilized wilderness, hates the people and Christianity that help define civilization, and wreaks havoc whenever he leaves his proper place in the mere. But he is just that – a monster – isn't he?

Grendel the Human

Were things so simple, Grendel would not be the abhorrent, repulsive monster he is. For perhaps the most disturbing thing about Grendel, to both Anglo-Saxon and modern audiences, is his humanity. As we have seen, for St Augustine, two things define a human, however monstrous in appearance, in *De civitate dei*:

> Whoever is born a man anywhere – that is, a rational, mortal animal – however extraordinary to our understanding the form of the body he carries, or his colour or his movement or his sound, or whatever part or power or quality in his nature: no one of the faithful might doubt that he draws his origin from that single protoplast [Adam].[50]

The essential defining features of a man to Augustine are descent from Adam and rationality. As such, Grendel's human ancestry is not up for debate:

> The grim spirit was called Grendel, the notorious boundary-walker [*mære mearcstapa*], he who ruled the moors, the fen and fastness; the miserable man [*wonsæli wer*] guarded the homeland of the monster race [*fifelcynnes eard*] for a while after the Creator had condemned him among Cain's kin. The Eternal Lord avenged that murder, because he slew Abel; [Cain] did not rejoice in that vengeance, but he, the Ruler, banished him far from the race of mankind because

> of that crime. From thence were born all the evil progenies, the giants [*eotenas*] and elves [*ylfe*] and wicked monsters [*orcneas*], [and] also the giants [*gigantas*] that fought against God for a long time; He repaid them a reward for that.[51]

Cain, of course, is the firstborn son of Adam and Eve, eternally condemned to wander the earth after murdering his brother Abel. This explains the note that Grendel lives *godes yrre bær* (bearing God's anger):[52] like his forefather Cain, Grendel is cursed. But although he has human ancestry and thus satisfies Augustine's definition of a man, the poem makes it clear that Grendel is still a monster.

Beowulf here alludes to a popular medieval belief that Cain was the father of monsters. This derived from a reading of Genesis 6:2, which recounts how 'The sons of God seeing the daughters of men, that they were fair, took to themselves wives of all which they chose.' Genesis 6:4–6 condemns this union, and mentions that giants were the result of the coupling:

> Now giants were upon the earth in those days. For after the sons of God went in to the daughters of men and they brought forth children, these are the mighty men of old, men of renown. And God seeing that the wickedness of men was great on the earth, and that all the thought of their heart was bent upon evil at all times, it repented him that he had made man on the earth.

In early medieval Christian exegesis, endorsed by Augustine, the 'daughters of men' were Cain's offspring, and the 'sons of God' the descendants of Seth, the third son of Adam and Eve.[53] This tradition existed alongside another interpretation, put forward in the apocryphal Book of Enoch, that the 'sons of God' were fallen angels whose sexual congress with mortals defiled the angelic essence, angering God.[54] The two traditions were commonly conflated, as in the *Vita sancti Guthlaci*, where the demons that attack the eremitic saint are called *semen Cain* (the seed of Cain).[55]

As well as carrying God's anger, Grendel, too, is an exile. To the Anglo-Saxons, the essential aspect of God's curse on Cain was his banishment: 'thus you must wander far-stretching tracks, hateful to your companions.'[56] Like Cain, Grendel lives in the wilderness, far from his fellow men, and *wræclastas træd* (walked the paths of exile).[57] In common with other Anglo-Saxon exiles, he is cut off from happiness (*dreamum bedæled*, deprived of joys),[58] and his rage at the sound of communal devotion and merriment in Heorot is an extreme version of the exile's lament in *The Wanderer*, who asks rhetorically, *hwær sindon seledreamas* (where are the hall-joys?).[59] The proximity of Grendel's home to the wolf-slopes (*wulfhleopu*) associates him with the animals, which we previously discussed as a common fate for the Anglo-Saxon exile, such as the friendless man of *Maxims* I. Grendel is even called a *heorowearh* (malicious *wearg*),[60] which fits neatly with our earlier discussion of people banished for abominable crimes who take on something of the wolf's identity, and also further links the mere to Blickling Homily XVII's Hell, where *weargs* also live. Grendel's mere is doubly a place of exile, for it resembles Hell, which at its core significance is exile from God.

The poem's vocabulary furthermore leaves no doubt that Grendel is a man. Not only is he *earmsceapen on weres wæstmum* (shaped in the form of a man),[61] but the poem uses numerous nouns meaning 'man' to describe him: *wer*, *rinc*, *guma*, *healðegnes* (hall-thane), *hilderinces* (warrior).[62] Although Grendel is simultaneously referred to as an *eoten* (giant),[63] and Beowulf's exploits against him see him called an *eotonweard* (guard against giants)[64] and compared to another *eoten*-slayer, Sigmund, we must remember that the *eotenas* are explicitly mentioned as descendants of Cain in the monstrous genealogy passage, and so this does not jeopardize his humanity. An Anglo-Saxon illustration of the giants mentioned in Genesis 6:4 indeed renders them as large, saturnine men in flowing robes, engaged in discussion and gesturing animatedly with enormous hands. Despite their size, these particular giants are recognizably human.

As for rationality, Augustine's other defining feature of a man, Grendel displays it in abundance. He mulls over the sound of the *scop* and communal fun coming from Heorot before deciding to attack, and laughs in gleeful anticipation of another feast. His attacks on Heorot, planned and premeditated, are far from bestial acts: '[Hroðgar] knew that the monster [*ahlæcan*] planned an attack on the high-hall.'[65] Furthermore, it is implied that Grendel could settle his feud with Heorot on human terms, but opts not to do so: 'he did not wish for peace with any man of the Danish army, to

Antediluvian giants depicted in Cotton Claudius B. IV, f. 13r.

withdraw his deadly evil [or] to settle payment [for the men he killed].'[66] The latter part of this statement refers to *wergild*, the Germanic system of paying compensation for murder to the victim's relatives, a measure intended to avoid violence and feuding. That this is a consideration for Grendel shows his innate rationality, his rejection of it his innate evil. Finally, although Grendel only ever kills with his bare hands, he does make use of human technology in the form of a bag to carry his dinner home, as Beowulf relates: 'his sack hung down, broad and strange, firmly fixed with cunning clasps; it was all adorned with skilful thought, with devil's crafts and dragons' skins. He, the ferocious doer of deeds, intended to put me, guiltless, in there, one of many.'[67]

Again, making this bag required forethought and skill with tools, both indications of rationality. Grendel, then, is equally man and monster, a *mearcstapa* who moves at will between both categories.

Grendel's Mother

After Grendel's death at the hands, quite literally, of Beowulf, Hroðgar thanks God for delivering him from Grendel's ravages, and immediately orders Heorot to be repaired:

> Then the order was quickly given so that Heorot was decorated inside with hands. There were many men and women who equipped the wine-hall, the guest-hall. The tapestries shone on the walls, adorned with gold, many wondrous sights for any of the men that gaze upon such things.[68]

Rebuilding Heorot is both a practical and symbolic act. For with nightly murders and the damage associated with Grendel ripping the door off its hinges at an end, the Danes can once again enjoy their majestic hall. At the same time, this is a gesture symbolically reasserting civilization, as God is praised once more and the hall, the very symbol and centre of Hroðgar's kingdom, is redecorated and repaired, making a strong statement of the defeat of the wilderness represented by Grendel. There is, once again, an emphasis on the communal, with the mention of the many men and women who helped decorate Heorot, and the description of it as a *gestsele* (guest-hall). Civilization, with its attendant values of Christianity, loyalty and fellowship, returns with the repair of Heorot.

However, the wilderness isn't done, just yet.

> It soon became manifest, widely known to men, that an avenger yet lived after the hostilities, after a long time, after the battle-sorrow. Grendel's mother, a female [*ides*], a monster-woman [*aglæcwif*], mindful of miseries, she who had to dwell in the dreadful water, the cold streams, after Cain became a sword-slayer to his only brother, his father's son; then he departed, doomed, marked by murder, fled from human joy, occupied the wilderness [*westen*]. From thence awoke many dire-spirits; Grendel was one of them, the malicious *wearg* [*heorowearh*], he who found at Heorot a watchful man awaiting battle [Beowulf].[69]

Grendel is very much his mother's son. She too is descended from Cain, and with the infamous fratricide found herself on the wrong side of God's anger. She shares the mere with Grendel in the *westen*, and, lest this symbolically charged home were not enough to confirm her status as a monster, she is explicitly called an *aglæcwif*,[70] a compound noun marrying 'monster' (*aglæca*) with 'woman' (*wif*). However, in among these monstrous facts, it is clear that she, too, is human: she is called an *ides*, and her descent from Adam via the evil line of Cain satisfies part of Augustine's definition of a human. Later, when Beowulf visits the mere, the home of the Grendelkin is described using domestic human terms. The nouns *hrofsele* (roofed hall) and *niðsele* (hostile hall)[71] parallel the numerous *-sele* compounds describing Heorot, such as *winsele* (wine-hall) and *gestsele* (guest-hall),[72] and both locations are called a *reced* (hall).[73]

Hroðgar's account confirms that she is, just about, physically recognizable as a woman:

> I have heard my people, counsellors inhabiting that country, say that they have seen two such great boundary-walkers [*micle mearcstapan*], alien spirits [*ellorgæstas*] that rule the moors. One of them was, so far as they might easily ascertain to know, in the likeness of a woman [*idese onlicnæs*]; the other walked the paths of exile, shaped in the form of a man, except that he was bigger than any other man; in the old days the country-dwellers named him Grendel. They did not know of any father, whether before any was born of secret spirits.[74]

This passage brings out further similarities with her son, beyond their humanoid taxonomy. They are both *micle mearcstapan*, moving between human and monster, and both are firmly associated with their wilderness environment, like all monsters. Grendel's mother is however perhaps associated with the wilderness even more firmly than her son. During her raid on Heorot she is a fish out of water and, unlike Grendel, gets in a panic when in a civilized space: 'she was in haste, wished to get out' after being seen. As soon as she has grabbed a sleeping warrior, *heo to fenne gang* (she went to the fen).[75] Grendel's mother's predicament recalls that of the 'king of terror' that flounders and dies when it leaves its native wilderness.

The *aglæcwif*'s raid on Heorot has a very human motivation, as Hroðgar explains to Beowulf: 'she avenged the feud, because you killed Grendel last night.'[76] Revenge in heroic poetry is a laudable activity – 'it is better for everyone that he avenges his friend than mourns too much,' as Beowulf says[77] – but Grendel's mother here is clearly in the wrong. After all, Beowulf killed Grendel after he committed over a decade of nightly murders, and we must remember that Grendel would not settle the feud with *wergild*. One life in exchange for the countless Danes that Grendel has eaten seems hardly fair to Hroðgar, let alone worthy of the other side's retaliation. Although there is a tendency among modern readers to sympathize with Grendel's mother for wanting to avenge her son's murder, a closer reading of the poem makes it clear that she has sinned by heinously renewing the feud, as we will see in the next chapter. Most importantly for our immediate purposes, by pursuing a vendetta Grendel's mother reveals herself to be a rational creature, satisfying Augustine's second stricture for the definition of a human.

Pursuing this feud aside, it is clear that Grendel's mother is less culpable than her son. She might perhaps indulge in eating the men Grendel brings home in his dragon-skin satchel, and she has been seen abroad by Hroðgar's counsellors with her son, presumably on some baleful mission or other. But although she knows where Heorot is, only Grendel is mentioned as perpetrating the reign of terror that lasts twelve winters; perhaps, until the feud, she merely eats, rather than kills, people. Our analysis of monsters in Anglo-Saxon thought however allows us to apprehend the true monstrosity of Grendel's mother. For her panic at Heorot after being spotted by the resting warriors is in direct contrast with her remarkable strength and bravery when fighting Beowulf in the mere, again recalling the whale.

> The weary-hearted one, the strongest of men, the foot-soldier [Beowulf], stumbled, so that he took a fall. She sat on the hall-guest and drew her *seax* [a small knife carried by Anglo-Saxon warriors], broad and shining-edged. She wished to avenge her son, her only offspring.[78]

Even the dragon does not manage to put the much older Beowulf on his backside. Wielding a *seax*, showing a facility with man-made weapons alien to her son, Grendel's mother continues to straddle the woman/monster boundary. In this encounter, Beowulf's armour protects him from the *seax*'s blows, but clearly Grendel's mother is a very different beast in her natural environment. Like all monsters, she ferociously defends her wilderness home against denizens of the civilized world. Her greater comfort and strength within the mere, the supreme statement of wilderness, demonstrates her sinful nature and essential monstrosity. In a civilized space, Grendel's mother is surprisingly timid, but in an uncivilized arena she shows herself stronger than the strongest man alive. The vocabulary describing her at the mere harmonizes with this reading. She is a *brimwylf* (sea-wolf),[79] associated with this most unsavoury of canine monsters, like her son, and is called *grim ond grædig* (grim and greedy),[80] the same epithet used for Grendel earlier in the poem, strongly suggesting that she, too, is guilty of man-eating. It is also clear from the passage quoted above that she is not desperately defending her own life but gleefully pursuing the feud resulting from Grendel's long overdue death. More than anything, it is Grendel's mother's strong association with the mere – the hellish, pagan, uncanny and most desolate and uncivilized of all wildernesses – that should define her in our eyes as a monster.

In the passage quoted above describing the sightings of the Grendelkin on the prowl together, it is intriguing that only Grendel is named. Despite her importance to the poem, Grendel's mother never receives a proper name of her own. In a sense, this makes her even more Other than her son. It is fairly common to give a feminist reading of this anonymity and see her defined only in terms of motherhood, a symptom of misogyny or patriarchal discourse. Without discounting this reading, it is clear from the poem's context that there is something specific to Grendel's mother that prevents her being given a proper name. Other women in the poem are named and given prominent roles: Hroðgar's queen, Wealhþeow, is frequently seen performing ceremonial deeds at Heorot, and like her husband doles out valuable advice about monarchical rule to Beowulf. Hygelac, Beowulf's uncle, is married to another praiseworthy and named individual, Hygd. Both Wealhþeow and Hygd distribute treasure, giving them a similar status to the kings in the poem, who are often described as treasure givers (for example as *goldwine*, gold-friend).[81] The narrative of the poem, moreover, suggests that people are far less familiar with Grendel's mother than with her son, since he is a fixture at Heorot every night for twelve years, and knowledge of her is contained within shadowy glimpses of the pair out on the moors. However, in the context of the importance of boundaries to the Anglo-Saxons, it is possible that she remains unnamed because she is even more unknowable than her son. For in being far less at ease with civilized spaces and more at home in the mere, Grendel's mother lies even further from the world of light and civilization than Grendel. To name something is to exert power over it, to confine it within a defined set of criteria: perhaps it is simply not possible to do so for Grendel's mother.

Micle mearcstapan

The Grendelkin are thus very aptly called *mearcstapan*. They are creatures of the wilderness able to enter civilized spaces, moving at will from mere to Heorot. They are physical beings, perpetrating bodily harm to people, and yet have murky associations with the incorporeal spirits that came about with Cain's exile, expressed in the term *ellorgæstas* (alien spirits) applied to them. But most disturbingly of all, they are both human and monster, and therein lies their most potent threat to the Anglo-Saxons, and the reason for their lingering ability to terrify a millennium after being immortalized in the Nowell Codex. Their peculiar horror lies in their confounding of the boundaries between seemingly opposing and mutually exclusive categories.

It is even possible that the Grendelkin had a life and reputation outside the poem. In the charter corpus, there are several possible references to Grendel living far from the legendary world of Scandinavia in the landscape of Anglo-Saxon England itself.[82] Four in particular are intriguing. In a grant of land from King Eadwig to Lyfing in Hertfordshire, dating to 957, among the boundaries of the land there is mention of a *gryndeles syllen* (Grendel's bog). Another grant, from King Eadgar, this time for land in Worcestershire to Pershore Abbey in 972, mentions a *Grindles bece* (Grendel's beck). Both becks and bogs are watery places, similar to Grendel's home in the poem, and were these the only references they would still be remarkable. However, there are also two references to an actual Grendel's mere: a *grendles mere* in Wiltshire, mentioned in King Æðelstan's grant to Wulfgar of 931, and a *grendlesmere* in Staffordshire in King Eadred's grant to Burhelm of 958. The Wiltshire reference is particularly intriguing as it comes from an area of land not far from Malmesbury Abbey, where the eminent scholar Michael Lapidge believes *Beowulf* may have been put into its recognizable form, some time before the Nowell Codex was created.[83] Grendel is not an Anglo-Saxon personal name, and neither was it used for anything apart from the first monster in *Beowulf* and minor places linked to the name in the charters. It seems abundantly possible, therefore, that Grendel was a monster thought to live in the watery places of Anglo-Saxon England. In the East Anglian dialect, the term 'grindle' means 'drain' or 'ditch' and could be a survival of the belief in a fen-dwelling monster.[84] Folklore from the same area tells of the Shuck (from the Old English *scucca*, demon), a huge dog with glowing red eyes that sometimes has an association with water: could this be a version of Grendel, a huge monster referred to as a *scucca* in the poem, with shining eyes and strong links to water?[85]

THIS FINAL EVIDENCE IS disturbing. Grendel and his mother, as we have seen, were both human and monster. However evil their deeds or disgusting their appearance, their descent from Adam and capacity for rational thought cannot be eradicated. This opens up the intriguing possibility that 'Grendel' was a name for any man-monster that lived in the uncivilized watery wastes of Anglo-Saxon England, not far from the tenuously maintained civilized spaces of mead hall and monastery. In the next chapter, this threat will be sharpened as we consider the possibility that the Grendelkin represented a type of monster that all men and women had the potential to become. Were Grendelkin born or made?

VII

MEARCSTAPAN, PART TWO: BEOWULF AND OTHERS

One of the functions we have seen monsters perform in Anglo-Saxon culture is confronting mankind with uncomfortable questions about its identity. The Grendelkin are both human and monster simultaneously, and this opens up some deeply disturbing possibilities for both the characters within *Beowulf* and the audience outside the poem. As by far the longest surviving Old English poem, *Beowulf* interrogates us on a more profound and distressing level than any other text discussed in this book. We will examine the questions that the monsters of *Beowulf* ask, and answer them, in this final chapter.

Nature versus Nurture

Through their ancestry, the Grendelkin are human, but cursed by God for Cain's crime. Grendel exists *godes yrre bær* (bearing God's anger), and his mother 'had to dwell in the dreadful water, the cold streams, after Cain became a sword-slayer to his only brother'.[1] Explaining that the Grendelkin are part of Cain's *untydras* (evil progenies) is more than sufficient as an origin story and indication of their species.[2] So why does the poem go to such lengths as to refer to them with words used for people, have them live in a hall carefully described with the same vocabulary used for Heorot and exhibit rational behaviour?

The *Beowulf* poet's technique is not tautological. The *Old English Boethius*, like Augustine, invokes rationality as a defining characteristic of mankind:

> We have great power. There is no rational creature [*gesceadwis gesceaft*] that does not have freedom. He who has rationality has the power to judge and separate what he ought to desire and what he ought to detest, and each man has freedom, so that he knows what he wants and what he does not want . . . There is no creature that has freedom and rationality except angels and men.[3]

Possessing rationality means that people have the choice to commit good or evil deeds, but with that comes culpability for one's actions and sins. This makes the Grendelkin doubly damned: as rational beings, they know that killing and eating people are immoral acts, and yet do both regardless. By constantly reminding readers of the Grendelkin's humanity, the poem keeps this context in the foreground. Most of the map monsters and dragons, along with wolves and whales, lack the requisite rationality to question whether their crimes against humankind are right or wrong. Although the demons that attack Guthlac and Cuthbert are former angels and thus have reason, they have already been eternally damned and, in tempting and afflicting the living, are carrying out God's will. Grendel and his mother, on the other hand, are human, and God is yet to sentence them for eternity, and so they have every reason to shun their evil inheritance and embrace their righteous, human side. Alas, they choose not to do so, and like Decius and the *weargs* their humanity remains but a footnote to their monstrosity.

This reading finds further support elsewhere in the poem. Emphasizing the Grendelkin's humanity suggests that they have the potential to be human rather than monster. Both the Danes and Grendelkin live in a *reced* (hall),[4] but whereas Heorot is a *gestsele* (guest-hall), the mere is a *niðsele* (hostile hall).[5] Physically, of course, a grand wooden building above ground has little in common with a natural chthonic cavern. However, the linked but contrasting *-sele* compounds suggest that the halls are abstractly identical but used for different ends: Heorot for keeping the peace and distributing treasure, the mere for pursuing war and strife. As we have seen across this book, wilderness and civilization are not merely physical spaces but locations defined by their occupant, and so the mere could, potentially, be the same sort of *sele* as Heorot were it not for the Grendelkin's outrageous behaviour. With a change in the conduct of its occupants, the mere could become a philosophically civilized dwelling like Heorot.

Likewise, when Grendel approaches Heorot for the final time, he is called a *rinc* (man), and yet within the hall he surveys *rinca manige* (many men), identifies them as prey, and seizes a *slæpendne rinc* (sleeping man) before eating him and drinking his blood.[6] The repetition here draws attention to the fact that Grendel is a man, just like his victims, but does not behave like one. Instead, he commits murder and cannibalism and becomes more monster than man. Cannibalism and murder are a moral boundary separating men from monsters, and another *mearc* that Grendel crosses. Like Decius and the *weargs*, it is this *rinc*'s crimes against *rinca manige* that make him a monster, and his potential to act like a man is implicit in the vocabulary.

The Grendelkin in this way find a foil elsewhere in the Nowell Codex. In the first chapter, we discussed how another monster-man, St Christopher, rises above his evil and deformed nature by embracing Christianity. Despite being a giant dog-headed cannibal from a heathen wilderness, Christopher is human, and his physical appearance does not change once he accepts the light of Christ. His monstrous body and homeland make him, like the Grendelkin, one of the *untydras* that are spawned after Cain's exile, and hence cursed by God. The Grendelkin, like Christopher, are aware of the message of Christianity: it is, after all, the *scop*'s song about Creation that causes Grendel to begin his vendetta against Heorot. That Christopher, aware of God's message, rises above his nefarious origins to become not only a Christian but a saint is further evidence that the Grendelkin could forsake their evil nature and become more human than monster.

Outside the Nowell Codex, the original readers of *Beowulf* would have known all about another race of people with evil, heathen origins living in an uncivilized wilderness who had forsaken their inauspicious beginnings, and civilized their homeland, by accepting Christianity: themselves. Before Augustine's mission landed in Kent in 597, they were pagans (and thus devil worshippers) living on a remote island in the far north, vilified as an uncivilized wilderness by the rest of Europe. As we have seen, the Anglo-Saxons were well aware of their heathen origins, even embracing a version of Woden as an ancestor, and were proud of their triumph over ancestral evil and the freezing, isolated island. But the conversion did not happen overnight, and nor was it a permanent, irreversible alteration: even in the late Anglo-Saxon period, legislation was being passed against people reverting to paganism, such as Cnut's second law code, dating to about 1020. So if the Anglo-Saxons had the potential to lapse into heathenism, or, in other words, embrace their evil origins, does this explain why several places in extant charters were associated with Grendel? Was becoming Grendel, through rejecting God and committing mortal sins, a real threat?

Men into Monsters

There is one ferocious monster from *The Wonders of the East* that we have delayed discussing until now. It is known as the Donestre.

> Then there is a certain island in the Red Sea where there is a race of men called among us Donestre, that are grown

> like soothsayers [*frihteras*] from the head to the navel, and the other part is like a man's body. And they know all human languages. When they see a man from a foreign nation, then they name him and his companions with the names of acquaintances, and with false words they deceive him and seize him, and then after that they eat all of him except for his head, and then sit and weep over the head.[7]

Like many of the text's wonders, the appearance of the Donestre is incomprehensible. It is unclear, to us at least, how a soothsayer differs in appearance from humans. Its behaviour, however, is comprehensibly malevolent. Using cunning and an uncanny flair for languages, the Donestre tricks strangers into friendship before eating them. The detail about the Donestre weeping over the body is likely to signal that it is conscious of committing a sin, for it is clear from its actions and linguistic prowess that this monster possesses reason and must be essentially human. We have deferred analysis of the Donestre until this point because the illustration accompanying its entry in the Tiberius version of *Wonders* has explicit parallels to our reading of the Grendelkin. Read sequentially in a clockwise direction, the Tiberius illustration is a clear demonstration of a man perverted into a monster through the sins of murder and cannibalism.[8]

At first, the Donestre stands on two legs, like a human. Although its head and chest are leonine, perhaps demonstrating what a soothsayer looked like to an Anglo-Saxon, the Donestre's face is human: we see a human nose, front-facing eyes, a mouth and a chin. Although the Donestre is naked, with large bright-red genitalia, and is eye-level with the man only because the latter is standing on a hummock, the overall impression is humanoid, and beyond the long, curly hair on its head and differently coloured shading on the soothsayer portion, there is nothing to make this individual unequivocally a monster. The pose is not hostile, and one of the Donestre's large, human hands seems to be gently touching the traveller's own gesticulating counterpart. The Donestre is evidently talking to the man, and in the next illustration this cunning linguist makes its attack. Now the Donestre's head has become altogether bestial: gone are the human nose, chin and mouth, replaced by a predator's muzzle into which half the man's arm has disappeared. Further, its stance is no longer bipedal: it crouches almost on all fours, using a large clawed hand like a paw to pin the man's head down. In the final image, the Donestre weeps over the traveller's severed head, looking again more human than monster in its face and hands. Its expression is one of human rationality as the Donestre acknowledges the meaning of what it has done, and despairs. However, that a change in the Donestre has taken place after the crossing of ethical boundaries is clear from the less distinct lines used to depict it in the final scene. Like Grendel, the Donestre is human, but becomes a monster by merit of committing murder and cannibalism.

As well as paralleling Grendel, the nightmarish Donestre has kin in the men of *Beowulf*. When Beowulf arrives at Heorot, he is met with instant antagonism from one of Hroðgar's retainers, Unferth. Unferth, who accuses Beowulf of vanity for challenging Breca to a swimming contest as a young man, clearly enjoys a privileged place at Heorot: *þe æt fotum sæt frean Scyldinga* ('he sat at the feet of the King of the Shieldings,' meaning Hroðgar).[9] However, after defending himself against accusations of vainglory and foolishness, Beowulf lands his own blow against Unferth's honour: 'you became a slayer to your brothers, close kinsmen: thus you must endure damnation in hell.'[10] Unferth is guilty of fratricide, the same crime for which God sentenced Cain to exile, and indeed the same word is used to describe the two murderers: Unferth is a *banan* (slayer), Cain an *ecgbanan* (sword-slayer).[11] Despite its civilized appearance, Heorot is not only sheltering a man stained with the same sin as Cain but honouring him. It is interesting to

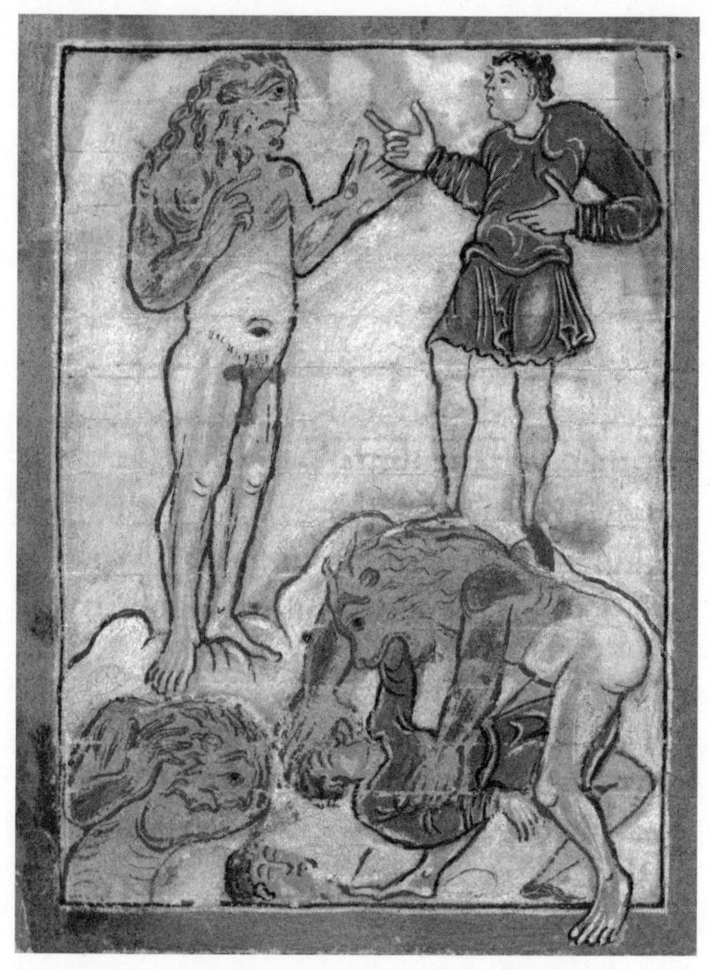

Donestre depicted in Cotton Tiberius B. V, Part I, f. 83v.

note that the chastened Unferth later lends Beowulf his sword for the fight with Grendel's mother, and it fails to cut her: 'that was the first time for the noble treasure that its glory failed.'[12] Since it belongs to a fratricide, perhaps the sword fails to harm another who has been cursed because of that awful crime. Given the life-long attachment of warriors to their swords in heroic poetry, it may even have been the very weapon with which Unferth killed his closest relations.

While the full implications of the garrulous Unferth's fratricide are not explored in *Beowulf*, another character's descent into sin is recounted at some length. Beowulf's defeat of Grendel sees him flatteringly compared to Sigmund the dragon slayer, but allusion is also made to another apparently relevant figure: Heremod, an early Danish king.

> He [Sigmund] was the most widely celebrated exile across the nations of men, the protector of warriors, for his great deeds; he had so prospered after Heremod's prowess in battle, strength and courage, came to an end. He was betrayed away among the giants [*mid eotenum*] in the power of fiends, quickly killed. Surging sorrows oppressed him for a long time; he became a cause for life-sorrows to his people, all the noblemen . . . evil entered into him.[13]

At this stage, Heremod's crime is not stated, but there are nonetheless a few crucial parallels to Grendel. First, because of his sin, Heremod is tricked into going to live *mid eotenum*. Grendel is at one point called an *eoten*, and *eotenas* are listed among the evil progeny that spring up after Cain is exiled.[14] Second, when he is sent there, he falls *on feonda geweald* (in the power of fiends), which is the precise phrase used to describe Grendel's death at the mere.[15] Furthermore, being sent to live *mid eotenum* is configured as an exile, like the punishment endured by Grendel because of Cain's offence. The specificities of Heremod's crimes are later outlined by King Hroðgar:

> [Heremod] did not grow up as they desired, but as the death and widespread slaughter of the Danish people. Swollen with rage at heart [*bolgenmod*], he destroyed his

> table-companions, his closest friends, until he, alone, the notorious king, departed from the joys of men. Although the Mighty God exalted him in the delights of strength [and] power, promoted him forth over all men, his spirit however grew bloodthirsty in his chest. By no means did he give [gold] rings to the Danes according to custom; he lived joyless, so that he suffered misery because of that conflict, from the long-lasting punishment by his people.[16]

Heremod is sent to live *mid eotenum* because he became a tyrant and, in a similarity to Unferth and Cain, killed the people closest to him; in fact, Heremod 'departed from the joys of men [*mon-dreamum*]', which is the same compound noun used to describe Cain's exile. An avaricious murderer, instead of protecting his subjects and using his strength and power wisely he became a torment to them until they could endure him no longer. Heremod's tyranny is also configured as ingratitude to God, who 'exalted him in the delights of strength [and] power, promoted him forth over all men'. A wise ruler, unlike Heremod, would use these gifts responsibly in honour of their divine bestower, rather than behave in a manner offensive to him like the Grendelkin. In the ideological landscape of the poem, to live *mid eotenum* is to live in the most uncivilized wilderness of all, for that is where Grendel the *eoten* has his home. As we have seen, living in such a wilderness can only mean one thing: evidently, through his horrible sins, Heremod became more monster than man, and no longer belonged in the civilized world of men. Like Grendel and the Donestre, Heremod's behaviour makes him a monster, and hence he must live in the wilderness. Between them, the *scop* who sings the song that introduces Heremod, and Hroðgar, who picks up the narrative thread, show how easily a man can become a monster.

In Hroðgar's description, Heremod becomes *bolgenmod* (swollen with rage at heart). This links him, again, to Grendel, who becomes *bolgenmod*[17] when he stands outside the doors of Heorot, and also the dragon, which becomes *gebolgen* (swollen with rage)[18] when its hoard is robbed. But there is one major character in the poem we have not yet discussed at length who, like Heremod, Grendel and the dragon, is also described as both *bolgenmod* and *gebolgen*: Beowulf himself. Is there a reason that two separate people lament the life and times of the king who became a monster with reference to the titular hero?

Beowulf, the Third *Mearcstapa*

From the moment he is introduced, the poem leaves us in no doubt as to the great size and strength of Beowulf: 'he was the strongest in might of mankind on that day of this life, noble and [physically] powerful.'[19] When the Geats arrive in Denmark, the coastguard challenges the foreign warriors and is immediately impressed by Beowulf's vastness: 'I have never seen a larger man across the earth than one of your number, the man in armour.'[20] Prodigal size and strength are important qualities for a warrior, but such characteristics can also make one a monster. Grendel is described as 'shaped in the form of a man . . . except that he was bigger than any other man'.[21] In the *Liber monstrorum*, mention is made of a character in *Beowulf* reckoned a monster by merit of his physical stature:

> And there are monsters of an awesome bulk [*monstra mirae magnitudinis*], like King Hygelac, who ruled the Geats and was killed by the Franks, whom no horse was able to carry from the age of twelve. His bones are preserved on an island in the River Rhine, where it bursts forth into the Ocean, and they are shown as a miracle to comers from a long way away.[22]

King Hygelac's size makes him worthy of inclusion in a text dedicated entirely to monsters. Beowulf, we must remember, is a blood relative of Hygelac: the great king is his maternal uncle. In both *Beowulf* and the *Liber monstrorum*, then, physical size is a symptom of monstrosity. Does it, therefore, take a monster to kill monsters?

Indeed, on closer inspection, there are numerous disturbing links between Beowulf and the Grendelkin. On his first frenzied attack on Heorot, Grendel 'carried away thirty thanes at rest',[23] suggesting that he is stronger than thirty warriors. The same is explicitly said of Beowulf: 'seafarers, those who carried gift-treasures to the Geats as thanks [diplomats], have said that he has the great power of thirty men strong in battle in his hand-grip.'[24] Along the same lines, the poet later recalls another astonishing feat of the young Beowulf: 'he had in his arms, alone, thirty [pieces of] armour, when he fled across the water.'[25] Beyond this overt numerological link, when Beowulf fights Grendel it is clear that he is not just a match for the cannibal but in fact possesses superior strength:

> Immediately the guardian of sins found that he had not met on the middle-earth, the earth's regions, with a stronger hand-grip in any other man. In his heart, his spirit, he grew afraid . . . the terrifying monster [*atol æglæca*] experienced bodily pain; a lasting wound became clear on his shoulder, the sinews sprung open, the bone-fastenings [*banlocan*] burst. Triumph in battle was granted to Beowulf; mortally wounded, Grendel had to flee from there under the fen-slopes [*fenhleoðu*] to seek the joyless dwelling-place.[26]

Grendel's death is appropriately as painful and bloody as that of the sleeping Geat warrior he has just torn apart and devoured. As for Beowulf, this incident shows that, as well as being more powerful than Grendel, his method of killing is somewhat monstrous, a display of brute strength without recourse to the weaponry favoured by men, and a technique not dissimilar to that of his fen-dwelling adversary. Beowulf in fact shares with Grendel a lifelong dislike for weapons, which rarely serve him well. When he kills Grendel's mother, Beowulf has to use a monstrous weapon after Unferth's human sword fails him:

> Then he saw a victory-blessed sword among the war gear, an old sword made by giants [*eald sweord eotenisc*] with strong edges, the glory of warriors; that was the best of weapons, except it was bigger than any other man could wield in battle, good and splendid, the work of giants [*giganta geweorc*].[27]

Although there is no suggestion that Beowulf is himself a giant, his ability to wield a sword made by giants for their own use, and far too big for other people, again suggests his monstrous size. Furthermore, describing the giant sword as *eotenisc* positions Beowulf yet closer to Grendel the *eoten*. The poet later explains why Beowulf generally has little luck with weapons: 'it was not granted to him that the edges of iron might help him in battle; the hand was too strong, so that, I have heard, it overstrained every sword too hard with its stroke.'[28] Weapons strong enough to cleave right through people are far too delicate for Beowulf: his strength is monstrous, primitive even. Beowulf is significantly more comfortable fighting with his hands alone, like Grendel, and his techniques for doing so are elsewhere as monstrous as the severing of Grendel's arm: 'before the veteran warriors I became a hand-slayer to Dæghrefn, the warrior of the Hugas . . . the sword's edge was not the killer, but the battle-grip broke the bone-house [*banhus*], the heart's surgings.'[29] The death of Dæghrefn is brutal and animalistic: Beowulf literally crushes him to death with his bare hands. As an instance of Beowulf's great strength, this feat is not one that can be accomplished by normal men: it signifies brutal monstrosity.

Beyond their strength and size, Beowulf and the Grendelkin are also linked by their flair for swimming. The Grendelkin live in a hall at the bottom of a mere, which though itself empty of water by a freak of the natural world is reachable only by the most proficient of swimmers. 'No one wise of the sons of men lives that knows the bottom [of the mere],' warns Hroðgar, and yet Beowulf comes to know it very well indeed: 'it was the whole of the day before he could perceive the bottom.'[30] It is perhaps no surprise to learn that the misshapen and uncanny Grendelkin can hold their breath for such an inconceivable length of time, but in Beowulf this ability is startling. Grendel's mother, in particular, is closely associated with the element of water: she is a *brimwylf* (sea-wolf), a *merewif mihtig* (mighty mere-woman), *se ðe floda begong heorogifre beheold hund missera* (she who had guarded the region of the waters, fiercely ravenous, for fifty years).[31] Though perhaps more closely associated with the moors and fens surrounding his *niðsele*, the mere still reacts viscerally to Grendel's moribund return and beheading, as we saw in the previous chapter. Beowulf has similarly strong associations with water. In Chapter Five we examined Beowulf's account of his swimming contest against Breca, in which he not only swims a great distance over an entire week but survives being dragged to the bottom of the sea and slays nine *niceras*. We also discussed how the sea was defined as the most hostile, misanthropic wilderness of all, a place that men dreaded for its awesome power and resident sea monsters. As such, Beowulf's swimming ability aligns him unflatteringly not only with the Grendelkin but with the terrifying monsters of the deep that he kills with great ease when racing Breca. Indeed, the *nicor*, the deadliest sea monster of all, lives in both the sea and the mere,[32] where, disturbingly, Beowulf is equally comfortable and deadly. For Beowulf is not just able in the water but apparently very much at home there: when he carries the thirty pieces of armour, he is crossing the sea, with no apparent diminution in his power, and is even able to drag the hilt of the *eotenisc* sword out of the mere along with Grendel's severed head. The latter alone requires four ordinary warriors to carry it on land.

Beyond the terms *gebolgen* and *bolgenmod*, there are further semantic and narrative similarities between Beowulf and his adversaries. Most famously, and much discussed, the term *aglæca* (literally 'the formidable one') is applied both to Sigmund and Beowulf and to the monsters the latter fights. *Aglæca* is an ambiguous noun: outside *Beowulf*, it is used both to describe the titular monster of *The Whale* and to praise the Venerable Bede in Byrhtferth's *Enchiridion* (Manual), an influential early eleventh-century text on numerology.[33] *Aglæca*'s meaning therefore varies according to context, and so we have been translating it as 'monster', when it has been applied to monsters, throughout the book. In *Beowulf*, Grendel is called an *aglæca* eleven times, and his mother an *aglæcwif* (monster-woman) once, with the sea monsters that live with them in the mere getting two dubbings and the dragon five.[34] Early critics quietly avoided any ambiguity about Beowulf's moral status by quietly translating it along the lines of 'hero' when applied to Sigmund and the Geat, and 'monster' when applied to the Grendelkin and the dragon.[35] However, its use within *Beowulf* is clearly meant to provide a layer of narrative uncertainty. Sigmund is called an *aglæca* after killing the dragon,[36] and the plural *aglæcan* likewise describes Beowulf and the basilisk locked in mortal combat.[37] What this seems to suggest is that the prodigiously strong Beowulf and Sigmund are *aglæcan* because of their physical might, which is a monstrous characteristic. The *Beowulf* poet leaves it up to the reader to decide whether physical monstrosity makes these heroes monsters like those they famously fight, something we will examine in the next section. For now, though, it is worth briefly considering the use of *aglæca* in *Andreas*, where its use has parallels to *Beowulf*. The term is applied to the cannibalistic Mermedonians, a devil and also the titular St Andrew.[38] In the case of the Mermedonians and the devil, *aglæca* can be translated as 'monster' and reflects the unforgiveable and transformative sins they share with Grendel: murder and cannibalism for the mortals, rebellion against God in the devil's case. As for Andrew, he is called an *aglæca* by the devil that attempts to lure him into sin, implying instead his powerful, nigh-on monstrous sanctity and danger to it: to the devil, he is indeed an *aglæca*.

There is a further important aspect of Beowulf that ties him closely to the Grendelkin. In the first half of the poem, only Beowulf and the Grendelkin are able to move between the civilized splendour of Heorot and the heathen wilderness of the mere. When the expedition to slay Grendel's mother reaches the mere, all except Beowulf stand shivering on its shores, unable to tread further. Like the Grendelkin, even when out of what is apparently his natural environment Beowulf is a deadly force: he survives the day-long deep dive into the unknown on his way to killing the *aglæcwif* in her own home. The narrative structure of the Grendelkin's attacks on Heorot and that of Beowulf's fight in the mere are emphatically parallel. Like Grendel, Beowulf travels to a *sele* intending to commit murder, where he grows *gebolgen*, kills an inhabitant, then returns to the space from which he came. The acts are structurally identical: Beowulf, like the Grendelkin, is very much a *mearcstapa*. In terms of topography, Beowulf moves easily between contrasting wilderness and civilization and shows himself to be equally deadly in both. He is a human – the poem leaves no doubt about that – but, through nuanced choices in vocabulary, repetition, the stress on his size and narrative parallels, Beowulf is shown to be physically monstrous. The same statement could be made about the Grendelkin. The poem's evident parallels thus ask difficult, uncomfortable questions of its readers. Since only Beowulf and the Grendelkin can move successfully between Heorot and the mere, does this mean they are all monsters? The question of whether Beowulf crosses another *mearc* violated by the Grendelkin – sin and cultural taboos – and thereby becomes a monster will occupy us for the rest of this chapter.

Which Side of the *Mearc*?

> The man who fights with monsters might be careful that he does not in doing so become a monster. And if you gaze into the Abyss for a long time, the Abyss also gazes into you.[39]

On the basis of his size and sheer physical power, Beowulf is indubitably a monster. He is stronger than the Grendelkin and, even as an old man, proves a deadly opponent for an enormous fire-breathing dragon. But Sigmund, to whom Beowulf is flatteringly compared, is also a heroic monster-slayer called an *aglæca* due to his physical strength. The question we must answer relates directly to the *scop*'s song after Beowulf kills Grendel: is he a monstrous man, like Sigmund, or a man perverted into a monster, like Heremod?

To help us determine on which side of the *mearc* Beowulf resides, we can consult the sermon Hroðgar delivers after Beowulf slays Grendel. After describing Heremod's downfall, Hroðgar uses the sorry tale to identify dangers that face every earthly ruler:

> He lives in abundance; illness and old age do not impair him, nor does dire sorrow turn his spirit dark, nor does violent hate manifest anywhere, but all the world goes according to his desire – he that does not know worse – until a measure of excessive pride [*oferhygda*] grows and flourishes within him. Then the guardian sleeps, the soul's protector; the sleep is too heavy, oppressed with cares, the

> killer very near, he who wickedly shoots [arrows] from a bow. Then the bitter arrow strikes in his heart beneath the armour – he who does not know how to guard himself – with the perverse mysterious promptings of the evil spirit. What he long possessed seems too little to him, the hostile-minded one becomes covetous, no longer does he honourably give decorated rings, and he forgets and disregards the future destiny [*forðgesceaft*] [and] the portion of worldly glories that God, the Lord of Glory, previously gave to him. At the end it comes to pass again, that the transitory body declines, falls fated to die . . . Guard yourself against this hateful affliction, dear Beowulf, best of men, and choose for yourself the better, eternal rewards; do not concern yourself with excessive pride [*oferhyda*], renowned warrior.[40]

To the notorious king's avarice, neglect of religious duties and wrathful, murderous crimes Hroðgar also adds the sin of excessive pride (*oferhygd*). Heremod's transformation from privileged king to monster comes from a nefarious cornucopia of all these offences. This passage shows also that, although cannibalism is very much one of the crimes that make Grendel a monster, it is not a prerequisite for the transformation. To determine whether Beowulf is, or becomes, a monster, we must analyse his character over the course of the poem to see whether he is guilty of any fault through which someone can lose their humanity.

It is an easy task to clear Beowulf of murderous wrath, a sin Heremod and the Grendelkin have in common. Although he becomes *bolgenmod* and *gebolgen* when fighting enemies, and exhibits horrifying combat techniques such as crushing Dæghrefn to death with his bare hands, Beowulf is explicitly not a tyrant or base murderer. The poet confirms the hero's innocence between Beowulf's return from Heorot and the arrival of the dragon:

> So the son of Ecgtheow [that is, Beowulf] showed himself brave, the man known for good deeds in battles, strove after glory; never, drunk, slew hearth-comrades; his heart was not fierce but, brave in battle, with the greatest strength of mankind, he held the great gift that God granted to him.[41]

The poet, it seems, wishes to exonerate Beowulf of becoming excessively wrathful. The crucial distinction between Heremod and Beowulf is that the latter exercises his physical (and legislative) power with discretion and moderation. It is his rationality, his ability to know the difference between right and wrong that he shares with all men, that prevents the fearful raw material of his physical bulk being used for evil. It is in order to highlight this contrast that the terms *bolgenmod* and *gebolgen* link Beowulf with Grendel, Heremod and the dragon. For there is another character in the poem with the capacity to become *gebolgen*: having been told of the dragon's appearance, 'the wise man [Beowulf] thought that he had made the Ruler, the Ancient Lord, bitterly swell with rage [*gebulge*] over an ancient law.'[42] God, the perfect being, cannot be morally wrong, and the use of the verb for him suggests that swelling with rage is acceptable in some circumstances but not others. Heremod grows *bolgenmod* before murdering his 'table-companions', Grendel when attacking innocent Christians, and the dragon when a tiny piece of treasure is stolen from the hoard it avariciously guards. Beowulf, on the other hand, exhibits this behaviour only when fighting monsters guilty of deadly crimes: he awaits Grendel *bolgenmod*,[43] and grows *gebolgen* when fighting Grendel's mother[44] and on the approach to the dragon's lair.[45] The fact that Beowulf swells with rage only on these particular occasions is significant: in these three fights, Beowulf is unequivocally in the right against foes who are ill-intentioned and insatiably furious, aligning him more with God than with the monsters he kills. That is, Beowulf uses his rationality to decide when such fury is appropriate and morally acceptable, and when it is not. Heremod, also a man and thus rational, has the same powers of discrimination but, crucially, gives way to terrible sin and hence becomes a monster, like the Grendelkin.

Hroðgar's emphasis on pride is a more compelling line of inquiry that again forces us to compare Beowulf to Grendel. To early medieval Christians like the Anglo-Saxons, great physical size was thought to equate to monstrous pride.[46] As we saw in Chapter Five, for example, Leviathan was interpreted allegorically as a symbol of repulsive pride and arrogance. The link between physical size and excessive pride also included giants: Gregory the Great described biblical giants as 'damned through the sin of pride'.[47] The Anglo-Saxons, specifically, adapted the popular line of thought from patristic theology that held giants responsible for the Tower of Babel recounted in Genesis 11:1–9, perhaps the most reprehensible act of pride against God besides Satan's rebellion: Ælfric explains that 'the giants [*entas*] wished to build a city and a tower so high that its roof rose up to heaven.'[48] In Old English poetry, wonderful ruins are commonly called *enta geweorc* (the work of giants), making a tangible link between giants and hubristic pride. The Exeter Book poem *The Ruin*, an elegy inspired by the sight of Roman ruins, for example, describes crumbling masonry as *enta geweorc*, and the narrator imagines a former inhabitant swaggering about them 'cheerful and bright with gold, adorned with splendours, proud [*wlonc*] and merry with wine'.[49] This tradition links directly to Grendel, who is described as an *eoten* and whose home contains an *eald sweord eotenisc*, which *Beowulf*'s narrator later describes using the poetic formula associating giants with arrogant pride: *enta ærgeweorc* (the ancient work of giants).[50] Grendel, remember, is not only an *eoten* but explicitly an enemy of God, and attacks Heorot after hearing a song in praise of the Lord: rebellion against God, as Satan found out, is the most heinous act of excessive pride, for it presupposes that the perpetrator can prevail against the omnipotent deity. This also adds another layer of meaning to the story of Heremod's descent into monstrosity, for after ruling his people tyrannically, he is exiled to live *mid eotenum*: among the giants, Heremod's excessive pride was in good company.[51]

Beowulf's great size, therefore, indicates that he might be too proud. Unferth, for all his many faults, seizes on this when he confronts Beowulf about his swimming contest early in the poem: 'for pride [*wlence*, a form of *wlonc*] you two tested the sea, and for vainglory [*dolgilpe*] you risked [your] lives in the deep water.'[52] Beowulf explains the incident away as childish sport, and it is not mentioned again. However, the *scop* and Hroðgar mentioning the over-proud Heremod may also be a cautionary response to Beowulf's physical size, for the notorious king was also prodigiously strong: 'the Mighty God exalted [Heremod] in the delights of strength [and] power'. Indeed, shortly before being upbraided by Unferth, Beowulf has been boasting of his physical achievements: 'I have undertaken many famous deeds in youth . . . I destroyed a family of giants [*eotena cyn*] and slew sea-monsters [*niceras*] at night on the waves.'[53] Has Beowulf already given way to *oferhygd*?

There are numerous mitigating factors here. In the first instance, boasting is an important part of heroic poetry: warriors boast about a deed they will do, and then fulfil it. In the *Dream of the Rood*, a mystical poem in which the tale of Christ's Crucifixion is told in the heroic idiom by the cross upon which he died, the holiest of all relics is similarly boastful of its strength.[54] It would be anachronistically harsh, therefore, to condemn Beowulf for being a character in a heroic poem. Furthermore, as he himself explains, Beowulf has come to Heorot to help Hroðgar and the Danes against an evil scourge, and in so doing is renewing his late father's cordial relations with Hroðgar. When he boasts of his achievements, Beowulf is in the midst of asking Hroðgar's permission to fight Grendel and is giving something of a verbal curriculum vitae. Killing Grendel is an act not of glory-seeking but of diplomacy and a communally spirited deed to improve the lot of Hroðgar's beleaguered men. The slaying of Grendel's mother is likewise carried out to help Hroðgar, not out of *oferhygd*. Killing Grendel has made Grendel's mother take up the feud between Heorot and the mere, and it is strongly implied that more murders will follow. As well as being directly responsible for the arrival of Grendel's mother, Beowulf is the only man strong enough to kill her.

The dragon fight, however, puts us back in uncertain waters. Given his now old age, Beowulf's insistence on fighting the dragon in single combat seems unbelievably stupid, even vainglorious. However, killing the basilisk is interpreted by Beowulf as a communal obligation. It has, after all, laid waste to his kingdom, killed his people and burned his hall to ashes. Moreover, he has a premonition that the contest will be the death of him: 'in him the mind was sad, restless and eager for slaughter; fate was immeasurably near, that must greet the old man, seeking the soul's treasure, separate asunder life from the body: it was not long that the noble's life would be bound in flesh.'[55] Fighting the dragon is an act of self-sacrifice for the benefit of Geatland. Although Beowulf says he will *mærðu fremman* (earn fame), he does so explicitly in his capacity as *frod folces weard* (old guardian of the people).[56] However it may offend modern sensibilities, Beowulf's fearsome reputation protects his people and ensures peace for his fifty-year reign until the dragon stirs: 'there was not a people's king from any of the neighbouring nations that dared to meet me with war-friends [that is, soldiers].'[57] Carrying out foolhardy deeds is just another communal obligation for kings in the world of *Beowulf*.

We cannot even burden Beowulf with the charge of avarice, a sin characterizing the dragon and one of the crimes that turns Heremod into a monster. Beowulf is an exceptionally generous king, with his hall described as *gifstol Geata* (gift-throne of the Geats),[58] and when he returns from Heorot laden with gifts from

Hroðgar he immediately gives them away to his uncle, Hygelac. As we have seen, sharing treasure helped to define a good king in heroic poetry and symbolized peace and fellowship among men. Though the thought of the dragon's treasure is a partial motivation for the fight ('I shall win the gold with courage, or war, perilous deadly evil, will take your king'), it is clear that Beowulf wants to win it for his people's use: 'for these treasures that I look upon here, such that I was able to acquire for my people before [my] death-day, I give thanks, speaking with words, to the Lord of All, the King of Glory, the Eternal Lord.'[59] Fighting the dragon and taking its treasure may bring Beowulf glory, but he does not perform the deed out of pride or greed: for this heroic king, the basilisk's death will save his people from a deadly scourge, and its treasure increase Geatland's wealth and help foster peace and fellowship when distributed.

Finally, against the charge of irreligiosity there can be no doubt that Beowulf, however anachronistically, is a devout Christian. Beowulf's motto throughout his heroic career seems to be *non nobis domine* (not unto us, O Lord). When he wins the treasure from the dragon, there is no egotistical smugness about his achievement: rather than revel in his selfless heroism, Beowulf attributes the victory and treasure to God. Likewise, before fighting Grendel, Beowulf states despite all his previous boasting that God will decide the victor: 'the wise God, the Holy Lord, will assign glory to whichever hand that seems worthy to Him.'[60] Relating his successful fight with Grendel's mother, Beowulf is also careful to attribute his victory to the Lord: 'the battle was almost ended, unless God shielded me . . . but the Ruler of Men allowed that I saw a mighty old sword hanging beautifully on the wall.'[61] Giving thanks to God is not only an act of humility but a fundamental Christian tenet.

It is one thing to trust in God, but another entirely when God is on your side. From Beowulf's earliest time in Heorot, he is seen as a divinely sent saviour: 'I have hope that Holy God has sent him to us, to the West Danes, against Grendel's terror out of kindness,' says Hroðgar.[62] His optimism is not misplaced, as the poet tells us before Grendel's fateful arrival: 'the King of Glory had appointed a hall-guardian [Beowulf] against Grendel, as men obtained knowledge of.'[63] During the fight with Grendel's mother, too, Beowulf is explicitly under God's protection: 'the Holy God brought about victory in war.'[64] God's favour to Beowulf here should remove any sympathy we have for Grendel's mother, for in backing the hero God simultaneously condemns the monster. With God on his side, Beowulf may very well grow *bolgenmod*. Beowulf's divine assistance is such that some critics have seen the fight at the mere as a metaphor for the Harrowing of Hell, when Christ descended into the abyss to defeat the Devil, as told in the apocryphal Gospel of Nicodemus.[65] For our discussion, what is most important to note is that Beowulf's Christianity is vital for the classic setting of Anglo-Saxon monster narratives to work. The chief distinction between the monstrous yet entirely human Beowulf and the human yet entirely monstrous Grendelkin is Beowulf's fervent Christianity – the defining aspect of the civilized world – which influences his conduct and his subsequent favour from God. Both Beowulf and Heremod are blessed with power and strength by God, but where Beowulf 'held the great gift that God granted to him', Heremod's 'spirit however grew bloodthirsty in his chest'. The hellish overtones of the mere and scent of a salvation narrative are fundamental to the success of this Anglo-Saxon monster story, for these associations are what make Beowulf the champion of the civilized world, fighting against the heathen, God-cursed monsters of the wilderness.

In the end, Beowulf's resemblance to the monsters he fights is revealed to be superficial. To defeat them, he needs to have monstrous strength, but the poem reveals victory in battle to be ultimately decided by God, and so Beowulf's Christian beliefs and morality are what make him the successful warrior he is. Thus

Nietzsche's famous warning to 'the man who fights with monsters', with which we began this section, is certainly apt, but Beowulf's faith, moderation and essential goodness ensure that he himself 'does not in doing so become a monster'.

Mearcstapan One and All

On the simplest, narrative level, *Beowulf* is an example to all its readers of the need to fight tooth and nail against the monsters, and the uncivilized values they symbolize, that threaten civilized society. *Beowulf* testifies not only to the Anglo-Saxon belief in monsters but to their awareness of the fragility of civilization. Without strong, confrontational action, monsters will progressively return civilized places to wildernesses suitable to their habitation. In this sense, *Beowulf* is a call to arms: faced with monsters, we should not be cowardly like the Geats who abandon their king to the dragon, or resort to heathenism like the Grendel-plagued Danes, but put our trust in God and protect Christian civilization, as Beowulf does.

The message of the poem is far deeper than a simple tale of good and evil, however. Beowulf is not, ultimately, a monster, but the poet's hints, implicit links and semantic choices are there for a reason. For what is Beowulf if not a man with the potential to become a monster, who does not succumb to the sins that would effect the transformation? Beowulf is indubitably a *mearcstapa*, but the side of the *mearc* on which he belongs is clear: the human, Christian, civilized side, as opposed to its monstrous, heathen and uncivilized binary opposite.

Yet *Beowulf* carries a dire warning. Heremod and the Grendelkin are humans perverted into monsters through sin: like all rational creatures, they have a choice to make between good and evil. This applies to the readers of *Beowulf*, too, and offers a chilling possibility for the origin of the Grendel names in charters. And with this dual human–monster potential inherent in us, all humans are, in a sense, *mearcstapan*. We are made in the image of God and yet often show ourselves to be of the Devil's party through our deeds. Thus we walk the *mearc* between man and civilization on the one hand, monster and wilderness on the other, and through sin can pass over permanently into the latter. Beowulf himself is in this sense the very image of Everyman: like him, we all have the potential for evil, and the poem's dire warning is that certain acts can turn us into a monster if we do not use our rationality to avoid them. The Anglo-Saxons were former pagans living on one of the most remote, naturally uncivilized islands on the map: reverting to pride, wrath, avarice and heathenism could turn them into monsters. Or at least get a swamp named after them.

CONCLUSION

Monsters were at the heart of the Anglo-Saxon world. Some challenged the very definition of a human or provided warnings about certain types of behaviour. Others were real animals whose size and mythological behaviour made them monsters in Anglo-Saxon eyes. But what is most interesting to note is that all were associated with the wilderness, the uncivilized opposite of civilization, with its attendant philosophical values: sin, heathenism, hostility to man. In some monster tales, civilization was shown to have only a tenuous hold on the wild island in the far north. But despite representing the terrifying power of nature and its uncivilized values, monsters performed the important role of reinforcing the very definition of civilization by highlighting its opposite. All Anglo-Saxon monsters strove to protect the integrity of their wilderness home, whether by killing interlopers or simply fleeing from them, to maintain the ideological boundary separating man and monster. Their behaviour straddled what was 'known' about the landscape of England and the abstract topography their homes represented.

In the twenty-first century, most monsters of the type encountered in Anglo-Saxon literature are by and large extinct in the wild. You would be hard pressed today to find anyone who lives in fear of dragons, and belief in demons is dwindling alongside the Christian faith in whose pantheon they operate. Both, however, are still very active in the worlds of literature and cinema, which is testament to their enduring appeal. To paraphrase Coleridge, unabashed monsters can still be enjoyed through 'the willing suspension of disbelief', and their resilience in the face of scepticism and scientific rationality demonstrates that they still have an important cultural role to play as manifestations of evil, our deepest fears or unacceptable modes of behaviour, even though we no longer believe them to be real.

The Grendelkin find a modern parallel in the various hominids studied by cryptozoologists. Like the Grendelkin, Bigfoot and the Yeti are humanoid creatures that are said to live in the wilderness, making occasional – and usually disastrous – forays into civilization and attacking people who stray into their home territory. Both are as closely related to the wilderness as their Anglo-Saxon forebears: Bigfoot is something of an icon for conservationists, a reminder of the wilderness lost when European settlers came to North America and began changing the continent's topography, and it is no coincidence that the Yeti lives in the Himalayas, one of the most inhospitable places on earth containing the world's highest mountain. Perhaps Bigfoot and the Yeti represent our longing for a lost world, pastoral symbols for a time when we, as a species, lived closer to nature and the world still held magic and mystery. Between them, the two big names in the mystery hominid world also resemble Grendel and his mother in challenging our understanding of what defines a human. Whereas before the advent of science such hairy bipeds would be discussed for evidence of rationality and their possible awareness of God, now their potential place in the evolutionary tree of *Homo sapiens* is vociferously debated. The world of Bigfoot researchers in particular is fiercely divided between those who believe shooting one would be unethical, or even murder, and those who see Bigfoot as just another animal and wish to secure a specimen. Despite scientific advances and deeper understanding of our species, there remains an anxiety about what defines a human and how much we differ from our close relations. Bigfoot and the Yeti also remind us of the endurance of myths about the wild places of the world. Evidence for their existence is, frankly, scant, and the vast majority of the world's population have never 'seen' one. Yet we all know their names, and every year thousands of people are pulled into their world in search of something that most likely does not exist. Philosophically speaking, you cannot prove a negative, and so long as there are unoccupied, uncivilized places, the legends will thrive.

Perhaps the closest modern equivalent to Anglo-Saxon monsters in the UK is the big cat. Thought to be escapees or deliberate releases from private menageries, stories of leopards and other exotic cats roaming Britain first became mainstream news in the 1960s, when an animal known as the Surrey Puma began terrifying people in London's rural commuter belt. Reports continue to the present day, often in slightly hysterical explosions of sightings ingeniously dubbed 'cat-flaps'. Although it is not our purpose to debate their existence here, it would be churlish not to mention that an increasing body of evidence for the creatures now sits alongside sceptical counter-arguments, including Felicity, a puma captured alive near Inverness in 1980, and a lynx shot by a gamekeeper in Norfolk in the early 1990s; recent advances in forensic archaeology have also suggested that some alleged instances of big cats preying on livestock may not be tall tales after all.[1]

Most relevant for our discussion, the behaviour of big cats in witness testimonies closely resembles that of Anglo-Saxon monsters. Wherever these cats are seen, they are a dangerous carnivore outside their natural range, and this is disconcerting in a similar manner to an Anglo-Saxon monster entering a civilized space. Typically, though, they are encountered in wild places, such as the desolate landscapes of Exmoor and Dartmoor or the few thick woodlands left in the UK, such as Cannock Chase in Staffordshire or the Forest of Dean in Gloucestershire. These environments are still those in which people feel uncomfortable and vulnerable to nature: the millennium or so separating us from the Anglo-Saxons is but a millisecond in the course of human evolution, and our brains are still pre-programmed to fear environments where we do not have a clear peripheral outlook or adequate cover, and to identify large carnivores that are not really there. Like the map monsters, big cats in most reports flee when they detect the presence of people, or more rarely adopt an aggressive attitude to them, seeking to ensure their immediate environment is free from human interference. The generally brief glimpses of these animals, which often take place at dusk or dawn, are not terribly far from the reports of shadowy giants seen in the murk of the fens given to Hroðgar in *Beowulf*. Many tales stop there, but far more graphic reports of livestock predation involving bestial forays into cultivated areas are not uncommon. An alleged melanistic leopard known as the Beast of Exmoor, for example, was blamed for thousands of sheep kills in the 1980s. The quantity and gruesome nature of these deaths terrified the local population, leading to mass hysteria and the Royal Marines being called in to find and kill the animal responsible. They were unsuccessful. People respond to alleged big cat kills in a similar manner to wolf–livestock predation: with the feeling of boundaries being violated by creatures that should respect them, followed by vociferous local reaction, entry of the events into the region's folklore, and every livestock killing being blamed on a single species.

So much for distant relatives and non-human creatures. But in the twenty-first century there are other monsters that some condemn in a manner familiar to the Anglo-Saxons. One section of *The Wonders of the East* is particularly uncomfortable for the modern reader: 'there is a kind of man that is of a black colour [*sweartes hiwes*] in their countenance, that people call Ethiopians [*silhearwan*, roughly 'sun-inhabitants'].'[2] Among the monsters and strange creatures of the mythological East, black people are included in the text by merit of their skin colour. Prejudice and discrimination against people based upon their skin colour remain a prevalent evil in the twenty-first century, but it would be unfair to label the Anglo-Saxons as knowingly racist here: the overwhelming majority would never have seen anyone non-Caucasian, and the thought of any other skin colour than white was naturally fascinating.[3] That said, although no particular monstrous behaviour is attributed to them, the text does locate the Ethiopians in the uncivilized, monster-ridden wilderness of the East, which is hardly flattering: they are strange not just because of their appearance but also because of their homeland. As briefly mentioned in the chapter on map monsters, the view of the East as uncivilized and odd has characterized colonial attitudes up to the present day.

Looking beyond the 'Ethiopians', it is noticeable that it is not just physical differences that make Eastern people strange in the *Wonders* and *Letter of Alexander to Aristotle*, but also sartorial choices, religious practices and diet. Exactly the same tools are used to marginalize minority groups in the West today. Certain areas of the media criticize Muslim people for their religious beliefs, halal diet and mode of dress: just think of the campaigns aiming to 'ban the burka' across Europe in the last few years. By highlighting how Muslims differ from the Western, Christian 'norm', rabble-rousing media platforms emphasize their difference to imply that they simply do not belong in Western society. Like the Anglo-Saxons, some people still want to assign people and things to one particular, unalterable location, as reflected in the furious outcry at the sight of refugees fleeing war-torn Syria in 2015 and some of the most obnoxious racial slurs associating a group of people with a specific environment. Some individuals and media organizations would have it that Muslims are unalterably foreign to Western countries and an inferior, uncivilized threat to the status quo of civilization. One need only read a newspaper to see how depressingly successful such attempts are, and that part of the Anglo-Saxon world-view has lasted to the present day.

Returning again to Grendel and the man-monsters of *Beowulf*, it is also interesting to note that there remain cultural taboos and crimes constituting a *mearc* that, when crossed, dehumanize the offender. The death penalty is still enforced for certain crimes in places across the world: commit murder or blasphemy in some countries, and you do not deserve to live, like the *weargs* and outlaws who carry the *caput lupinum*. Popular consensus on certain wrongdoers furthermore suggests a worldwide belief that certain deeds can make or break a human being. As a result of the #MeToo movement, people found guilty of the heinous offences of rape, sexual assault and harassment have lost their former positions and often their social networks, being essentially outcast and precluded from parts of human society as a result of their deeds. The term 'monster' is often thrown at these individuals without elaboration, but when we analyse such usages more closely, it is clear that in modern society, as much as Anglo-Saxon England, it is possible to become a monster by breaking cultural taboos, crossing a moral *mearc* like Grendel, Heremod and the *weargs*. At that point, the monster in question no longer has a place in civilized society and is cast out, a *mearcstapa* carrying not a wolf's head but an evil, irreparably damaged reputation.

TO CONCLUDE, THEN, THE philosophical mechanisms underlying the Anglo-Saxon world-view still characterize our own. The need to create monsters lies deep in the human psyche: people may not believe in the same monsters as before, but then, as now, the figure of the monster, the outsider, the unforgiveable one who has forsaken their humanity, is a cultural necessity. With a greater sense of our individuality, we identify monsters based on our idiosyncratic outlook and the sources of information we consult. As an Anglo-Saxon proverb has it, however, *soð bið swicolost*, 'truth is most deceptive':[4] the challenge to us in the modern day is not only to avoid becoming a monster ourselves but to ensure that those we identify as haunting our world really are monsters.

REFERENCES

All translations in this book are my own except where otherwise stated.

INTRODUCTION

1 Gildas, *De excidio et conquestu Britanniae*, Book I, Chapter xiv, in *Patrologia Latina*, ed. J. P. Migne (Turnhout, 1844–65), vol. LXIX, cols 329–92. All subsequent translations are prepared from this edition, and all citations made hereafter refer to the numbering in PL LXIX.

2 Heinrich Härke, 'Anglo-Saxon Immigration and Ethnogenesis', *Medieval Archaeology*, LV (2011), pp. 1–28.

3 For more on Anglo-Saxon paganism, see David N. Wilson, *Anglo-Saxon Paganism* (London, 1992), and E. G. Stanley, *The Search for Anglo-Saxon Paganism* (Cambridge, 1975).

4 The classic discussion of the conversion is Henry Mayr-Harting, *The Coming of Christianity to Anglo-Saxon England*, 3rd edn (University Park, PA, 1991).

5 For a thorough discussion of the early Anglo-Saxon kingdoms, see F. M. Stenton, *Anglo-Saxon England*, 3rd edn (Oxford, 1971).

6 Sarah Foot, 'The Making of *Angelcynn*: English Identity before the Norman Conquest', in *Old English Literature: Critical Essays*, ed. R. M. Liuzza (New Haven, CT, 2002), pp. 51–78.

7 On Alfred, see Richard Abels, *Alfred the Great: War, Kingship and Culture in Anglo-Saxon England* (London, 1998).

8 *The Old English Boethius: With Verse Prologues and Epilogues Associated with King Alfred*, ed. and trans. Susan Irvine and Malcolm Godden (Cambridge, MA, 2012), Prose 29. All subsequent translations are prepared from this edition.

9 I will be following the numbering of the Latin Vulgate, the version known to the Anglo-Saxons, for all scriptural references. Where the numbering of verses differs from the more familiar King James Bible, I will add a footnote with the abbreviation 'KJV + [reference]'.
10 *Genesis A*, 805–812a, in G. P. Krapp and E. V. Dobbie, eds, *The Anglo-Saxon Poetic Records: A Collective Edition*, 6 vols (New York, 1931–53), vol. I. All Old English poetry is translated from the editions prepared by Krapp and Dobbie, and will hereafter be referenced with the relevant line numbers and the volume of ASPR in which the quoted text appears.
11 On the Anglo-Saxon view of nature, see Jennifer Neville, *Representations of the Natural World in Old English Poetry* (Cambridge, 1999).
12 The standard discussion of the Anglo-Saxon landscape is Oliver Rackham, *The History of the Countryside* (London, 1986).
13 Oliver Rackham, 'Woodland', in *The Wiley Blackwell Encyclopedia of Anglo-Saxon England*, ed. Michael Lapidge et al., 2nd edn (Chichester, 2014), pp. 507–8.
14 D. P. Kirby, 'The Old English Forest: Its Natural Flora and Fauna', in *Anglo-Saxon Settlement and Landscape: Papers Presented to a Symposium, Oxford 1973*, ed. Trevor Rowley (Oxford, 1974), pp. 120–30, at 125.
15 On Anglo-Saxon woodland, see Della Hooke, *Trees in Anglo-Saxon England: Literature, Lore and Landscape* (Woodbridge, 2010).
16 On the purse-lid, see R.L.S. Bruce-Mitford, *The Sutton Hoo Ship Burial* (London, 1978), pp. 512–14.
17 Ralph L. Slotten, 'The Master of Animals: A Study in the Symbolism of Ultimacy in Primitive Religion', *Journal of Bible and Religion*, XXXIII/4 (1965), pp. 293–302.
18 C. S. Lewis, *The Discarded Image: An Introduction to Medieval and Renaissance Literature* (Cambridge, 1964), p. 10.
19 Charles Thomas, *The Early Christian Archaeology of North Britain: The Hunter Marshall Lectures Delivered at the University of Glasgow in January and February 1968* (London, 1971), p. 29.
20 Bede, *Historia ecclesiastica*, III.9, in *Bede's Ecclesiastical History of the English People*, ed. and trans. Bertram Colgrave and R.A.B. Mynors (Oxford, 1969). All subsequent translations are prepared from this edition, and all citations hereafter refer to the numbering it uses.

21 For examples, see Helena Hamerow, *Rural Settlements and Society in Anglo-Saxon England* (Oxford, 2012), pp. 73–8.
22 *Maxims* II, 1b; 3a, ASPR VI.
23 Eddius Stephanus, *The Life of Bishop Wilfrid*, 45, quoted from J. F. Webb, trans., *The Age of Bede* (Harmondsworth, 1965).
24 *Maxims* II, 27b–28a; 29b–30a, ASPR VI.
25 *Old English Boethius*, Meter 13, 35–39a.
26 On grotesquery and later medieval art, see Michael Camille, *Image on the Edge: The Margins of Medieval Art* (London, 1992).
27 Originally published in 1968, the Sawyer Catalogue has been expanded and made available for free online at https://esawyer.lib.cam.ac.uk.
28 Walter de Gray Birch, ed., *Cartularium Saxonicum* (London, 1885–93), vol. III, Charter no. 1331.
29 F. L. Attenborough, ed. and trans., *The Laws of the Earliest English Kings* (New York, 1963), pp. 42–3.
30 Paolo Squatriti, 'Offa's Dyke between Nature and Culture', *Environmental History*, IX/1 (2004), pp. 37–56.
31 W. G. Hoskins, *The Making of the English Landscape* (London, 1977), p. 66.
32 *Old English Boethius*, Prose 9.
33 Roger S. Ulrich, 'Biophilia, Biophobia, and Natural Landscapes', in *The Biophilia Hypothesis*, ed. Stephen R. Kellert and Edward O. Wilson (Washington, DC, 1993), pp. 73–137.
34 Augustine, *De civitate dei*, Book XVI, Chapter viii, in *Sancti Aurelii Augustini, hipponensis episcopi, opera omnia*, ed. J. P. Migne (Paris, 1861–5), vol. VII, cols 13–804. All subsequent translations are prepared from this edition, and all citations hereafter refer to the numbering it uses.
35 Isidore of Seville, *Etymologiae*, Book XI, Chapter iii, 1–2, 12, in *Patrologia Latina*, ed. J. P. Migne (Paris, 1844–65), vol. LXXXII, cols 9–723. All subsequent translations are prepared from this edition, and all citations hereafter refer to the numbering in PL LXXXII.

1 THE MAP MONSTERS

1 For a concise discussion of the origins of map monsters, see John Block Friedman, *The Monstrous Races in Medieval Art and Thought* (Syracuse, NY, 2000), pp. 5–25.
2 Pliny the Elder, *Historia naturalis*, Book XI, Chapter ii, in *C. Plini Secundi naturalis historiae libri* XXXVII, ed. Karl Friedrich Theodor

Mayhoff, 6 vols (Lipisae [Leipzig], 1870–98). All subsequent translations are prepared from this edition, and all citations hereafter refer to the numbering it uses.

3 Also found in KJV, Psalms 74:12.

4 *De civitate dei*, Book XVI, Chapter xvii.

5 Edward W. Said, *Orientalism* (London, 2003), p. 1.

6 This theory is expounded by Andy Orchard in his *Pride and Prodigies: Studies in the Monsters of the Beowulf-Manuscript* (Cambridge, 1995).

7 On the three manuscripts, see Asa Simon Mittman, *Maps and Monsters in Medieval England* (London, 2006), pp. 70–80.

8 *The Wonders of the East*, 2, ed. Andy Orchard in *Pride and Prodigies*, Appendix 1b. All subsequent translations are prepared from this edition, and all citations hereafter refer to the numbering it uses.

9 *Wonders of the East*, 3.

10 Asa Simon Mittman and Susan M. Kim, *Inconceivable Beasts: The Wonders of the East in the Beowulf Manuscript* (Tempe, AZ, 2013), p. 146.

11 *Wonders of the East*, 4.

12 Ibid.

13 *Wonders of the East*, 9.

14 *Wonders of the East*, 15.

15 For an in-depth discussion of the Blemmyae, see Mittman and Kim, *Inconceivable Beasts*, pp. 133–4.

16 *Wonders of the East*, 21.

17 *Wonders of the East*, 8.

18 Friedman, *Monstrous Races*, pp. 26–9.

19 *Wonders of the East*, 13.

20 *Wonders of the East*, 18.

21 *Wonders of the East*, 26.

22 Plutarch, *Moralia*, 329B, quoted in Ian Worthington, ed., *Alexander the Great: A Reader* (London, 2003), p. 58.

23 *The Letter of Alexander to Aristotle*, 3, ed. Andy Orchard, in *Pride and Prodigies*, Appendix IIb. All subsequent translations are prepared from this edition, and all citations hereafter refer to the numbering it uses.

24 *Letter of Alexander to Aristotle*, 8.

25 *Letter of Alexander to Aristotle*, 9.

26 Ibid.

27 *Letter of Alexander to Aristotle*, 15.

28 *Letter of Alexander to Aristotle*, 16.
29 Ibid.
30 *Letter of Alexander to Aristotle*, 17.
31 *Letter of Alexander to Aristotle*, 18.
32 *Letter of Alexander to Aristotle*, 20.
33 Orchard, *Pride and Prodigies*, pp. 116–39.
34 *Letter of Alexander to Aristotle*, 35.
35 Richard J. Schrader, 'Sacred Groves, Marvellous Waters, and Grendel's Abode', *Florilegium*, v (1983), pp. 76–84.
36 *Letter of Alexander to Aristotle*, 22.
37 *Letter of Alexander to Aristotle*, 33.
38 Orchard, *Pride and Prodigies*, p. 86.
39 Michael Lapidge, '*Beowulf*, Aldhelm, the *Liber Monstrorum* and Wessex', *Studi medievali*, 3rd ser., XXIII (1982), pp. 151–92.
40 *Liber Monstrorum*, Prologue, ed. Andy Orchard, in *Pride and Prodigies*, Appendix IIIa. All subsequent translations are prepared from this edition. I have consulted Orchard's accompanying translation for the trickier sections of this arcane text.
41 *Liber monstrorum*, Prologue.
42 Ibid.
43 *Liber monstrorum*, I.1.
44 *Liber monstrorum*, I.17.
45 *Liber monstrorum*, II.16.
46 *Wonders of the East*, 7.
47 *Letter of Alexander to Aristotle*, 29.
48 *Liber monstrorum*, I.16.
49 *Liber monstrorum*, II.13.
50 S. C. Thomson, 'Telling the Story: Reshaping Saint Christopher for an Anglo-Saxon Lay Audience', *Open Library of Humanities*, IV/2 (2018), pp. 1–31.
51 Translated from Christine Rauer, ed., *The Old English Martyrology: Edition, Translation and Commentary* (Cambridge, 2013), no. 73.
52 Augustine, *De civitate dei*, Book XVI, Chapter viii.
53 Joyce Tally Lionarons, 'From Monster to Martyr: The Old English Legend of St Christopher', in *Marvels, Monsters, and Miracles: Studies in the Medieval and Early Modern Imaginations*, ed. Timothy S. Jones and David A. Sprunger (Kalamazoo, MI, 2002), pp. 167–82.
54 *The Passion of St Christopher*, ed. R. D. Fulk, in *The Beowulf Manuscript: Complete Texts and the Fight at Finnsburg* (Cambridge, MA, 2010), p. 2.

55 This ingenious observation was made by Mittman and Kim, *Inconceivable Beasts*, pp. 17–18.
56 On classical geography's placement of Britain, see Martin K. Foys, *Virtually Anglo-Saxon: Old Media, New Media, and Early Medieval Studies in the Late Age of Print* (Gainesville, FL, 2007), pp. 135–6; Kathy Lavezzo, *Angels on the Edge of the World: Geography, Literature, and English Community, 1000–1534* (Ithaca, NY, 2006), pp. 1–26.
57 Isidore, *Etymologiae*, Book XIV, Chapter vi, 2.
58 Gildas, *De excidio*, Book I, Chapter i; vi.
59 Bede, *Historia ecclesiastica*, Book I, Chapter I.
60 Bede, *Historia ecclesiastica*, Book III, Chapter 25.
61 Martin K. Foys, 'The Virtual Reality of the Anglo-Saxon *Mappamundi*', *Literature Compass*, I (2004), pp. 1–17.
62 *Wonders of the East*, 25.

II OF WOLF AND MAN

1 On the wolf's survival and extinction in Britain, see James Edmund Harting, *British Animals Extinct within Historic Times* (London, 1880), pp. 115–205; Oliver Rackham, *The History of the Countryside* (London, 1986), pp. 34–5.
2 *Maxims* II, 18b, ASPR VI.
3 L. E. Webster, 'The Iconographic Programme of the Franks Casket', in *Northumbria's Golden Age*, ed. Jane Hawkes and Susan Mills (Stroud, 1999), pp. 227–46.
4 Ibid., p. 239.
5 Ælfric, *Passio St Eadmundi regis*, in *Ælfric's Lives of Saints*, ed. W. W. Skeat (London, 1881–1900), vol. II, pp. 314–35. All subsequent translations are prepared from this edition.
6 *Elene*, 28a; 113a, ASPR I.
7 *Battle of Brunanburh*, 65a, ASPR VI; *Judith*, 206a, ASPR VI.
8 C. Aybes and D. W. Yalden, 'Place-name Evidence for the Former Distribution and Status of Wolves and Beavers in Britain', *Mammal Review*, XXV/4 (1995), pp. 201–27.
9 *Fortunes of Men*, 13a, ASPR III.
10 This information is taken from a BBC documentary that aired in 2001: BBC2, *Transylvania: Living with Predators*, 25 March 2001.
11 Aleksander Pluskowski, *Wolves and the Wilderness in the Middle Ages* (Woodbridge, 2006), p. 39.
12 Ibid., p. 32.

13 *Exodus*, 168a, ASPR I.
14 Bede, *Historia ecclesiastica*, Book II, Chapter 6.
15 George Norman Garmonsway, ed., *Ælfric's Colloquy* (New York, 1965), p. 22.
16 Steven H. Fritts et al., 'Wolves and Humans', in *Wolves: Behaviour, Ecology and Conservation*, ed. L. David Mech and Luigi Boitani (Chicago, IL, 2003), pp. 289–316.
17 Pam J. Crabtree, 'Sheep, Horses, Swine, and Kine: A Zooarchaeological Perspective on the Anglo-Saxon Settlement of England', *Journal of Field Archaeology*, XVI/2 (1989), pp. 205–13.
18 This pattern began to change in the later Anglo-Saxon period, when hunting deer became an elite sport and herds of deer were preserved in large tracts of countryside. For an account of Anglo-Saxon deer hunting, see Tim Flight, 'Aristocratic Deer Hunting in Late Anglo-Saxon England: A Reconsideration, Based upon the *Vita S. Dvnstani*', *Anglo-Saxon England*, XLV (2016), pp. 311–31.
19 Sam Bradpiece, 'French Farmers Howl as Wolf Attacks on Livestock Soar', *Sunday Times*, 2 September 2018.
20 L. David Mech and Rolf O. Peterson, 'Wolf–Prey Relations', in *Wolves: Behaviour, Ecology and Conservation*, pp. 131–57, at 145.
21 Fritts et al., 'Wolves and Humans', p. 306.
22 Quoted from Harting, *British Animals*, p. 124.
23 Isidore, *Etymologiae*, Book XII, Chapter ii, 23.
24 *Christ* I, 256–258a; 259b–260, ASPR III.
25 See charters no. 453 and no. 1056 in *The Electronic Sawyer*, https://esawyer.lib.cam.ac.uk.
26 Richard Morris, ed., *The Blickling Homilies* (London, 1967), pp. 209, 211. All subsequent translations are prepared from this edition, and all citations hereafter refer to its page numbers.
27 *Fortunes of Men*, 12b–14a, ASPR III; *The Wanderer*, 82b–83a, ASPR III.
28 Malcolm Godden, ed., *Ælfric's Catholic Homilies: The Second Series* (London, 1979). All subsequent translations are prepared from this edition.
29 Winchester (Old Minster) no. 88, in *The Corpus of Anglo-Saxon Stone Sculpture in England* (Oxford, 1984–), vol. IV, pp. 314–22.
30 Martin Biddle, 'A Late Saxon Frieze Sculpture from the Old Minster', *Antiquaries Journal*, XLVI (1966), pp. 329–32.
31 Pluskowski, *Wolves and the Wilderness*, p. 102.
32 Preceding statistics are taken from Fritts et al., 'Wolves and Humans', p. 303.
33 John Pollard, *Wolves and Werewolves* (London, 1991), pp. 57–9.

34 C. E. Wright, ed., *Bald's Leechbook* (Copenhagen, 1955).
35 Fritts et al., 'Wolves and Humans'.
36 Ibid., pp. 302–4.
37 *Judith*, 205b–209a, ASPR IV.
38 Pollard, *Wolves and Werewolves*, pp. 23–6.
39 Pluskowski, *Wolves and the Wilderness*, p. 20.
40 Charter no. 1180 in William Farrer, ed., *Early Yorkshire Charters* (Edinburgh, 1914–16), vol. II, pp. 468–9.
41 Æthelweard, *Chronicle*, entry for the year 596, translation quoted from *The Chronicle of Æthelweard*, ed. and trans. A. Campbell (London, 1962).
42 *Maxims* I, 146–147a, ASPR III.
43 *The Wanderer*, 50b–53a, ASPR III.
44 *Maxims* I, 147b; 149–51, ASPR III.
45 Translated from the Latin quoted in Michael E. Moore, 'Wolves, Outlaws, and Enemy Combatants', in *Cultural Studies of the Modern Middle Ages*, ed. Eileen A. Joy (New York, 2007), pp. 217–36.
46 Exeter Riddle 55, 12a, ASPR III.
47 *Old English Boethius*, Prose 26.
48 Mary R. Gerstein, 'Germanic *Warg*: The Outlaw as Werewolf', in *Myth in Indo-European Antiquity*, ed. Gerald James Larson (Berkeley, CA, 1974), pp. 131–56.
49 *Maxims* II, 55b–57a, ASPR VI.
50 Gerstein, 'Germanic *Warg*', p. 133.
51 Ibid., p. 135.
52 Ibid., p. 134. See this article as a whole for the full history of the term.
53 Blickling Homily XVII, p. 209.
54 Translated from the text quoted in Montague Summers, *The Werewolf in Lore and Legend* (London, 1933), p. 4.

III *HIC SUNT DRACONES*

1 See Adrienne Mayor, *The First Fossil Hunters: Dinosaurs, Mammoths and Myth in Greek and Roman Times* (Princeton, NJ, 2011).
2 David E. Jones, *An Instinct for Dragons* (New York, 2000).
3 Pliny, *Historia naturalis*, Book VIII, Chapter xxxiii; Isidore, *Etymologiae*, Book XII, Chapter iv, 6–9.

4 Aldhelm, 'Riddle LXXXII', in *Aldhelmi opera*, ed. Rudolf Ehwald (Berlin, 1913).

5 Robert Stanton, *The Culture of Translation in Anglo-Saxon England* (Cambridge, 2002), p. 46.

6 *Beowulf*, 3042a, ASPR IV.

7 *Beowulf*, 2273a, ASPR IV; Aldhelm, poetic *De virginitate*, 2399, quoted from the Latin reproduced in Paul Sorrell, 'The Approach to the Dragon-fight in *Beowulf*, Aldhelm and the "traditions folkloriques" of Jacques Le Goff', *Parergon*, XII/1 (1994), pp. 57–87.

8 *Maxims* II, 26b–27a, ASPR VI.

9 *Beowulf*, 2411, ASPR IV.

10 *Beowulf*, 2298a, ASPR IV.

11 *Beowulf*, 1410, ASPR IV.

12 Aldhelm, poetic *De virginitate*, 2400; 2406, quoted from Michael Lapidge and James Rosier, trans., *Aldhelm: The Poetic Works* (Woodbridge, 2009). All subsequent translations are quoted from this edition, and all citations hereafter refer to the numbering it uses.

13 Isaiah 35:7 via Bede, *Historia ecclesiastica*, Book III, Chapter 23.

14 Aldhelm, poetic *De virginitate*, 2387–90.

15 *Solomon and Saturn* II, 206–10, in *The Old English Dialogues of Solomon and Saturn*, ed. Daniel Anlezark (Woodbridge, 2009).

16 *Beowulf*, 2213a, ASPR IV.

17 *Beowulf*, 2275b–2276a, ASPR IV.

18 Sarah Semple, 'A Fear of the Past: The Place of Prehistoric Burial Mounds in the Ideology of Middle and Later Anglo-Saxon England', *World Archaeology*, XXX (1998), pp. 109–26; Margaret Gelling, *Signposts to the Past: Place-names and the History of England*, 3rd edn (Chichester, 2010), pp. 143–4.

19 Alfred K. Siewers, 'Landscapes of Conversion: Guthlac's Mound and Grendel's Mere as Expressions of Anglo-Saxon Nation-Building', *Viator*, XXXIV (2003), pp. 1–39.

20 For a concise overview, see Martin Carver, *Sutton Hoo: Burial Ground of Kings?* (London, 1998).

21 Gelling, *Signposts to the Past*, pp. 150–51.

22 Ibid., p. 152.

23 Semple, 'A Fear of the Past'.

24 Ibid.; Della Hooke, *Trees in Anglo-Saxon England: Literature, Lore and Landscape* (Woodbridge, 2010), p. 173.

25 Siewers, 'Landscapes of Conversion', pp. 16–17; Semple, 'A Fear of the Past', p. 113.

26 Aldhelm, poetic *De Virginitate*, 549.
27 *Beowulf*, 2276b–2277a, ASPR IV.
28 *Christ and Satan*, 97–98a, ASPR I.
29 Translated from Donald G. Scragg, ed., *The Vercelli Homilies and Related Texts* (Oxford, 1992).
30 Matt Kaplan, *The Science of Monsters: Why Monsters Came to Be, and What Made Them So Terrifying* (London, 2012), pp. 109–14.
31 *Beowulf*, 2282a, ASPR IV.
32 *Beowulf*, 2231b–2232, ASPR IV.
33 *Beowulf*, 2287–2289a; 2293b–2297a; 2299b–2300a, ASPR IV.
34 *Beowulf*, 2302b–2310a; 2314b–2315, ASPR IV.
35 *Beowulf*, 2280b–2281a, ASPR IV.
36 A. Kristina Cherryson, 'Disturbing the Dead: Urbanisation, the Church and the Post-burial Treatment of Human Remains in Early Medieval Wessex, c. 600–1100 AD', *Anglo-Saxon Studies in Archaeology and History*, XIV (2007), pp. 130–42.
37 Gelling, *Signposts to the Past*, p. 134.
38 *Beowulf*, 2324–2327a, ASPR IV.
39 Kathryn Hume, 'The Concept of the Hall in Anglo-Saxon Poetry', *Anglo-Saxon England*, III (1974), pp. 63–74.
40 Kathryn Hume, 'The Theme and Structure of *Beowulf*', *Studies in Philology*, LXXII/1 (1975), pp. 1–27.
41 *Beowulf*, 2525b–2527a, ASPR IV.
42 *Beowulf*, 2555a, ASPR IV.
43 *Beowulf*, 2688–2693, ASPR IV.
44 *Beowulf*, 2713a; 2714–2715a, ASPR IV.
45 Bede, *Vita sanctorum abbatum monasterii in Wiramutha et Girvum*, in *Patrologia Latina*, ed. J. P. Migne (Paris, 1844–65), vol. XCIV, cols 711–30.
46 Christine Rauer, *Beowulf and the Dragon: Parallels and Analogues* (Cambridge, 2000), p. 44.
47 Gosforth no. 01, in *The Corpus of Anglo-Saxon Stone Sculpture in England* (Oxford, 1984–), vol. II, pp. 100–104.
48 *Beowulf*, 2329–2331a, ASPR IV.
49 *Beowulf*, 3001–3004; 3021–3027, ASPR IV.
50 Translated from *The Anglo-Saxon Chronicle: A Collaborative Edition*, ed. David Dumville and Simon Keynes (Cambridge, 1983–), vol. VII, p. 43.
51 *Battle of Finnsburh*, 3b, ASPR VI.
52 *The Wanderer*, 73–7, ASPR III.
53 *Beowulf*, 427a; 1171a, ASPR IV.

54 *Beowulf*, 71–2, ASPR IV.
55 *Beowulf*, 838a; 2327a; 168a, ASPR IV.
56 *Beowulf*, 2277b, ASPR IV.
57 *Beowulf*, 1719b–1722a, ASPR IV.
58 *Beowulf*, 1384b–1385, ASPR IV.
59 *Beowulf*, 2298b; 2307a; 2561, ASPR IV.
60 *Beowulf*, 2232a; 2410a, 2515a; 2719a, ASPR IV.
61 *Beowulf*, 485a; 767a; 2320a, ASPR IV.
62 *Beowulf*, 2288b; 2552a; 1047a; 1852a; 2293b; 2302b; 2554b; 2593a, ASPR IV.
63 *Beowulf*, 884b–895a, ASPR IV.
64 Roberta Frank, 'Skaldic Verse and the Date of Beowulf', in *The Dating of Beowulf*, ed. Colin Chase (Toronto, 1997), pp. 123–40.
65 Klaus Düwel, 'On the Sigurd Representations in Great Britain and Scandinavia', in *Languages and Cultures: Studies in Honour of Edgar C. Pollard*, ed. M. A. Jazayery and W. Winter (Berlin, 1988), pp. 133–56.
66 *Beowulf*, 2231b–2270a, ASPR IV.
67 Raymond P. Tripp Jr, *More about the Fight with the Dragon: Beowulf, 2208b–3182: Commentary, Edition, and Translation* (Lanham, MD, 1983).
68 Hilda R. Ellis Davidson, 'The Hill of the Dragon: Anglo-Saxon Burial Mounds in Literature and Archaeology', *Folklore*, LXI/4 (1950), pp. 169–85.
69 Martin Biddle and Birthe Kjølbye-Biddle, 'The Repton Stone', *Anglo-Saxon England*, XIV (1985), pp. 233–92.
70 Ibid., p. 251.
71 Ibid., p. 250.

IV SAINTS AND *SATANAS*

1 J. W. Lever, '*Paradise Lost* and the Anglo-Saxon Tradition', *Review of English Studies*, XXIII/90 (1947), pp. 97–106.
2 *Christ and Satan*, 269–71, ASPR I.
3 *The Life of Antony*, 5, quoted from Carolinne White, trans., *Early Christian Lives* (Harmondsworth, 1998). All subsequent translations are quoted from this edition.
4 James E. Goehring, *Ascetics, Society, and the Desert: Studies in Early Egyptian Monasticism* (Harrisburg, PA, 1999), p. 74. This rather pithy comment is not reproduced in Evagrius' translation.

5 Derwas J. Chitty, *The Desert a City: An Introduction to the Study of Egyptian and Palestinian Monasticism under the Christian Empire* (London, 1966), p. 3.
6 *Life of Antony*, 8.
7 Catherine A. M. Clarke, *Literary Landscapes and the Idea of England, 700–1400* (Cambridge, 2006), p. 50.
8 *Vita sancti Guthlaci*, Chapter XXIV, ed. Bertram Colgrave, in *Felix's Life of Saint Guthlac* (Cambridge, 1985). All subsequent translations are prepared from this edition, and all citations hereafter refer to the numbering it uses.
9 Ibid.
10 Ibid.
11 Oliver Rackham, *The History of the Countryside* (London, 1986), p. 382.
12 Ibid., p. 383.
13 Aleksander Pluskowski, *Wolves and the Wilderness in the Middle Ages* (Woodbridge, 2006), p. 56; Rackham, *History of the Countryside*, p. 384.
14 Katherine O'Brien O'Keeffe, 'Guthlac's Crossings', *Quaestio*, II (2001), pp. 1–26.
15 *Letter of Alexander to Aristotle*, 27.
16 *Vita sancti Guthlaci*, XXV; *Guthlac A*, 174a, ASPR III.
17 *Vita sancti Guthlaci*, XXVIII; *Guthlac A*, 101b–102a, ASPR III.
18 *Vita sancti Guthlaci*, XXV.
19 *Guthlac A*, 140b–146a, ASPR III.
20 *Liber monstrorum*, Prologue.
21 Sam Newton, *The Origins of Beowulf and the Pre-Viking Kingdom of East Anglia* (Cambridge, 1993), pp. 143–4.
22 *Vita sancti Guthlaci*, XXIX.
23 *Guthlac A*, 273–277a, ASPR III.
24 *Guthlac A*, 271–272a, ASPR III.
25 Translated from text quoted in Sarah Semple, *Perceptions of the Prehistoric in Anglo-Saxon England: Religion, Ritual, and Rulership in the Landscape* (Oxford, 2013), p. 147.
26 For a fuller discussion, see L. E. Webster, 'The Iconographic Programme of the Franks Casket', in *Northumbria's Golden Age*, ed. Jane Hawkes and Susan Mills (Stroud, 1999), pp. 227–46.
27 Ibid.
28 *Guthlac A*, 148a, ASPR III.
29 *Vita sancti Guthlaci*, XXIX.
30 *Vita sancti Guthlaci*, XXX.

31 *Vita sancti Guthlaci*, XXVIII.
32 Sarah Downey, 'Too Much of Too Little: Guthlac and the Temptation of Excessive Fasting', *Traditio*, LXIII (2008), pp. 89–127.
33 Jerome Kroll and Bernard S. Bachrach, *The Mystic Mind: The Psychology of Medieval Mystics and Ascetics* (London, 2005), p. 85.
34 *Vita sancti Guthlaci*, XXXVI.
35 *Vita sancti Guthlaci*, XXXI.
36 *Guthlac A*, 208b–213, ASPR III.
37 *Vita sancti Guthlaci*, XXXI.
38 *Guthlac A*, 557–63; 587–9, ASPR III.
39 *Vita sancti Guthlaci*, XXXVIII.
40 *Guthlac A*, 733b–746, ASPR III.
41 *Vita sancti Guthlaci*, XXXIV.
42 Clarke, *Literary Landscapes*, p. 31.
43 Bertram Colgrave, ed. and trans., *Two Lives of Saint Cuthbert: A Life by an Anonymous Monk of Lindisfarne and Bede's Prose Life* (New York, 1969), pp. 13, 16.
44 Ibid., pp. 17–50.
45 *Anonymous Life of St Cuthbert*, Book III, Chapter i, in *Two Lives*, ed. Colgrave. All subsequent translations are prepared from this edition.
46 Bede, *Prose Life of Cuthbert*, Book XVII, in *Two Lives*, ed. Colgrave. All subsequent translations are prepared from this edition.
47 *Anonymous Life*, III.i.
48 Bede, *Prose Life*, XVII.
49 *Anonymous Life*, III.v.
50 Bede, *Prose Life*, XIX.
51 *Anonymous Life*, III.i.
52 Bede, *Prose Life*, XVII.
53 *Juliana*, 321–323a; 325–327a; 382–391a; 393b–397a; 403b–409a, ASPR III.
54 *Juliana*, 483b–486a, ASPR III.

V THE DEVIL AND THE DEEP BLUE SEA

1 Gildas, *De Excidio*, Book I, Chapter 3.
2 Pliny, *Historia naturalis*, Book XIX, Chapter i.
3 *The Seafarer*, 1–12a, ASPR III.

4 *Andreas*, 369b–377a, ASPR II.
5 Sebastian I. Sobecki, *The Sea and Medieval English Literature* (Woodbridge, 2008), pp. 34–5.
6 Ibid., p. 38.
7 Gregory the Great, *Moralia in Iob*, IX.50, in *Patrologia Latina*, ed. J. P. Migne (Paris, 1844–65), vols LXXV–LXXVI, cols 509–1162, 9–781. All subsequent translations are prepared from this edition.
8 Translated from Thomas A. Carnicelli, ed., *King Alfred's Version of St Augustine's Soliloquies* (Cambridge, MA, 1969), pp. 67–8.
9 Nicholas Howe, *Writing the Map of Anglo-Saxon England: Essays in Cultural Geography* (New Haven, CT, 2008), p. 50.
10 *Exodus*, 81b; 105b–106a; 494a; 504b, ASPR I.
11 *Beowulf*, 549a; 554a, ASPR IV.
12 *Beowulf*, 558a, ASPR IV.
13 *Beowulf*, 3131b–3133, ASPR IV.
14 Translated from *The Anglo-Saxon Chronicle: A Collaborative Edition*, ed. David Dumville and Simon Keynes (Cambridge, 1983–), vol. VII, p. 43.
15 Gregory via Bede, *Historia ecclesiastica*, Book I, Chapter 30.
16 Alcuin, *Versus de patribus, regibus et sanctis Eboracensis ecclesiae*, 1325–6, quoted from Alcuin, *The Bishops, Kings, and Saints of York*, ed. and trans. Peter Godman (Oxford, 1982).
17 Mick Aston, 'Early Monasteries in Somerset – Models and Agendas', in *The Land of the Dobunni: A Series of Papers Relating to the Transformation of the Pagan, Pre-Roman Tribal Lands into Christian, Anglo-Saxon Gloucestershire and Somerset, from the Symposia of 2001 and 2002*, ed. Martin Ecclestone (King's Lynn, Norfolk, 2004), pp. 36–48.
18 On the appearance of hermitages in the UK and Ireland, and the place of hermits in the Anglo-Saxon Church, see Tim Flight, 'Apophasis, Contemplation, and the Kenotic Moment in Anglo-Saxon Literature', DPhil thesis, Magdalen College, Oxford, 2016, pp. 1–75.
19 Gillian R. Hutchinson, 'Ships', in *The Wiley Blackwell Encyclopedia of Anglo-Saxon England*, ed. Michael Lapidge et al., 2nd edn (Chichester, 2014), pp. 432–4.
20 *Beowulf*, 540b, ASPR IV.
21 Mark Gardiner and John R. Stewart, 'Anglo-Saxon Whale Exploitation: Some Evidence from Dengemarsh, Lydd, Kent', *Medieval Archaeology*, XLII (1999), pp. 96–101.

22 George Norman Garmonsway, ed., *Ælfric's Colloquy* (New York, 1965), pp. 29–30. All subsequent translations are prepared from this edition.
23 Gardiner and Stewart, 'Anglo-Saxon Whale Exploitation'.
24 *The Whale*, 53a, ASPR III.
25 Inscription from the Franks Casket, cited from L. E. Webster, 'The Iconographic Programme of the Franks Casket', in *Northumbria's Golden Age*, ed. Jane Hawkes and Susan Mills (Stroud, 1999), pp. 227–46, at 232.
26 *The Seafarer*, 63a; 60a, ASPR III; *Andreas*, 274b, ASPR II; *Death of King Edgar*, 28a, ASPR VI.
27 Riddle 2, 5a, ASPR III; *Andreas*, 370a, ASPR II.
28 *The Meters of Boethius*, Meter 5, 10a; *Andreas*, 266a; 634a, ASPR II; *Beowulf*, 10a, ASPR IV; *Andreas*, 821a, ASPR II.
29 *Beowulf*, 2805b; 3136b, ASPR IV.
30 Garmonsway, *Ælfric's Colloquy*, p. 29.
31 Isidore, *Etymologiae*, Book XII, Chapter vi, 7.
32 Vicki Ellen Szabo, '"Bad to the Bone"? The Unnatural History of Monstrous Medieval Whales', *Heroic Age*, VIII (2005), at www.heroicage.org/issues/8/szabo.html.
33 I. N. Wood, 'Ripon, Francia and the Franks Casket in the Early Middle Ages', *Northern History*, XXVI (1990), pp. 1–19.
34 *Beowulf*, 421b–422a; 574b–575a, ASPR IV.
35 *Beowulf*, 845b, ASPR IV.
36 *Beowulf*, 847b, ASPR IV.
37 *Beowulf*, 1426a, ASPR IV.
38 Augustine, *De civitate dei*, Book XVIII, Chapter XXX.
39 Isidore, *Etymologiae*, Book XII, Chapter vi, 8.
40 *The Whale*, 4–17a; 24–32a; 44b–49a, ASPR III.
41 Jeremy DeAngelo, '*Discretio spirituum* and *The Whale*', *Anglo-Saxon England*, XLII (2013), pp. 271–89, at 280.
42 *The Voyage of Saint Brendan*, 10, quoted from J. F. Webb, trans., *The Age of Bede* (Harmondsworth, 1983).
43 *The Whale*, 49b–62a; 67b–70; 76–81, ASPR III.
44 Isidore, *Etymologiae*, Book XI, Chapter iii, 2.
45 KJV Job 41:26–7; 29; 33.
46 *Moralia in Iob*, XXXIII.17.
47 Translated from the Old English quoted in Thomas D. Hill, 'The Devil's Forms and the *Pater Noster*'s Powers: "The Prose Solomon and Saturn" *Pater Noster* Dialogue and the Motif of the Transformation Combat', *Studies in Philology*, LXXV/2 (1988), pp. 164–76, at 166.

48 *Moralia in Iob*, XXXIII.44.
49 KJV Job 41:19.
50 *Moralia in Iob*, XXXIII.59.
51 KJV Job 41:22.
52 *Moralia in Iob*, XXXIV.2.
53 KJV Job 41:34.
54 DeAngelo, '*Discretio spirituum*', p. 282.
55 *Moralia in Iob*, IV.16.
56 KJV Job 41:31.

VI *MEARCSTAPAN*, PART ONE: THE GRENDELKIN

1 Andy Orchard, *Pride and Prodigies: Studies in the Monsters of the Beowulf-Manuscript* (Cambridge, 1995), p. 2.
2 Ibid.
3 See, for example, *The Dating of Beowulf*, ed. Colin Chase (Toronto, 1981).
4 J.R.R. Tolkien, '*Beowulf*: The Monsters and the Critics', in *The Monsters and the Critics and Other Essays*, ed. Christopher Tolkien (London, 2006), pp. 5–48, at 7–8.
5 John Halverson, 'The World of *Beowulf*', *English Literary History*, XXXVI/4 (1969), pp. 593–608.
6 *Beowulf*, 64–72; 74–82a, ASPR IV.
7 Kathryn Hume, 'The Concept of the Hall in Anglo-Saxon Poetry', *Anglo-Saxon England*, III (1974), pp. 63–74, at 64.
8 See, for instance, Daniel G. Calder, 'Setting and Ethos: The Pattern of Measure and Limit in *Beowulf*', *Studies in Philology*, LXIX/1 (1972), pp. 21–37; Alvin A. Lee, *The Guest-hall of Eden: Four Essays on the Design of Old English Poetry* (New Haven, CT, 1972).
9 Mircea Eliade, *Cosmos and History: The Myth of the Eternal Return*, trans. Willard R. Trask (New York, 1959), p. 10.
10 Bede, *Historia ecclesiastica*, Book II, Chapter 13.
11 *Beowulf*, 1357b–1376a, ASPR IV.
12 *Beowulf*, 847b, ASPR IV.
13 Orchard, *Pride and Prodigies*, pp. 39–42; Lars Malmberg, 'Grendel and the Devil', *Neuphilologische Mitteilungen*, LXXVIII (1977), pp. 241–3.
14 *Beowulf*, 845b, ASPR IV.
15 See Richard J. Schrader, 'Sacred Groves, Marvellous Waters, and Grendel's Abode', *Florilegium*, V (1983), pp. 76–84.

16 Ibid., pp. 80–81.
17 Sarah Lynn Higley, '*Aldor on ofre*, or the Reluctant Hart: A Study of Liminality in *Beowulf*', *Neuphilologische Mitteilungen*, LXXXVII (1986), pp. 342–53.
18 *Maxims* II, 42b–43a, ASPR VI.
19 *Beowulf*, 102–4, ASPR IV.
20 *Beowulf*, 86a, ASPR IV.
21 *Beowulf*, 160a; 161b–162a, ASPR IV.
22 *Beowulf*, 450a, ASPR IV. *fenhopu* (764a, 'fen-retreat'), *fenfreoðu* (851a, 'fen-refuge').
23 *Beowulf*, 764a; 851a, ASPR IV.
24 *Beowulf*, 845b–849, ASPR IV.
25 *Beowulf*, 1591–1594a, ASPR IV.
26 *Beowulf*, 426a, ASPR IV.
27 *Beowulf*, 710–716a; 721b–724a, ASPR IV.
28 *Beowulf*, 144–146a, ASPR IV.
29 *Beowulf*, 413a, ASPR IV; *Genesis A*, 106a, ASPR I.
30 *Beowulf*, 175–189a, ASPR IV.
31 Wihtred's laws are discussed and translated in Lisi Oliver, ed. and trans., *The Beginnings of English Law* (Toronto, 2002).
32 *Beowulf*, 852a; 986a, ASPR IV.
33 *Beowulf*, 101b, ASPR IV.
34 *Beowulf*, 164b; 1276a, ASPR IV.
35 *Juliana*, 317b; 630a; 523a, ASPR III.
36 *Beowulf*, 786b; 1682b, ASPR IV; *Guthlac A*, 210a, ASPR III.
37 *Beowulf*, 1776a, ASPR IV.
38 *Beowulf*, 1680a, ASPR IV.
39 *Beowulf*, 1274a, ASPR IV; *Juliana*, 457a; 615a, ASPR III. For full discussion of these verbal links, see Marie Padgett Hamilton, 'The Religious Principle in *Beowulf*', *Proceedings of the Modern Language Association*, LXI/2 (1946), pp. 309–30; Orchard, *Pride and Prodigies*, p. 39.
40 *Beowulf*, 86–98, ASPR IV.
41 *Vita sancti Guthlaci*, XXIX.
42 *Beowulf*, 740–745a, ASPR IV.
43 *Beowulf*, 726b–727, ASPR IV.
44 For a list of Anglo-Saxon prohibitions on blood-drinking, see Orchard, *Pride and Prodigies*, p. 64.
45 *Genesis A*, 1518–20, ASPR I.
46 *Beowulf*, 730b, ASPR IV.
47 *Beowulf*, 122b–123a, ASPR IV.

48 *Beowulf*, 1637b–1639, ASPR IV.
49 *Beowulf*, 984b–990, ASPR IV.
50 Augustine, *De civitate dei*, Book XVI, Chapter viii.
51 *Beowulf*, 102–14, ASPR IV.
52 *Beowulf*, 711b, ASPR IV.
53 Ruth Mellinkoff, 'Cain's Monstrous Progeny in *Beowulf*: Part I, Noachic Tradition', *Anglo-Saxon England*, VIII (1979), pp. 143–62, at 147.
54 R. E. Kaske, '*Beowulf* and the Book of Enoch', *Speculum*, XLVI/3 (1971), pp. 421–31, at 426–7.
55 *Vita sancti Guthlaci*, XXXI.
56 *Genesis A*, 1020b–1021, ASPR I.
57 *Beowulf*, 1352b, ASPR IV.
58 *Beowulf*, 721a, ASPR IV.
59 *The Wanderer*, 93b, ASPR III.
60 *Beowulf*, 1267a, ASPR IV.
61 *Beowulf*, 1351b–1352a, ASPR IV.
62 *Beowulf*, 105a; 1352a; 720b; 1682a; 141a; 986b, ASPR IV.
63 *Beowulf*, 761a, ASPR IV.
64 *Beowulf*, 668b, ASPR IV.
65 *Beowulf*, 646b–647, ASPR IV.
66 *Beowulf*, 154b–156, ASPR IV.
67 *Beowulf*, 2085b–2091a, ASPR IV.
68 *Beowulf*, 991–6, ASPR IV.
69 *Beowulf*, 1255b–1268, ASPR IV.
70 *Beowulf*, 1259a, ASPR IV.
71 *Beowulf*, 1515a; 1513a, ASPR IV.
72 *Beowulf*, 771b; 994a, ASPR IV.
73 *Beowulf*, 770b; 1572b, ASPR IV.
74 *Beowulf*, 1345–1357a, ASPR IV.
75 *Beowulf*, 1295b, ASPR IV.
76 *Beowulf*, 1333b–1334, ASPR IV.
77 *Beowulf*, 1384b–1385, ASPR IV.
78 *Beowulf*, 1543–1547a, ASPR IV.
79 *Beowulf*, 1599a, ASPR IV.
80 *Beowulf*, 1499a, ASPR IV.
81 *Beowulf*, 1171a, ASPR IV.
82 Michael Lapidge, '*Beowulf*, Aldhelm, the *Liber Monstrorum* and Wessex', *Studi medievali*, 3rd ser., XXIII (1982), pp. 151–92, at 179–84.
83 Ibid.

84 Sam Newton, *The Origins of Beowulf and the Pre-Viking Kingdom of East Anglia* (Cambridge, 1993), p. 144.
85 Ibid.

VII *MEARCSTAPAN*, PART TWO: BEOWULF AND OTHERS

1 *Beowulf*, 711b; 1260–2, ASPR IV.
2 *Beowulf*, 111b, ASPR IV.
3 *Old English Boethius*, Prose 31.
4 *Beowulf*, 770b; 1572b, ASPR IV.
5 *Beowulf*, 994a; 1513a, ASPR IV.
6 *Beowulf*, 720b; 728b; 741a, ASPR IV.
7 *The Wonders of the East*, 20. I follow Orchard's translation here for the slightly arcane *cuðra manna naman* (with the names of acquaintances).
8 This ingenious reading is taken from Jeffrey Jerome Cohen, *Of Giants: Sex, Monsters, and the Middle Ages* (Minneapolis, MN, 1999), p. 2.
9 *Beowulf*, 500, ASPR IV.
10 *Beowulf*, 587–589a, ASPR IV.
11 *Beowulf*, 587b; 1262a, ASPR IV.
12 *Beowulf*, 1527b–1528, ASPR IV.
13 *Beowulf*, 898–906; 915b, ASPR IV.
14 *Beowulf*, 761a; 112a, ASPR IV.
15 *Beowulf*, 903a; 808a, ASPR IV.
16 *Beowulf*, 1711–22, ASPR IV.
17 *Beowulf*, 723b, ASPR IV.
18 *Beowulf*, 2220b; 2304a, ASPR IV.
19 *Beowulf*, 196–198a, ASPR IV.
20 *Beowulf*, 247b–249a, ASPR IV.
21 *Beowulf*, 1351b–1352a; 1353, ASPR IV.
22 *Liber monstrorum*, I.2.
23 *Beowulf*, 122b–123a, ASPR IV.
24 *Beowulf*, 377–381a, ASPR IV.
25 *Beowulf*, 2361–2, ASPR IV.
26 *Beowulf*, 750–754a; 815b–821a, ASPR IV.
27 *Beowulf*, 1557–62, ASPR IV.
28 *Beowulf*, 2682b–2686a, ASPR IV.
29 *Beowulf*, 2501–2; 2506b–2508a, ASPR IV.
30 *Beowulf*, 1366b–1367; 1495b–1496, ASPR IV.
31 *Beowulf*, 1599a; 1519a; 1497b–1498, ASPR IV.

32 *Beowulf*, 421b–422a; 845b, ASPR IV.
33 Alex Nicholls, 'Bede "Awe-inspiring" not "Monstrous": Some Problems with Old English *aglæca*', *Notes and Queries*, XXXVIII (1991), pp. 147–8.
34 Doreen M. E. Gillam, 'The Use of the Term æglæca in *Beowulf*', *Studia Germanica Gandensia*, III (1961), pp. 145–69, at 145.
35 Nicholls, 'Bede "Awe-inspiring"'.
36 *Beowulf*, 1000b, ASPR IV.
37 *Beowulf*, 2592a, ASPR IV.
38 Gillam, 'The Use of the Term æglæca', pp. 163–4.
39 '*Wer mit Ungeheuern kämpft, mag zusehn, dass er nicht dabei zum Ungeheuer wird. Und wenn du lange in einen Abgrund blickst, blickt der Abgrund auch in dich hinein*': Friedrich Nietzsche, *Jenseits von Gut und Böse*, in *Werke in drei Bänden*, ed. Karl Schlechta (Munich, 1973), vol. II, p. 636.
40 *Beowulf*, 1735–1755a; 1758–1761a, ASPR IV.
41 *Beowulf*, 2177–2183a, ASPR IV.
42 *Beowulf*, 2329–2331a, ASPR IV.
43 *Beowulf*, 709a, ASPR IV.
44 *Beowulf*, 1539b, ASPR IV.
45 *Beowulf*, 2401b; 2550b, ASPR IV.
46 David Williams, *Deformed Discourse: The Function of the Monster in Medieval Thought and Literature* (Exeter, 1999), p. 119.
47 Orchard, *Pride and Prodigies*, p. 80.
48 Ælfric, 'For the Holy Day of Pentecost', translated from the text quoted in Cohen, *Of Giants*, p. 24.
49 *The Ruin*, 2b; 33–34a, ASPR III.
50 *Beowulf*, 761a; 1558a; 1679a, ASPR IV.
51 R. E. Kaske, 'The *eotenas* in Beowulf', in *Old English Poetry: Fifteen Essays*, ed. Robert Creed (Providence, RI, 1967), pp. 285–310.
52 *Beowulf*, 508–11, ASPR IV.
53 *Beowulf*, 408b–409a; 421–422a, ASPR IV.
54 For more on this fascinating poem, see Tim Flight, '*The Dream of the Rood*: A Neglected Contemplative Text', in *Mystical Doctrines of Deification: Case Studies in the Christian Tradition*, ed. John Arblaster and Rob Faesen (Abingdon, 2018), pp. 72–88.
55 *Beowulf*, 2419b–2424, ASPR IV.
56 *Beowulf*, 2514a; 2513a, ASPR IV.
57 *Beowulf*, 2733b–2735, ASPR IV.
58 *Beowulf*, 2327a, ASPR IV.
59 *Beowulf*, 2535b–2537; 2794–8, ASPR IV.

60 *Beowulf*, 685b–687 ASPR IV.
61 *Beowulf*, 1657b–1658; 1661–1663a, ASPR IV.
62 *Beowulf*, 381b–384a, ASPR IV.
63 *Beowulf*, 665b–667a, ASPR IV.
64 *Beowulf*, 1553b–1554a, ASPR IV.
65 M. B. McNamee, '*Beowulf*: An Allegory of Salvation?', *Journal of English and Germanic Philology*, LIX/2 (1960), pp. 190–207. According to Christian theology, all mortals who died before the Crucifixion were unredeemed by Christ and thus logically went to Hell. Unlikely residents back then included Abel, Noah and the Old Testament Prophets. The Gospel of Nicodemus describes Christ going to Hell after his death, defeating the Devil and releasing all worthies who died before him.

CONCLUSION

1 See, for instance, Ros Coard, 'Ascertaining an Agent: Using Tooth Pit Data to Determine the Carnivore/s Responsible for Predation in Cases of Suspected Big Cat Kills in an Upland Area of Britain', *Journal of Archaeological Science*, XXXIV/10 (2007), pp. 1677–84.
2 *Wonders of the East*, 32.
3 On this passage of *Wonders of the East*, see Asa Simon Mittman, 'Are the "Monstrous Races" Races?', *Postmedieval: A Journal of Medieval Cultural Studies*, VI (2015), pp. 36–51, at 43–5.
4 *Maxims* II, 10a. I follow here the manuscript's *swicolost* as per Tom Shippey's edition of the text in *Poems of Wisdom and Learning in Old English* (Cambridge, 1976).

BIBLIOGRAPHY

PRIMARY TEXTS

Birch, Walter de Gray, ed., *Cartularium Saxonicum*, 3 vols (London, 1885–93)

Colgrave, Bertram, ed. and trans., *Felix's Life of Saint Guthlac* (Cambridge, 1985)

—, ed. and trans., *Two Lives of Saint Cuthbert: A Life by an Anonymous Monk of Lindisfarne and Bede's Prose Life* (New York, 1969)

Colgrave, Bertram, and R.A.B. Mynors, eds and trans., *Bede's Ecclesiastical History of the English People* (Oxford, 1969)

Dumville, David, and Simon Keynes, eds, *The Anglo-Saxon Chronicle: A Collaborative Edition*, 17 vols (Cambridge, 1983–)

Garmonsway, George Norman, ed., *Ælfric's Colloquy* (New York, 1965)

Irvine, Susan, and Malcolm Godden, eds and trans., *The Old English Boethius: With Verse Prologues and Epilogues Associated with King Alfred* (Cambridge, MA, 2012)

Krapp, G. P., and E. V. Dobbie, eds, *The Anglo-Saxon Poetic Records: A Collective Edition*, 6 vols (New York, 1931–53)

Lapidge, Michael, and James Rosier, trans., *Aldhelm: The Poetic Works* (Woodbridge, 2009)

Migne, J. P., ed., *Patrologia Latina*, 221 vols (Turnhout, 1844–65)

—, ed., *Sancti Aurelii Augustini, Hipponensis episcopi, opera omnia*, 11 vols (Paris, 1861–5)

Orchard, Andy, ed. and trans., *The Letter of Alexander to Aristotle*, in *Pride and Prodigies: Studies in the Monsters of the Beowulf-Manuscript* (Cambridge, 1995), Appendix IIb

—, ed. and trans., *Liber Monstrorum*, in *Pride and Prodigies: Studies in the Monsters of the Beowulf-Manuscript* (Cambridge, 1995), Appendix IIIa

—, ed. and trans., *The Wonders of the East*, in *Pride and Prodigies: Studies in the Monsters of the Beowulf-Manuscript* (Cambridge, 1995), Appendix 1b

Webb, J. F., trans., *The Age of Bede* (Harmondsworth, 1965)

SECONDARY TEXTS

Biddle, Martin, and Birthe Kjølbye-Biddle, 'The Repton Stone', *Anglo-Saxon England*, XIV (1985), pp. 233–92

Bruce-Mitford, R.L.S., *The Sutton Hoo Ship Burial* (London, 1978)

Camille, Michael, *Image on the Edge: The Margins of Medieval Art* (London, 1992)

Chase, Colin, ed., *The Dating of Beowulf* (Toronto, 1981)

Cramp, Rosemary, ed., *The Corpus of Anglo-Saxon Stone Sculpture in England*, 12 vols (Oxford, 1984–)

Eliade, Mircea, *Cosmos and History: The Myth of the Eternal Return*, trans. Willard R. Trask (New York, 1959)

Foot, Sarah, 'The Making of *Angelcynn*: English Identity before the Norman Conquest', in *Old English Literature: Critical Essays*, ed. R. M. Liuzza (New Haven, CT, 2002), pp. 51–78

Friedman, John Block, *The Monstrous Races in Medieval Art and Thought* (Syracuse, NY, 2000)

Gelling, Margaret, *Signposts to the Past: Place-names and the History of England*, 3rd edn (Chichester, 2010)

Gerstein, Mary R., 'Germanic *Warg*: The Outlaw as Werewolf', in *Myth in Indo-European Antiquity*, ed. Gerald James Larson (Berkeley, CA, 1974), pp. 131–56

Härke, Heinrich, 'Anglo-Saxon Immigration and Ethnogenesis', *Medieval Archaeology*, LV (2011), pp. 1–28

Hooke, Della, *Trees in Anglo-Saxon England: Literature, Lore and Landscape* (Woodbridge, 2010)

Howe, Nicholas, *Writing the Map of Anglo-Saxon England: Essays in Cultural Geography* (New Haven, CT, 2008)

Hume, Kathryn, 'The Concept of the Hall in Anglo-Saxon Poetry', *Anglo-Saxon England*, III (1974), pp. 63–74

Lapidge, Michael, '*Beowulf*, Aldhelm, the *Liber Monstrorum* and Wessex', *Studi medievali*, 3rd ser., XXIII (1982), pp. 151–92

—, John Blair, Simon Keynes and Donald Scragg, eds, *The Wiley Blackwell Encyclopedia of Anglo-Saxon England*, 2nd edn (Chichester, 2014)

Mayr-Harting, Henry, *The Coming of Christianity to Anglo-Saxon England*, 3rd edn (University Park, PA, 1991)
Mech, L. David, and Luigi Boitani, eds, *Wolves: Behaviour, Ecology and Conservation* (Chicago, IL, 2003), pp. 289–316
Mittman, Asa Simon, and Susan M. Kim, *Inconceivable Beasts: The Wonders of the East in the Beowulf Manuscript* (Tempe, AZ, 2013)
Neville, Jennifer, *Representations of the Natural World in Old English Poetry* (Cambridge, 1999)
Newton, Sam, *The Origins of Beowulf and the Pre-Viking Kingdom of East Anglia* (Cambridge, 1993)
Orchard, Andy, *Pride and Prodigies: Studies in the Monsters of the Beowulf-Manuscript* (Cambridge, 1995)
Pluskowski, Aleksander, *Wolves and the Wilderness in the Middle Ages* (Woodbridge, 2006)
Rackham, Oliver, *The History of the Countryside* (London, 1986)
Semple, Sarah, *Perceptions of the Prehistoric in Anglo-Saxon England: Religion, Ritual, and Rulership in the Landscape* (Oxford, 2013)
Sobecki, Sebastian I., *The Sea and Medieval English Literature* (Woodbridge, 2008)
Stanley, E. G., *The Search for Anglo-Saxon Paganism* (Cambridge, 1975)
Stenton, F. M., *Anglo-Saxon England*, 3rd edn (Oxford, 1971)
Ulrich, Roger S., 'Biophilia, Biophobia, and Natural Landscapes', in *The Biophilia Hypothesis*, ed. Stephen R. Kellert and Edward O. Wilson (Washington, DC, 1993), pp. 73–137
Webster, L. E., 'The Iconographic Programme of the Franks Casket', in *Northumbria's Golden Age*, ed. Jane Hawkes and Susan Mills (Stroud, 1999), pp. 227–46

ACKNOWLEDGEMENTS

I would like to thank David Watkins at Reaktion Books, who was instrumental in making this project happen in the first place and has been tirelessly helpful ever since its commission. I am also very grateful to Kate Wiles at *History Today* for kindly publishing several of my articles, including that which became this book.

I owe a huge debt of gratitude to my wonderful DPhil supervisors, professors Vincent Gillespie and Andy Orchard, to whose tutelage I hope my work does credit. One way or another, I did not get to say a proper goodbye when I left Oxford in 2016, and I hope that this book goes some small way in thanking Vincent and Andy for making my doctorate so fulfilling and among the best years of my life. I would also be remiss not to thank my Master's supervisor, Dr Jennifer Neville, whose great erudition and passion for Old English literature inspired me to specialize in the Anglo-Saxon period for my doctorate.

Finally, I must thank my mother, Mary Flight, for a lifetime of support and encouragement, and my wife, Martina Wise, for tolerating and assisting my eremitic approach to scholarship and love for the Anglo-Saxons, whom she thinks are boring.

ACKNOWLEDGEMENTS

PHOTO ACKNOWLEDGEMENTS

The author and publishers wish to express their thanks to the below sources of illustrative material and/or permission to reproduce it. Every effort has been made to contact copyright holders; should there be any we have been unable to reach or to whom inaccurate acknowledgements have been made, please contact the publishers, and full adjustments will be made to subsequent printings.

Bodleian Libraries: pp. 120, 121, 122; British Library, London: pp. 38, 57, 60, 187, 202; British Museum, London: p. 91; Cambridge University Library: p. 92; Ethan Doyle White: p. 95; Geni: p. 17; Tony Grist (Polipholo): p. 115; Alex Healing: p. 96; Midnightblueowl: p. 15; Mike Peel: p. 133; Rosser1954: p. 24; Gary Todd: p. 63; Winchester City Museum: p. 75.

INDEX

Page numbers in *italics* refer to illustrations